American Women of Letters and the Nineteenth-Century Sciences

Styles of Affiliation

Nina Baym

Rutgers University Press
New Brunswick, New Jersey, and London

Library of Congress Cataloging-in-Publication Data

Baym, Nina.
    American women of letters and the nineteenth-century sciences : styles
of affiliation / Nina Baym.
      p.   cm.
    Includes bibliographical references (p.) and index.
    ISBN 0–8135–2984–0—(cloth : alk. paper)—ISBN 0–8135–2985–9
(pbk. : alk. paper)
    1. American literature—19th century—History and criticism. 2. Literature and
science—United States—History—19th century. 3. Women and literature—
United States—History—19th century. 4. American literature—Women authors—
History and criticism. 5. Women in science—United States—History—19th century.
6. Science—United States—History—19th century. 7. Women scientists—United
States. 8. Science in literature. I. Title.

PS217.S34 B39 2001
810.9'356—dc21

          2001019805

British Cataloging-in-Publication information is available from the British Library.

Quotations from *The Poems of Emily Dickinson*, edited by Ralph W. Franklin (Cambridge, Mass: The Belknap Press of Harvard University Press), copyright © 1998 by the
President of the Fellows of Harvard College; copyright © 1951, 1955, 1979 by the
President and Fellows of Harvard College; reprinted by permission of the publishers and
the Trustees of Amherst College.

Copyright © 2002 by Nina Baym
All rights reserved
No part of this book may be reproduced or utilized in any form or by any means,
electronic or mechanical, or by any information storage and retrieval system, without
written permission from the publisher. Please contact Rutgers University Press, 100 Joyce
Kilmer Avenue, Piscataway, NJ 08854–8099. The only exception to this prohibition is
"fair use" as defined by U.S. copyright law.

Manufactured in the United States of America

To Nancy, Rex, Zane, and Eli; to Geoff and Jen; and, especially and always, to Jack

CONTENTS

ACKNOWLEDGMENTS

Friends and colleagues have helped, advised, and encouraged me as I worked on this book. At the University of Illinois I thank in particular Dennis Baron, Bill Maxwell, Bob Parker, Rick Powers, and Julia Walker. Among a larger number of friends in a time of need than I could ever have imagined, they, along with Iryce Baron, Stephanie Foote, Paul Friedman, Peter Garrett, Pat Gill, Philip Graham, Achsah Guibbory, Jim Hurt, David Kay, Bobbi Klein, Joan Klein, Miles Klein, Laurence Lieberman, Michael Madonick, Bruce Michelson, Carol Neely, Judy Rowan, Dick Schacht, Myron Salamon, Sonya Salamon, Julia Saville, Joseph Valente, Leon Waldoff, Emily Watts, and Dick Wheeler, were there before I had a chance to ask. I am forever grateful to Janet Lyon and Zohreh Sullivan.

I thank Hugh MacDougall of the James Fenimore Cooper Society for information about Susan Fenimore Cooper; my lifelong friend Bobbi Klein for discussions about home economics; Dan Peck for chats about Maria Mitchell; Susannah Shmurak for leads on Mary Lyon of Mount Holyoke; Elizabeth Renker for information about early school curricula; Lillian Hoddeson for the loan of books; Tim Dean for useful talk about Emily Dickinson; Myron Salamon for much talk over the years about science and the scientific worldview; Julia Saville for help with estheticism; and, especially, Lawrence Buell for his continued and continuing affirmation of my work. Leslie Mitchner of the Rutgers University Press has been a good friend as well as a great editor; her early interest in this project motivated me to make a book out of what was, when she first heard about it, only a vague idea.

I have found much useful material in the wonderful library of the University of Illinois. I was also able to borrow books from other Illinois libraries, including those of the University of Chicago, Illinois State University,

Northern Illinois University, Roosevelt College, Southern Illinois University at Carbondale, Southern Illinois University at Edwardsville, the University of Illinois at Chicago, the University of Illinois at Springfield, Western Illinois University, and Wheaton College. The libraries of Harvard University, Northwestern University, Yale University, Iowa State University, the University of Minnesota, Occidental College, and Princeton University also loaned materials. I was able to acquire some otherwise unavailable texts through the on-line used book services, in which context I want gratefully to acknowledge support by the Swanlund Endowment and the Center for Advanced Study.

I am enormously grateful to the American Literature Section of the MLA for awarding me the Hubbell Lifetime Achievement Medal in the year 2000, a gesture that took me completely by surprise, while doubling and redoubling my determination to make this the best book I possibly could. I am forever indebted to the energy, amiability, patience, and enthusiasm of three graduate student assistants: Liesl Ward and Melissa Tedrowe worked with me at the start, and Catherine Waitinas has helped me finish up. My greatest debt is to Jack Stillinger—for always, and still, sticking around.

American Women of Letters
and the Nineteenth-Century Sciences

CHAPTER 1

Print and Women's Scientific Affiliations

Over the course of the nineteenth century, the content and institutions of science in the United States altered dramatically. At the century's beginning—when Timothy Dwight appointed Benjamin Silliman to Yale's first professorship of chemistry even though Silliman had no scientific training—one encounters a few catchall categories (natural history, natural philosophy).[1] The word *scientist* had yet to come into general use; "men of science" were independent "savants" searching for new species to classify according to Linnaean taxonomy and to exhibit in their private "cabinets of curiosities."[2]

Few colleges offered science courses except as preparation for medical practice. In small schools, one man would teach all the sciences; in larger institutions, the instructors responded to curricular need by teaching chemistry, astronomy, natural history, geology, botany, or natural philosophy as circumstances dictated. All scientific instruction assumed that science would bolster piety because it would show the universe as governed by regular laws that could only have been installed by a Creator.[3] The miniscule number of antebellum scientific professionals is variably estimated from a high of 475 (Bruce) to a low of 138 (Beaver).[4] Thomas Jefferson's funding of the Lewis and Clark expedition in 1801 initiated governmental involvement in science, which continued in such enterprises as the Fremont and Stansbury expeditions in the West, the Wilkes naval expedition, and above all the U.S. Coast and Geodetic Survey.[5]

Around 1880, the number of scientists began to increase dramatically. By century's end, a range of tightly demarcated (albeit provisional) scientific fields requiring expensive and continually updated equipment had been firmly installed in academic institutions. These institutions, designed to create knowledge, transmitted the knowledge they created to professionals in training. The previously loose connections among academic, industrial, and governmental science had fused. Cabinets of curiosities and private museums still existed, but they were no longer of scientific importance compared to such institutional collections as Harvard's museum of comparative zoology or the Smithsonian in Washington. Individual scientists might be pious, but now they separated their science from their religious practice.

The increasing mathematizing of all the sciences furthered their development but estranged them irrevocably from the general public. Persons sweeping the skies with crude telescopes had been eclipsed by centralized, costly observatories. Those on the lookout for birds or butterflies or plants now ventured into nature for the fun of imagining themselves as scientists, or simply for the love of natural beauty. There was no longer any pretense that such people were doing "real" science.

This turn-of-the-century configuration is what we continue to recognize today as "science."[6] The sciences never dominated antebellum American popular discourse as politics, history, or entertainment did; but before the Civil War they figured more prominently in such discourse than they do now. For many reasons and to many thinkers, it seemed vital both that the national self should become scientific and that scientists be firmly connected to the general public.

Practicing scientists and their advocates defined scientific abstraction as the highest expression of human intellect while declaring that the technologies derived from abstract science—steam power, telegraphy, fertilizer, metallurgy, anesthesia—were the pinnacle of human progress. Nationalists who imagined the United States as an especially modern, especially progressive, especially entrepreneurial nation made the fruits of scientific knowledge central to American values. As John Kasson observes, dominant antebellum political ideology easily accommodated technological developments, which were in turn theorized as the concretization of scientific knowledge.[7] Chapter 10 of Toqueville's *Democracy in America*, even while it proposed that Americans were "more addicted to practical than to theoretical science," also opined that

> the more democratic, enlightened, and free a nation is, the greater
> will be the number of these interested promoters of scientific ge-
> nius and the more will discoveries immediately applicable to pro-

ductive industry confer on the authors gain, fame, and even power. For in democracies the working class take a part in public affairs; and public honors as well as pecuniary remuneration may be awarded to those who deserve them.

Advocates of science in the antebellum United States, whether familiar with Toqueville's pronouncements or not, worked to bring his vision into being. From a more global, imperialistic perspective, ideas about scientific advance fitted seamlessly into the Protestant-republican synthesis whereby a free people would inevitably reach the greatest intellectual as well as political and religious heights. The obvious superiority of Old World to U.S. science—an anomaly in a generally untroubled narrative of New World superiority (of course the presence of slavery was another "trouble" here)—could be used by scientific nationalists to argue for the widest possible dissemination of scientific knowledge among the people, as well as the greatest possible funding from all levels of government.[8]

To educate the public in science, presumably, would simultaneously introduce the subjects to scientists of the future while instilling in nonscientists the appreciation of science necessary to gain popular support. That a scientifically educated populace could be brought into being seemed possible in an era when, as I have observed, the sciences were not yet highly mathematical; when scientific intelligibility "did not exceed the reach of amateurs and laymen" (Bozeman, xiii); when scientific theories, based on familiar data, could often be expressed in vernacular language (Kohlstedt, *Formation* 59); when there existed a "common language of scientific prose and literary prose" in Anglo-America such that Darwin could write *The Origin of Species* not only for "the confraternity of scientists but with the assumption that his work would be readable by any educated reader" (Beer, 41). As well as reaching educated readers, science advocates in the United States could appeal to auditors, who packed halls across the nation for popular lectures on science.

𝒯he question my study seeks to answer is how and why the sciences were made available to women, by women. From the start, science posed a special case for the female intellect. The term "men of science" really meant men (Hugh Slotten, 8). Searchers for female precedent found virtually no women of science in the historical record. Only one woman—Maria Mitchell, who discovered a comet in 1847 (see chapter 7)—was recognized for scientific achievement before the Civil War. Margaret Rossiter, the historian of U.S. women scientists, starts the clock in 1870, when the opening of true higher education to women coincided with the vast expansion of the scientific professions themselves.

But there are of course ways to be involved in science without being a scientist. Even here, however, it was a particularly vexed question whether the sciences lay not only beyond the limits of a woman's allotted labors, but also beyond the limits of her intellect—and what, if this were so, it meant about her mind.

Throughout the century, gender conservatives became increasingly willing to cede belles lettres and language-centered subjects to women, and also to accept the wisdom of instructing women in the political ideologies that would explain the advantages of life for women in a republic. But science seemed to be different. The most reactionary thinkers claimed outright that women were not intelligent enough to understand it. More subtle critics proposed on the one hand that women's immersion in detail made them incapable of rigorous scientific abstraction. That is, women were too earthy to do science. They claimed on the other hand that women were too physically delicate to descend into mines, hack at rocks, or work with dangerous chemicals—and were at the same time too fanciful to focus on science's gritty details. That is, women were not earthy enough to do science.

Many women, attracted to an image of themselves as ethereal and otherworldly, agreed. The intensely intellectual Margaret Fuller, for example, told students in 1837 that it was "not to be expected that women would be good Astronomers or Geologists or Metaphysicians" but "they could and are expected to be good historians" (Capper, 235); she was attracted to the idea of women's nervous, electrical kind of intellectuality (Magner, 67) versus men's more muscular, mechanical mode of thinking. These arguments retain appeal; they explain in part why, at the outset of the twenty-first century, as the saying still goes, "girls (still) don't do science."[9]

Nevertheless, the Enlightenment-inspired project of demonstrating the intellectual parity of women and men assumed that, properly instructed, women could understand anything that men could understand. And it dictated that women ought to be so instructed. Thus—because the sciences represented the highest instantiation of the human mind (Isaac Newton held the place that Albert Einstein holds today), and because many men of high culture were incorporating ideals of scientific literacy into the mental equipment of the U.S. citizen—a small but assertive and influential group of nineteenth-century women of letters used their access to print to argue energetically that women ought to know the sciences. Their work conjoined an optimistic belief that science, the highest expression of human intellect, was on the march, with the pessimistic concession that women, notwithstanding their equal intellects, might never under any circumstances expect to do original science themselves the way men might. The advocates described and exhibited a variety of affiliative styles, simultaneously insisting that women could comprehend science and that they had to remain on what Sally Kohlstedt has aptly called the scientific "periphery." The advocacy of science always had an element of melancholy in it, because its recommendations so clearly conceded secondary status to women even as they tried to argue otherwise.

This work of affiliation made its mark on the culture, partly because of the women's public eminence, and partly because the compromise suited the culture at that time. Advocates of science for women claimed no more than what many by this time were ready to give them, reflecting as much as they initiated a general vogue for science among white women from the middle, upper-middle, and upper classes. Kohlstedt observes that such women are on record from an early moment in national history as promoters of the natural sciences, a fact she takes to indicate "the diffusion of the subject" (*Formation*, 10). Robert Bruce, who makes a point of women's systematic exclusion from professional science before 1876, also notes that by the second quarter of the nineteenth century it had become appropriate for women to take up science "as a polite study," which they might pursue formally in numerous academies and seminaries that had "invested in expensive telescope, physical and chemical apparatus, and natural history collections" (78).

Thomas Woody, the great scholar of women's education, finds chemistry offered in women's schools as early as 1798; his survey of antebellum texts turns up books of astronomy, botany, chemistry, geography, geology, mechanics, meteorology, mineralogy, natural history, natural philosophy, and zoology (229, 552–562). Of course a list of science courses in school bulletins does not indicate how much science any particular woman studied, nor does it speak to the quality of instruction she would have received. But at the least, all these science offerings bespeak an intention.

In "Ladies' Record," Sarah Hale's editorial roundup of curricular offerings in the *Ladies' Magazine,* one discovers, for March 1833, that women could study mathematics, geography, natural philosophy, chemistry, botany, and astronomy at Ipswich Female Academy (6:142); for April 1833, that Catharine Beecher's Hartford seminary taught botany, mineralogy, geology, natural history, geography, chemistry, natural philosophy, and astronomy (6:176); for December 1833, that "Miss Fiske's School for Young Ladies" included geography, natural philosophy, astronomy, geology, chemistry, botany, and natural history (6:552); and for February 1836, that Dr. Webber's female seminary has "a fine chemical, philosophical, electrical, and other apparatus" (9:116–120). In 1937, in Hale's later "Ladies' Mentor" column in *Godey's Lady's Book*, one learns that the "Female Seminary at New Hampton" taught algebra, botany, geometry, physiology, natural history, and geography (14:46–47]); and the St. Louis Female Seminary taught algebra, geography, botany, chemistry, mineralogy, geology and astronomy, and anatomy and physiology (14:140]).

Deborah Warner, summarizing a variety of sources, describes an antebellum scene of women studying astronomy, natural philosophy, chemistry, natural history, human biology (i.e., physiology and anatomy) in formal curricula, in popular lectures, and at home ("Science Education"). Barbara Gates and Ann Shteir, who posit popular science as its "own form of knowledge, shaped in relation to the needs of audiences" (4), have described work by English women who wrote popular science texts, finding that such writers seldom thought they were "hampered by their gender"; they "had an audience, liked the job of informing it, and were appreciated" (4). In *Cultivating Women*, Shteir writes specifically about genteel Englishwomen's longstanding interest in botany; Patricia Phillips chronicles a tradition of general scientific interest among English ladies—the class marker is significant—emerging in the seventeenth century in tandem with modern science itself, and continuing strongly throughout the eighteenth and nineteenth centuries.[10]

For the particular case of medical discourse in the United States, Susan Wells finds women participating actively from an early date. And while Gates and Shteir find (for England) that a previously fluid gender situation solidified at the close of the nineteenth century (10), Wells theorizes (for the United States) that uninformed though well-meaning feminists today, erroneously assuming that women have been excluded from public culture until recently, have misread the record. In short, there is growing awareness that a broad range of nonprofessional and quasi-professional scientific activities were pursued by U.S. women. More evidence is likely to emerge.

The English precedent served American women both as authorization and challenge. The immensely influential educational theorist Maria Edgeworth, along with her father, had written scientific textbooks—the "Harry and Lucy" series—for youths of both sexes. By far the most important English example was the Swiss-English Jane Marcet, spouse of a professor of medicine, whose *Conversations on Chemistry* (first published in 1805, pirated, reissued, updated numerous times thereafter) educated at least two generations of practicing chemists in the United States. Michael Faraday, who called Marcet a "good friend to me, as she must have been to many of the human race," said he was drawn to chemistry by encountering her book (Tyndall, 7; Gillispie, *Edge,* 436). Her case allowed Hale, in *Woman's Record,* to condemn men who spurned "the idea of a female philosopher, while the foundation of their own science has been made by the 'Conversations on Chemistry,' which book has for more than thirty years been the general text-book for young men in Great-Britain and the United States" (732).[11]

Marcet, who also wrote texts on natural philosophy and vegetable physiology, composed her books as dialogues among a teacher, Mrs. B., and two students, Caroline and Emily, whose different ages allowed the author to represent stages in mental development. Mrs. B.'s pedagogy, which encouraged open discussion and question asking, defined its protocols as unmistakably female, even while tackling male subject matter. For example, when Mrs. B. says, "You have seen the manner in which sulphuric acid decomposes all combustible substances, whether animal, vegetable, or mineral, and burns them by means of its oxygen," Caroline responds, "I have very unintentionally repeated the experiment on my gown, by letting a drop of the acid fall upon it, and it has made a stain, which, I suppose, will never wash out"; to which Mrs. B. answers in turn, "No, certainly; for before you can put it into water the spot will become a hole, as the acid has literally burnt the muslin" (83–84).

Marcet's example inspired many imitative "familiar" textbooks on diverse subjects. These include not only the conventionally "feminine" schoolbook floras that merged flower lore and poetry with elementary botanical information (e.g., Lucy Hooper and Sarah Hale herself), but also more obviously pedagogical scientific texts for young people and those charged with their education. These books were perhaps especially geared to anxious mothers who had to introduce their children to subjects in which they themselves had no background. Among these U.S. women writers are Margaret Coxe on conchology; Mary Townsend on entomology (*Life in the Insect World; or, Conversations upon Insects, Between an Aunt and Her Nieces*); Mary Hall, Louisa Tuthill, Catharine Beecher, and Harriet Beecher Stowe on geography; Mary Swift on natural philosophy; Mary Griffith on optics; Jane Kilby Welsh on geology and mineralogy (*Familiar Lessons in Mineralogy and Geology: Designed for the Use of Young Persons and Lyceums*); Laura Johnson on botany (*Botanical Teacher for North America*); Elizabeth Cary Agassiz on radiates (*A First Lesson in Natural History*—see chapter 6). None of these women claimed expertise as an original scientist, but each promised to convey findings of scientific men accurately and in language appropriate for their intended audience.

These books found a niche in a complicated system of scientific print artifacts ranging from the journals of elite science designed to communicate and publicize original findings on down, occupying probably the lowest rung on the educational print ladder. Almost without exception they were based on more advanced science textbooks written by men—textbooks used in women's as well as men's schools. Course offerings in the women's schools are typically represented by naming the textbooks: the St. Louis seminary that Hale noticed in "Ladies' Mentor" announced such courses as "Comstock's Chemistry," "Comstock's Mineralogy," "Smith's Anatomy and Physiology," and "Burritt's Geography of the Heavens" (14:140). These are all male-authored texts. The women's textbooks simplified the men's textbooks for primary school use and for the home instruction of young children. In fact, among American women apparently only Almira Phelps (see chapter 2)—and then only in the case of her botany—wrote a textbook that competed successfully against male-authored books.

Students and teachers wanted authoritative textbooks, and the authority of science was male. Poorly paid professional scientists in the antebellum era augmented their incomes and extended their influence through widely circulated textbooks based on their college courses. These were the books used by women in the advanced schools, a fact that reminds us that women had access to the whole print array, including but by no means limited to materials produced expressly for women. This meant it was far easier for a woman to pursue scientific interests as a consumer than as a producer.

William Gilmore notes the range of science books available in rural Vermont libraries: books on mathematics, botany, agricultural science, chemistry, geology, meteorology, zoology, mineralogy, astronomy, natural philosophy, and electricity. He observes that newspapers, periodicals, pamphlets, and broadsides reported constantly on the rapid developments in scientific knowledge, conveying not only content but also the aura of scientific advance (472). The *Scientific American* began life as an illustrated weekly about invention and technology in 1845. Frequent allusions and many editions suggest that popular science books by important European scientists were much in demand—for example, the astronomer John Herschel's *Preliminary Discourse on the Study of Natural Philosophy*; the organic chemist Justus Liebig's *Familiar Letters on Chemistry, and its Relation to Commerce, Physiology, and Agriculture*; above all, the first two volumes of *Cosmos*, by the great physical geographer Alexander von Humboldt. Only one woman figured in this group—Mary Somerville—but her *Connexion of the Physical Sciences* and *Physical Geography* were conceded by all to equal any similar books by men.

The holdings of circulating libraries and the evidence of curricular bro-
chures convey only part of the picture, for many popular science books were
bought by individuals and families. The Peter Parley textbook industry organized by Samuel G. Goodrich included a twenty-volume octavo "Cabinet Library"—"the only library that has been expressly written for a School and
Family Library" according to its publicity—that contained fourteen books of
biography and history, along with three of geography and three on the other
sciences.[12] Parley's 352–page *Glance at the Physical Sciences* covers astronomy; natural philosophy including properties of matter, mechanical powers, hydrostatics, hydraulics, pneumatics, optics, acoustics, electricity,
galvanism, magnetism and electromagnetism, mathematics, meteorology,
chemistry, geology, mineralogy, botany, and zoology. A book on geology and
another on zoology completed the "Cabinet's" science offerings.

Magazines were available to women and men, young and old; specialized journals in such fields as horticulture and agriculture appealed directly
to both genders. Popular journals, including some specifically designed for
women (above all, the *Lady's Book*, which Sarah Hale edited for forty years
beginning in 1837), featured articles about science. Women as well as men
attended the scientific lectures offered in lyceums, mechanics' institutes, and
other public venues. Popular lecturers on science—always men—included
Benjamin Silliman, chemistry professor from Yale, who is said to have delivered over five hundred public science lectures around the nation; Amos
Eaton, geologist and botanist from the Rensselaer school (a Silliman student),
an early advocate of women's scientific literacy who tutored Emma Willard,
Almira Phelps, and Mary Lyon; Edward Hitchcock, geologist (another
Silliman product); Dionysius Lardner, a Scotsman whose lectures on natural
philosophy in the United States were extremely well attended and, when published in this country as well, ran through eleven editions by 1849; Benjamin
Silliman Jr., who followed his father at Yale and on the circuit; and above
all, perhaps, the zoologist Louis Agassiz of Harvard, the best-known scientist in the United States before the Civil War. His charismatic proselytizing
for natural history inspired the formation of hundreds of "Agassiz Clubs"
around the nation in the wake of his appearances—clubs to which women as
well as men belonged.

Through the pursuit of recreational natural history—botanizing and
birding above all, for which the best guidebooks were available (Welch)—a
great many women managed to make science a living presence in their lives.
Sarah Alden Ripley of Massachusetts, whose passion was identifying mush-
rooms, testified to a botanical "mania" in her town as early as 1813, following

a series of public lectures by William Dandridge Peck, at that time Harvard's professor of natural history and director of the Cambridge botanical gardens. Ripley attended these lectures with her father (Goodwin, *Remarkable*, 49). She wrote to Mary Moody Emerson of her pleasure in seeing "so rational an amusement in fashion; by exciting a taste for nature it may perhaps render the country supportable to some of our fine ladies" (Goodwin, "Botanic Mania," 20)—by which she meant that botany might make living in the country bearable to ladies of fashion who would otherwise be horribly bored there.

Throughout the century, especially after the 1870s, illustrations from newspapers and magazines depicting public scientific lectures regularly show women in the audience. Representations of scientists at work, and of technological and scientific exhibits, often show women spectators, as though to fix women as the receivers, not producers, of scientific knowledge and yet to verify that a woman was gazing appreciatively at male achievement.[13] Even the decorative "accomplishments" of drawing and watercolor painting were made more sophisticated by science. Scientific illustration developed early on as a profession that women may have dominated (Norwood). Women's flower painting evolved from impressionism toward skilled draftsmanship. The geologist Edward Hitchcock's wife, Orra White—like so many wives of scientists his silent partner—drew geological charts for his Amherst College courses; these were reproduced in his popular textbooks. Hitchcock dedicated his *Religion of Geology* to his wife, thanking her for self-denying labors, sympathies, and cheering counsels; for relieving him "in great measure" from "the cares of a numerous family"; and for what he praises as her much more vivid scientific depictions with her pencil than his with the pen (iii).

If U.S. women of letters working for science figure within a print initiative, they also participate in the work of women doing and learning science in various nonprint ways. But one returns to print as the vehicle most capable of disseminating a perspective, engaging dispersed people in a common activity, and demonstrating—precisely—the literacy of its practitioners. One returns to it also as the vehicle through which women claimed the right to participate in a specifically public discourse; for publication is, precisely, public.

The special status of the sciences as test cases for women's intellect imparted a sense of urgency to this work. Margaret Fuller believed women were not apt to be good scientists, invoking a "female Newton" in "The Great Lawsuit" (repeated in its expansion, *Woman in the Nineteenth Century*) to illustrate the truly extraordinary lengths to which nature might, some day, go in gender bending. In the imagination of possibly the most eloquent spokeswoman of the age for female intellectuality, Newton and the female were polar opposites. Hale's *Woman's Record* singled out Mary Somerville as "the most learned lady of the age, distinguished alike for great scientific knowledge and all womanly virtues; she may well be esteemed an honour to England, her native country, and the glory of her sex throughout the world" (789). For Hale to choose a learned scientific lady as the "glory of her sex" speaks to her sense of what might constitute the ultimate expression of female intellectuality; but she never claimed that Somerville was a female Newton.

Throughout her career, Hale took the line—which after all might be considered more radical than Fuller's, which imagines a parallel gender-freak of nature in the creation of a male Siren—that women should set themselves to learn exactly the subjects they were *not* expected to be good at. She argued early on that for women to study only what was deemed appropriate for them would inevitably produce the gender disparities they took for granted. To advance this argument she featured a (possibly invented) letter to the editor in the *Ladies' Magazine* for May 1833 that complained about women studying science—in order to answer it the next month. "Do you not believe," the complainer wrote, "that one page, devoted to the cause of moral improvement, or which elevates the mind above the dull and insipid concerns of this dirty globe, is worth more than a thousand quires of foolscap written over with descriptions of stones, rocks, and the particles of which they are composed? . . . Science degrades and stupefies the mind. What shall we have to do with mineralogy, cogwheels, trigonometry, and acid gas, in another world?" (6:227–228). Hale's response, in the June issue, titled "Science and Sentiment," maintains that "the best and most sure means of permanently elevating the female mind" requires learning the sciences. Even more daringly she proposes that "the disparity (*inferiority*, as men, perhaps rightly, call it) which is observable between the minds of the sexes, is perpetuated (if not wholly induced) by the almost exclusive attention of women in her mental pursuits to subjects of taste, sentiment, and devotion" (6:273).

In identifying taste, sentiment, and devotion as the hallmarks of the feminized subject (both the person and what she learns), Hale makes clear that if the sciences masculinize the intellect, they also make it more human; the process produces something better than the stereotypically fantasy-prone female mind. In her educational writings, Hannah More, the Englishwoman beloved in the United States for her combination of reformism and conservatism, advocated teaching chemistry to women as a good, solid, unpretentious science, guaranteed therefore to overcome tendencies toward frivolity, fantasy, and self-display. Educators of women also urged the specific value of one or another science for women's practical duties: arithmetic for household accounts; chemistry for cooking and cleaning; natural philosophy for heating and ventilating; physiology for diet and clothing; botany and horticulture for gardening. Science was thus both progressive and conservative: it was progressive because it elevated women's minds and launched them into modernity; it was conservative because it assimilated women to the domestic sphere and valued frugality over finery.

Given that no influential women of letters in the United States ever dared dispute the centrality of piety in an admirable female character, and that a longstanding history of conflict between religion and science is often assumed today, it is important to stress again that antebellum Americans tended to see religion and science as partners. The geographer David Livingstone along with many other historians of science argues that Western science in general has been inspired, not impeded, by religion (69–70, 183–184, 351–352).

The idea that the universe is "regular" and that all its regularities converge toward a single theory is manifestly an article of faith, one easily aligned with the belief in one God characteristic of Judeo-Protestantism. In the nineteenth-century United States there seems to have been consensus at least until the 1870s that religion gave science an ultimate intellectual goal—to discover as much of God's mind as God permitted[14]—while, conversely, science rationalized religion in accordance with the Enlightenment belief in human agency. Under the aegis of an approach loosely labeled "Baconian," according to which science at best was merely descriptive, antebellum scientists did not question the priority of a Divinity who was identified with creative mind. To be sure, particular denominations might be threatened by one or another scientific hypothesis—for example, those biblical literalists for whom the six days of Creation could only mean exactly six successive twenty-four-hour days. But, as scholars like Charles Gillispie (*Genesis*) and Herbert Hovenkamp point out, across a range of public opinion, science and theology coexisted comfortably. In Theodore Bozeman's words, "Antebellum America, marked by a lively and growing interest in natural science, widely nurtured the comfortable assumptions that science and religion, Baconianism *and* the Bible, were harmonious enterprises cooperating toward the same ultimate ends" (xv). Louise Stevenson has described the evangelicalism of Yale's scientific faculty; Bruce cites James D. Dana's observation that in the mid–nineteenth century, the most religious group after the ministers were the scientists (119).

Of course, there were people of skeptical temperament, and it was recognized that a skeptical scientist had powerful support for his views. Timothy Dwight had appointed Benjamin Silliman as Yale's first professor of chemistry precisely because he was "resolved to meet squarely the Enlightenment's challenge to Christian faith by introducing chemistry and natural history into the curriculum and placing them in the care of one whom he himself had imbued with sound Christian understanding" (Greene, 11). But, by the time that science study became a fixture of higher education, it had been made safe for Protestantism.

Therefore, since antebellum science rightly understood posed no threat to religion rightly understood, women of letters who advocated the sciences spent little time explaining why they comported with religious belief. On the contrary, they freely offered science as an aid to piety. If there was concern that scientists themselves might drift away from religion, then people with unshakable faith needed to discipline them, which they could do only if they could impress scientists with their command of the material. Women thus were not only to become rationally pious by studying science, but their piety, being rational, would combat skepticism in a way that a fuzzier, less instructed emotionality might not. As Hale put it: "Woman has a quicker capacity for comprehending moral truth or sentiment than man, but she cannot explain this truth, nor expose error to *his comprehension*, unless her intellect has been, in some measure, trained like his. Men have little sympathy with intuitive knowledge, or feeling—'pure Reason'—in the doctrine of Kant: hence they must have the truth set before them in its relations with 'practical Reason'" (*Woman's Record*, xlvii).

Too, in an atmosphere fraught with sectarian discord, the global acceptability of the kind of nondoctrinal piety engendered by contemplation of the lawful universe worked to teach religion without teaching dogma. Woody notes that even in sectarian schools, women's curricula increasingly featured moral philosophy, natural theology, and science over Bible study and direct religious teaching. "The advance of science, and its rapid extension into schools, was doubtless a great factor in promoting this tendency to explain Christian religion rationally" (414–415).

Of course, the group of women who advocated science would not have been inclined to attack it. More generally, however, few women taking up the cause of female intellect were prepared to invoke the images of witchcraft, superstition, irrationality, unpredictability, or earthbound embodiment with which women had so long been associated. The age of reason, which was identical to the emergence of a scientific approach to the natural world, meant precisely the end of superstition. Given this premise, nineteenth-century

U.S. women's writing about science seldom queries its findings or its premises, and thus has little connection to today's range of antiscience feminisms. Certainly, a large number of women declined to interest themselves in science altogether or argued along stereotypical lines that women were interested in beauty rather than facts (see chapters 6 and 9). But the most extensively developed opposition to science-as-such among nineteenth-century women came from fundamentalist Christians and futuristic Spiritualists. Obviously, neither group deployed anything remotely like the antiscience approaches of contemporary postmodern or social constructionist feminism.[15]

In their own time, nineteenth-century women of letters speaking for science represented themselves as the voice of "woman" at her most politically progressive and liberal. Therefore it is important to iterate that their strategies all accepted the reality of sexual difference in the ultimate relation of women to science. Affiliation was their way of negotiating this difference. Cannily drawing on widely held cultural assumptions, they presented the occupational gender divide in science as women's opportunity. Ceding most of the doing of science—the production of new scientific knowledge in the field, laboratory, or study—to men, they allotted tasks like disseminating, popularizing, appreciating, and consuming it to women, thereby linking the genders in a constructive division of labor. Women, by bringing science to the people, made a market for the scientist and his product. Without that market, science could not survive the rigors of democratic competition. If women needed science to launch them into the modern world, science needed women equally to help them maintain the position it was seeking to occupy in the nation's intellectual and material life.

These ideas of course implied a middle-class view of the two sexes—working man and leisured woman, utilitarian man and decorative woman. But the aim was never to restrict middle-class status to those who happened, at any particular historical juncture, to inhabit the middle social rank. On the contrary, these women imagined a coming day when brawny laboring women would vanish from the earth. They dreamed of a Protestant republic in which the status and comforts of middle-class living were available to all. They dreamed of a time when all women would be genteel women. Indeed, the very possibility that women might pursue scientific interests could be seen as a benefit of middle-class leisure. In turn, because middle-class leisure—especially for women whose domestic destiny involved kitchens, sewing rooms, nurseries, and sickrooms—was unthinkable without the enabling conveniences of technology, science was signally responsible for the production of the middle-class woman herself. Ultimately, even the intuitive spirituality that might distinguish ideal women from ideal men could be understood as the outcome of applied science. Science had not invented female spirituality, but it had created the social conditions in which such spirituality might flourish.

A long segment from Harriot K. Hunt's 1856 memoir *Glances and Glimpses* provides a rich example of science advocacy from the woman's point of view I have been outlining here. Hunt (1805–1875) was a Boston doctor who practiced successfully among women and children for years before medical schooling or licensing became available to women. (She figures in chapter 10.) Late in her career she applied unsuccessfully to Harvard for permission to attend medical lectures, but in the very memoir where she vents her frustration ("General and special anatomy,—shall I ever forgive the Harvard Medical College for depriving me of a thorough knowledge of that science?" [122]), she methodically celebrates the scientific advances that had transformed life for the better since 1800. She begins by pointing to the interrelated impact of leisure and goods on ordinary lives in an agricultural economy:

> Every improvement in agriculture tends to set free mother earth, and enables her to bring forth her treasures more and more abundantly to bless her children. Every invention in agricultural machinery proves the internal resources of man to aid her in yielding up her vegetation with less and less labor to himself, whilst other inventions are constantly increasing his comforts and supplying him with conveniences, elegancies, and luxuries of which former generations never dreamed. (240–241)

Alluding next to urban life, she observes that "within the last fifty years, science has supplied all our large cities with water, and has furnished them with sewers for the draining off of all impurities" and that, even more impressively perhaps, also "during the last fifty years a mineral which had been regarded as wholly useless, has been dug from the earth and forced by the ingenuity of science, in giving up its imprisoned caloric, to warm millions of people by grates, stoves, furnaces, and batteries of steam pipes. This same mineral, by parting with its hydrogen and carbon in another form, dispels the darkness of night, for the most brilliant light is, by science, elaborated from the blackest substance" (241).

Moreover, "during this period science has, through the agency of steam, provided the most rapid and convenient modes of travelling by land and water;

thus bringing distant countries and States into near proximity, introducing nations to each other and increasing their resources of knowledge and intelligence, by affording opportunities to all to examine the natural curiosities and works of art which each contain; thus stimulating the social elements and promoting those friendly relations, which will ultimately bind all peoples, nations, and tongues into one great brotherhood" (241–242). The vision of a world linked by commerce and travel is at once Utopian universalist and imperially Western, unselfconsciously advanced as self-evidently better than a world ruled by suspicion and divided by national hatreds.

If, to Hunt, science has been good for the general population, it has especially helped women, and poor women above all: "Constructiveness watched the weary hours spent by indigence and worth in plying the needle to clothe mankind, and invented the sewing machine. She looked into the kitchen and substituted first, stoves for the inconvenient pot-hooks of former years; then she invented cooking ranges. . . . Science looked into the laundry also and pitied the laborers there—when behold! the invention of washing and wringing machines and mangles, and conveniences for heating, without smutting irons" (242). Hunt also mentions photography, telegraphy, and anesthesia, this last of particular significance to a doctor: science "has walked our hospitals, and whilst weeping tears of sympathy over the sufferings of those who are carried to the operating-room, discovered the means of producing insensibility to every pain" (243).

When she writes about gaslight, Hunt uses the transformation of black coal into light as a metaphor for the advent of modernity: "the most brilliant light is, by science, elaborated from the blackest substance, thus symbolizing those scintillations of light which are now emanating from minds once in the darkness of ignorance" (241). The Cartesian implications for women in this symbolizing are explicit: scientific advance promises "the complete triumph of mind over matter, and the obliteration of that strongest of all distinctions which characterize the sexes, making it possible for woman to *share* in the duties and responsibilities, honors and profits of every employment and office" (244). As machinery increasingly does the "heavy work of the world," men as well as women "will rule by intellectual, and *moral*, and religious power, not by physical strength and material force" (244–245). The brilliant light emanating from minds once in the "darkness of ignorance" also alludes obliquely to the gender-specific issues of superstition and witchcraft I have mentioned earlier. The supposed aptness of men's minds for abstract, instrumental scientific thinking as opposed to women's preference for the irrational—if true—puts women at exceptional disadvantage in a world making haste toward a rationalized future. From Hunt's standpoint, science rightly understood actually gives more to women than it does to to men. And it is therefore more important for women than for men to achieve this right understanding.

To be sure, in talking about "women's" acquisition of scientific knowledge, one is not talking about all women. The women who did this work for science hailed mainly from the northern states, especially from New England. They imagined themselves addressing those who were already or potentially much like themselves. As we know, throughout the century New England women had the highest literacy rates and the most education of any group of women in the nation; teachers around the country were chiefly recruited from their ranks. As for science, its earliest American flowering had been in Philadelphia, but according to Bruce, Boston surpassed Philadelphia around 1840 as the residence of the largest number of U.S. scientists even though Philadelphia was twice as large as Boston at that time. By 1850, "with less than 5% of the nation's population, Massachusetts produced more than 20% of the leading scientists"; this "per capita lead" remained "undiminished into the last quarter of the century" (Bruce, 33).

Thus science and New England women converged to their mutual benefit, although especially to the benefit of women like themselves. Science helped them see themselves as the advance guard—by no means arrived at the highest point the sex would eventually reach, but leading the way through their acquisition of scientific habits of mind and scientific knowledge. These habits and this knowledge distinguished them from the unenlightened, the happily ignorant, and—more invidiously—from primitive or uncivilized peoples. Some of these women believed that other races could never achieve the heights of science, while some believed that reason was a universal human attribute. All believed in the ideal of reason, whose success had, they thought rightly or no, improved the lives of women everywhere.

CHAPTER 2

Almira Phelps and the Discipline of Botany

*A*lmira Hart Lincoln Phelps (1793–
1884) enjoyed a long professional life as a women's educator, assisting her
older sister Emma Willard at Willard's Troy Female Seminary and later serving for years as principal of the Patapsco Female Institute in Maryland. Not
only did she make science the centerpiece of a curricular program designed
to transform unruly girls into self-disciplined women, her work figured centrally in making natural science a school subject around the nation. Her *Familiar Lectures on Botany*, published first in 1829, ran through at least
twenty-eight editions over some forty-four years (the last came out in 1872),
selling possibly 350,000 copies in all (Bolzau, 357). It also appeared in various abridgments, of which *Botany for Beginners* was the best known.[1] She
also wrote science texts in geology, chemistry, and natural philosophy.[2] The
chemistry text sold some 50,000 copies; the natural philosophy went through
fourteen editions (Bolzau, 257, 323). Sarah Hale wrote in *Woman's Record*
that "no woman in America, nor any in Europe, excepting Mrs. Marcet and
Mrs. Somerville, has made such useful and numerous contributions to the
stock of available scientific knowledge" (771).

Hale's word "available" hits exactly the right note, for Phelps's second
public purpose after reconstructing feckless femininity through subjection to
rational discipline was to channel science from experts to the populace, to
make the populace more scientific and the scientists more popular. An ad-
herent of early national ideology long after the early national period, she believed in a republican government by statesmen chosen by an instructed,
enlightened people. She yoked her traditional politics to scientific literacy.

"The time has been, that knowledge was confined to a very few, who were regarded by the ignorant world around them with superstitious dread, and who ruled over the minds of their fellow beings with the most despotic sway: indeed it was thought that men must be kept in ignorance in order that they might be governed. It is now found to be the case, that the most enlightened people are the most willing to submit to such laws as are necessary for the public good" (Phelps, *Chemistry*, 7–8).

Throughout the second third of the nineteenth century, thousands of schoolchildren encountered botany and were indoctrinated in the general idea of pervasive order in the natural world through Phelps's text. They also learned to substitute the evidential testing of hypotheses for the magical thinking supposedly characteristic of childhood and unenlightened nations. As Frederick Rudolph puts it, "because she wished to use texts that would lend themselves to inductive, objective teaching, she had to write them, and in doing so she supplied American schools with some of the tools that brought the sciences into the standard course of study" ("Almira Hart," 3:59).

Phelps used her own success forthrightly although modestly as evidence of the particular fitness of women as science popularizers. Though she never claimed to have discovered even one new species—the achievement that throughout the era signified botanical originality—her textbook success made her one of the science's intellectual leaders in the United States for more than twenty years. The American Association for the Advancement of Science (AAAS)—which had been organized in 1848—elected her to its membership in 1859, making her only the second woman (the first was Maria Mitchell) in the association. From this platform she argued passionately for the superiority of her traditional kind of taxonomical botany over newer, more specialized models of the science. For her this was no mere academic debate, but a struggle for the very soul of science.

Before Phelps, botany in the United States was formally taught only in colleges, under the rubric *materia medica*, a survey of medicinal plant properties for medical students. After her book came out, the number of courses in botany in U.S. schools increased more than in any other science, although botany never caught up with chemistry, natural philosophy, and astronomy (Keeney, 56–57). According to Thomas Woody, between 1830 and 1870 some 82 percent of the women's schools began to offer botany; 90 percent offered natural philosophy, 90 percent chemistry, 85 percent astronomy, and 60 percent geology (58). But these other sciences were not about the living world; thanks in large part to Phelps's work, botany became the school science that denoted the whole domain of natural history and hence, after the Civil War, opened the door to biology.[3] Gathering plants on botanizing expeditions, students learned to do fieldwork; dissecting and analyzing their finds under a microscope, they learned laboratory techniques.

It was Phelps, too, who articulated and circulated what became the standard rationale for teaching botany, making it paradigmatic for all natural science. Botany was "a means of improving mental function through developing the powers of observation, memory, and reasoning"; it encouraged analytic thinking and "love of the Creator" (Keeney, 44, 52); it would "enlarge the mind" and "render life more happy, and more correspondent to the dignity of our nature" because its objects are "the *real existences*, with which the great Author of our own being has surrounded us" (Phelps, *Fireside*, 222).[4]

*P*helps began her lifelong educational career as a teacher with the general aim of disciplining and transforming the imperfect female character. She saw women (herself included) as a particularly unruly and vulnerable population with, therefore, an especially strong need for rational discipline. She selected botany as her tool not because of women's likeness to delicate, beautiful flowers, but because the Linnaean taxonomy through which the vegetable world was systematized could be used as a vivid example of universal law and order. Conceding that flowers were indeed "beautiful and delicate," she reminded students that "these beautiful creations of Almighty Power are designed not merely to delight by their fragrance, colour, and form, but to illustrate the most logical divisions of Science, the deepest principles of Physiology, and the goodness of God" (*Familiar Lectures*, 1836, 8).

Thus her approach to botany differs from the English tendency (as described in Ann Shteir's *Cultivating* and Londa Schiebinger's *Mind Has No Sex?*) to recommend botany for women on the grounds that their natural affinity for flowers would make the subject delightful and easy. Phelps wrote often about overcoming initial student resistance to a subject whose Latinate terminology made it seem dry and difficult (*Familiar Lectures,* 1836, 190). She asked: Why are you, students, "of more value than the lilies of the field and the sparrows"? and she answered: Because of "the very principle within you which enables you to make this inquiry" (*Fireside*, 118–119). She used science as an implement precisely to pry women out of nature and move them into culture.

Her devotion to Linnaean taxonomy as the end as well as the beginning of the subject was what brought her into conflict with some of the newer developments in botanical science over the decades. She never lost her sense that God had implanted taxonomical principles in human minds to enable them to make sense of their environment by classifying its features, and that this systematizing was—or ought to be—the whole of science. "To watch Nature in her operations, to note the processes by which these operations are carried on, and from particular cases to form general conclusions, is now the professed aim of men of science" (170). The purpose of science was to identify—to observe rightly, and group properly, natural objects that were already there.

It was inconceivable to Phelps that the God who had invented history so as to enable human progress through general enlightenment would then further this aim through sciences whose difficulties put them beyond almost everybody's reach. Thus, the very simplicity of Linnaean rules—plants were identified by counting the number of pistils and stamens in the flower—recommended its approach to her as better comporting with what science ought to be than more complex models. If, however, Linnaean taxonomy offered a device for imposing order on the world whose reliability guaranteed that law and order really existed in the universe, yet, because its rules were so plainly "artificial"—the system was called "artificial" by advocates and detractors alike—it allotted to science a descriptive, not creative, function. "Questions as to the essence of matter, the secret springs of the machinery of the universe, and the first causes of things" are, she claimed "by common consent, exploded as pointless and unfathomable" (170). "No systems of man can change the laws and operation of Nature; though by systems, we are enabled to gain a knowledge of these laws and relations" (13). "To study the compound nature of substances, to classify, arrange, and by various combinations to beautify the world of matter, to cultivate the faculties of mind, until stronger and brighter the mental vision sees facts and principles before invisible; these are the high privileges bestowed on man;—but to *add one particle to matter, or one new faculty to the mind, is beyond the power of the whole human race*" (*Familiar Lectures*, 1836, 123).

For Phelps, botany had practical as well as ideological advantages. Among natural sciences it was the most taxonomically developed of the natural sciences; objects for study were plentiful, close at hand, and easy to work with. Because plants were presumably insentient, they could be dissected without guilt; but because at the same time they were "organized"—that is, were living wholes composed of organs with distinctly different functions contributing to the whole—they introduced students to the basic idea of organic nature underlying all anatomical and physiological study. And because the animating principle of the flower was no less mysterious than the animating principle of the human being, botany could instill a rational, nondoctrinaire piety in a way that study of inert matter could not.

If Phelps thought the benefits to students of studying botany were incalculable, she did not think the current of science flowed exclusively from the scientist to the student. She believed that the benefits to scientists of popular science study were also incalculable in a republic, where no courts existed to supply patronage. The public support that scientists needed involved the support of knowledgeable women; women not only comprised half the population but also (she believed) exerted enormous influence on the national character as instructors of sons and companions of husbands.[5] The United States would not take its rightful place as the most modern nation, she thought, until its women understood the importance of science to modernity well enough to appreciate and disseminate it.

This mutual need of women for science and science for women, in her view, called for an intermediary to handle the transaction between them. This was the scientific popularizer, whom Phelps represented both as its embodiment and its advocate. She argued effectively that scientific popularizing was a necessary field and also especially suited to female capacities, experience, and interests.

Emma Willard's Troy Female Seminary, established in 1821, was probably the most celebrated girls' academy in the country before the Civil War. Designed mainly for a wealthy clientele (although up to 10 percent of its students at any time were teacher trainees on scholarship), the school offered an alternative curriculum to the music, dancing, drawing, and French—the so-called accomplishments—typical of elite girls' education in the early republic. Rather than aiming to duplicate what she saw as the corrupt pretensions of this pseudoaristocratic education, Willard tried to create a women's education suitable for the wives and mothers of enfranchised republican men. Constantly aware of developments in the men's schools, she saw from the first how important it was to teach science to girls. Known for her work as a historian, and committed to history as the most important subject for women, she made science a close second and installed a strong science component in the Troy curriculum from the start.

Almira, her younger sister, joined the Troy faculty in 1823 when she was widowed and left with two small children to support. Natural history was one of her teaching assignments. (Willard, who was mathematically talented, handled natural philosophy and astronomy herself in the early years, as well as chemistry.) While Phelps had no background in the subject, she had one of the era's foremost science teachers and popularizers, Amos Eaton (1776–1842), as a neighbor. Eaton, who had studied briefly with Benjamin Silliman at Yale, pursued botany, geology, chemistry, mineralogy, and zoology.[6] Stephen Van Rensselaer, the great *patroon* of the Hudson Valley, successively appointed him geological and agricultural surveyor of Albany County (summer 1820), geological and agricultural surveyor of Rensselaer County (summer 1821), director of the survey preceding the building of the Erie Canal (summer 1822), and finally professor at the new Rensselaer Scientific School at Troy (1824).

This school, an early version of the agricultural and mechanical colleges established after the Civil War through the Morrell Act, was designed—in Eaton's words—to qualify "teachers for instructing the sons and daughters of farmers and mechanics, by lectures or otherwise, in the application of experimental chemistry, philosophy and natural history, to agriculture, domestic economy, the arts and manufactures." As these words show, Eaton's vision encompassed women equally with men; he wanted women to learn mathematics, geology, physical geography, botany, and "that part of chemistry, which illustrates by experiments, the principles of domestic operations as they regard health and economy" (McAllister, 368, 490).

Eaton's public lectures in New York and New England were always open to and heavily attended by women. He encouraged students and staff at Willard's school to attend his lectures at Rensselaer. He tutored many women privately, including Willard, Phelps, and Mary Lyon, founder of Mount Holyoke Seminary (see chapter 9). He even allowed some women to lecture on science—to men—at Rensselaer itself (McAllister, 484, 414). Committed to the Linnaean botanical system as a way of mastering the natural world, he said in 1819 that "it is among the hobbies of the Troy folks (and I ride it the hardest) to make botany a part of the common school learning in the summer season. We intend to have our Yankee girls teach it" (McAllister, 220). Eaton's particular interest in botany helps explain Phelps's decision to focus on botany in her natural history classes; but equally clearly, the "hobby" of the "Troy folks" points to a popular interest on which both Phelps and Eaton depended for success.

Eaton's (or Rensselaer's) desire to educate a population in the technologies that were relentlessly reshaping their lives involved in part a desire to forestall social unrest. Again, for Eaton this population included women, as this excerpt from an 1835 document makes clear:

The education of all girls should be adapted to some useful employment. After our factories had driven girls from the spinning wheel, and thereby put an end to two-thirds of their labor, the important question occurred: what employment should be substituted? Before the question was decided, the great evil of suddenly throwing into a state of idleness one third of the youthful population of our country, was most severely felt. . . . Being continually dressed in a style above the duties of the kitchen, and being enervated by inaction, and habituated to "gadding abroad," and planning schemes for amusement, every kind of labor was irksome and odious. (McAllister, 488–489)

Eaton's fear of what a horde of idle, rampaging, overdressed girls might do did not correspond exactly to the dangers posed by Willard's students, who hailed from a higher social stratum. But from Phelps's and Willard's perspective, this group—destined to be wives and mothers of influential men—needed discipline no less than women of the working class. No matter their social position, all women possessed surpluses of "the faculty of imagination, and the affections of the heart," which called for a compensatory or countervailing development of the "reasoning faculty which distinguishes the human species from the brutes. If woman is, in reality, devoid of this noble faculty, then is she a kind of intermediate link, between man and the brute creation" (Phelps, *Fireside*, 223).

Phelps's educational writings abound with laments over women's turbulent emotionality, irrationality, and addiction to escapist fantasies. Women, therefore, ought to study subjects that "sober the imagination, develop the reasoning powers, and strengthen the understanding, so apt in the female character to be biased by prejudice, or borne on the gossamer wing of a lively fancy, into the regions of error and folly" (306–308). "Not without reason," Phelps writes, have women been seen as

fluctuating in purpose, desultory in action, and unsettled in principle. Possessing vast power over the destinies of the world, by their influence over the other sex, they have often been the cause of contention and misery among nations, and of agitation and disquiet in the more limited domestic sphere. Of how much importance, to the well-being of mankind is it, that this fickle, restless, yet powerful, being should become consistent and reflecting, and learn how to exercise her influence for the good of society! (211)

To Phelps, these female qualities are ultimately physiologically determined, and thus to some extent ineradicable, by women's lesser physical strength and finer nerves compared to men. These lacks produce a sensitive heart, and spirits "easily elated or depressed"; woman is subject to "caprice" and "agitations, to which man, favored by greater physical strength, and more firmness of nerve, is exempt" (15). "Alas for woman's lot!" she writes toward the end of her career: "often gifted with lofty powers of intellect, and capable of high moral purpose, but possessing strong impulses, an excitable imagination, and capable of emotions which, left to act without restraint, carry her into the wildest excesses of passion" (*Hours*, 239); "what the Almighty has created her, that she is, with all her physical weakness, her nervous excitability, and her desire of loving, and of being loved" (324).

From this perspective, the best woman's education would always constitute a kind of "cure for femininity," an idea that, according to John Mullan, arose in late seventeenth-century England exactly in connection with advocacy of science instruction for women (41). Phelps assured her students that science would redeem the whole sex: "The daughters of Eve may eat of the tree of knowledge, without danger, or sin. No law, divine or human, forbids that the female mind should seek to penetrate the mysteries of science; and may we not hope, that the sad consequences of the disobedience of the first woman will, in some degree, be averted from the earth, by enlightening the minds of her daughters?" (*Fireside*, 224).

Phelps's invidious idea of the female is evident when she compares "two young persons, of different sexes, unaccustomed to travelling," who "find themselves, for the first time, on board a ship or a steam-boat. The female, probably, occupies herself with thoughts of the friends from whom she has parted, or of those whom she expects to meet; memory and imagination are busy, but her powers of observation slumber, unless, perhaps, exercised in noticing the dresses of those around her, their peculiarities of manners, and probable standing in society. The young man, very likely, examines the construction of the ship or steam-boat, its size, the velocity with which it moves, and the scenery which presents itself" (175).

Thus to learn botany, as to learn any science, was to learn to see the world, which meant both to engage with it instead of escaping it, and to master it. To obliterate fantasy by interesting women in the real world was by no means to advocate unmediated contact with "nature." In sharp contrast to the visionary romantic, Phelps insisted that untrained eyes could make nothing of their surroundings; in fact, inability to deal with the chaos of unsystematized reality was a major reason why people turned to fantasy. God, however, "has given human minds the power of reducing an almost infinite variety of objects into classes, so as to form beautiful and regular systems" allowing for comprehension—taking in—of what would "otherwise present to our bewildered minds a confused and indiscriminate mass" (*Familiar Lectures,* 1836, 13). In using this mental power, in becoming rational beings, humans demonstrate a power that sets them apart from nature and approximates them to God. The more they develop this power, the more distanced from the one, and the closer to the other, they become.

Ultimately, therefore (as Vera Norwood observes), Phelps cannot be deemed a pioneer in any tradition of women's nature writing that seeks epiphanies of "direct communion with nature" (22) through which one experiences the divinity of nature itself rather than the evidence, through nature, of divine laws installed by a lawgiver who is not equivalent to the creation itself. If, however, Phelps reveres the Creator, not nature's "magical world" (Norwood, 23), it is not least because magic, for her, was a sinister concept. Women had for too long been identified with witchcraft, superstition, and an irrational, primitive devotion to magical—pagan—thinking. Phelps is trying to introduce the concept of scientific law at least in part to override precisely women's residual belief in magic, not to mention a residual belief in women's susceptibility to the irrational. "Superstition," she opines, "dwells with ignorance; the more mankind are enlightened, the more they understand that the changes which take place in the physical world, are the effects of general laws, established by God for the regulation of the universe. Even what seem to be irregularities, or exceptions, when traced to their causes, are found to result from these very laws" (*Fireside*, 123).

The more aspects of nature that were brought under the rule of secondary causes, the better Phelps liked it. She admired Charles Lyell's uniformitarian geology for subjecting yet another previously mysterious domain of the natural world to the rule of reason. "A long period must have been required, to bring the materials of these primitive rocks into the compact and hardened state in which we now find them; for, although the Deity could, in an instant, have changed the most subtle gases into rocks and stones, we have no reason to believe, that he did not operate by second causes, as much in the formation of the world, as he has since done" (*Fireside*, 201).

Indeed, Phelps is not a nature writer but a science writer, something quite different. She urged other women with literary ambitions to write as she did: to turn out serious, improving, pedagogically useful works rather than the fictional and poetic literary frivolities that gave women authors a bad reputation and harmed their female readers. Both of her conduct novels contain women characters with literary ambitions who choose the useful over the frivolous, even though frivolous work is better paid and better publicized. In *Ida Norman* her exemplar "became known as a writer, not of vitiating novels or vapid poetry, but of useful and instructive books; some of which she wrote more particularly, for the benefit of a large family of younger brothers and sisters, and of numerous nephews and nieces" (1:305).

In one of her few poems Phelps justified her own literary choice in a similar way. "Fair truth," she says,

> With her pure, steady light, has seemed more bright
> Than Fiction's flickering torch, and gilded ray.
> To study nature, and God's providence,
> As manifest in these material things,
> And having learn'd, t'impart to other minds,
> Knowledge so wondrous, this, I've better deem'd
> Than pencilling fantastic imagery.
> There's poetry in science, when it leads
> To gaze upon the rainbow's glorious arch,
> To follow Echo to her grottos wild,
> To trace the circling planets in their course,
> And watch the bud first bursting into bloom. (*Hours*, xxiv)

The poem alludes efficiently to several sciences: the rainbow to optics, Echo to acoustics, the circling planets to astronomy, the blooming bud to botany. In each case, the meager poetic trope signifies a topic that is implicitly much more richly comprehended by science than by poetry.

*B*ut if, in deciding to write science over fiction and poetry, Phelps meant to elevate her work over conventional female literary production, she also located herself on a lower rung of the ladder of science than the actual producer of scientific knowledge. The science pedagogue who writes for a student audience is not a scientist writing for peers; she is not reporting on knowledge that she has discovered or produced but is recycling or translating what is already known. Her attainments are distinctly secondary to those of "professors in Colleges and universities" who "ought not to be expected to devote their time to teaching the *a b c* of Chemistry; those can do this as well, who have not made the attainments they have done, and who are not therefore as capable of being useful in the higher walks of science" (*Chemistry*, iii).

Opening a gap between lower and higher walks of scientific attainment that nevertheless allowed for—indeed was designed to foster—constant bridging, Phelps cannily secures a place for scientific educators while leaving the strongly gendered hierarchies of science in place. The popularizer need not be a man, but those who are content to remain on the lower rungs are more likely to be women than men. "There may be among the young persons who are gaining from this book the first elements of the science of Chemistry, those who are destined to make discoveries even greater than any preceding chemist has yet done," she says. "Hopes like these encourage the author who labours to prepare simple works of instruction for the young," who, without "honour and fame" is nevertheless cheered by the thought that these "humble efforts may be the means of raising up among the children of our country, those who are, hereafter, to add to her glory and prosperity" (211–212).

Not to be overly obsequious to scientists, however, Phelps defends the affiliates of lesser scientific attainments who free a professor's time as probably better qualified to teach the subject at an introductory level than he. A "brilliant course" of experiments in college might demonstrate "the skill and knowledge of the experimenter, but rather confuse than assist" a pupil who was "ignorant of the language and first principles of the science. These should have been acquired before" (iii). Conceding that popular knowledge alone would never make a scientist, Phelps argued both that popular knowledge was just what the populace needed, and also that even those who would eventually make their mark as professional scientists needed to begin their learning at the beginning. To fill these needs required skills that ought to be thought of as professional: an understanding of cognitive development (to argue that such a thing as cognitive development in the young existed was the sisters' reason for translating Saussure's treatise on children), a sense of how to distribute knowledge in a graded or progressive fashion (a theory that would become the basis for all education in the United States over time), the skill to write accessibly for nonspecialized audiences, and the ability to understand the specialized knowledges that she was transmitting. Thus, if Phelps theorized scientific popularizing as an affiliative activity, she also described it as the very essence of education in terms that would eventually dominate education at every level, and deliver all education except that provided in the elite men's college into women's hands.

"The few master minds to whom is given a key to unlock the secrets of nature, should not indeed be hindered in their researches;—they are not called on to stoop to humble capacities; to teach the rudiments of science;—they are to furnish materials for other minds to elaborate. There should be a division of labor in science, as in the arts and manufactures" (*Reviews and*

Essays, 284). Although Phelps says here that only a few of either gender might become original scientists, the fact is that she took it for granted that women were foundationally incapable of original science. The rare creative scientist was always male. This position was entirely conventional; even the era's icon of scientific womanhood, Mary Somerville, whose mathematical abilities clearly surpassed those of most men in her day, appears to have thought that women were not naturally endowed with original scientific powers. In a draft of her memoirs she expressed melancholy awareness of her own shortcomings, which she attributed to her sex: "I have perseverance and intelligence but not genius, that spark from heaven is not granted to the sex, we are of the earth, earthy, whether higher powers may be allotted to us in another state of existence God knows, original genius in science at least is hopeless in this" (Elizabeth Patterson, 89).

With no knowledge of Somerville's unpublished rumination, but in the same vein, in a passage loaded with metaphors of women as spectators and consumers, not producers of science, Phelps wrote that a woman might "not aspire to add, to the stock of chemical science, discoveries of her own; but, gifted with intellectual power to trace the relations of cause and effect, and comprehend the wonderful properties of matter which science reveals, she may dare to raise the curtain, which conceals the operations of Nature, and entering her laboratory, behold the grand experiments there exhibited: nor should it be considered a small privilege, that she is permitted to share in the sublime discoveries of science, and to feast on the banquet of knowledge, prepared by others" (*Fireside*, 185).

A representation of popularizing as a profession indeed, but one dependent on and celebratory of a specifically male achievement, a profession directed mainly toward women's work with other women and young people, a depiction of the popularizer herself as law abiding, serviceable, self-effacing, hard working, useful, and good—this picture probably helped to neutralize in advance whatever gender-based objections might have been raised against Phelps's work. The substantial recognition she received from practicing scientists may have reflected their satisfaction with her feminine deportment as much as it conveyed appreciation of her contributions. Even her intractable commitment to a dated kind of botany might have pleased a masculine scientific establishment, insofar as that establishment was eager to keep women out of the professional ranks. From this perspective, Phelps's project, if successful, would sideline women forever. For her part, Phelps would have responded that professionals who shortchanged the populace or supposed that popular knowledge was not real knowledge were gravely in error. For her, the only way to keep science vital in the U.S. polity was to keep it popular; American women who did that work were doing as much or more for science than the professionals themselves.

𝒫helps's botany text followed the same organization throughout its many editions. It was designed for the classroom, but its idea of classroom involved the field and the laboratory, referring often to botanical excursions or procedures with the microscope and dissecting knife. Always well illustrated and containing numerous diagrams—these were featured by author and publisher as important selling points—the text's discourse assumed that students would be working with real plants, not merely absorbing information from the book. Phelps took care to explain that the role of the book in scientific education was to serve, not dictate. Bibliophilia to her smacked too much of the medieval scholasticism that Protestant Baconianism had successfully overcome. She advised students in her textbook of natural philosophy to "turn your thoughts to the real appearances of Nature around you; consider the knowledge of books as nothing, but as it serves to explain the changes which are constantly taking place" (175). But this assurance told only half the story and was perhaps somewhat disingenuous, since it was precisely the book that communicated the system and permitted the identification. Nature did not—this was basic to Phelps's idea about the central place of reason in the human endowment—organize itself in a way that could be intuited. The scientific organization of nature, on the other hand, did not duplicate the divine mind; Linnaean latinity served as a constant reminder of the human origins of science.

Each section of Phelps's botany text takes a different approach to the plant. A "practical botany" describes the parts of a plant and shows how to identify a species through the Linnaean system, including discussions of plant anatomy and physiology; a flora helps make identifications; a section on vegetable physiology describes the life cycles of plants; a section on physical geography lays out their global distribution; a botanical glossary gives definitions. Along the way Phelps introduces poetry, plant lore, etymologies, and descriptions from travel accounts and histories to make her work "familiar," and though she rejects Marcet's dialogue form, she writes accessibly and conversationally. (The book, however, becomes increasingly impersonal over its publication span.) By 1836, just seven years after its first appearance, the text was already in its fifth edition and Phelps could claim with some justice that it had "removed the obstacles which formerly impeded the progress of botanical information, in schools, and among our own sex. We have seen that even children may become botanists" (*Familiar Lectures,* 1836, 235). Later she would propose more aggressively that she had "in some degree been made instrumental by means of her various works on the physical sciences, in diffusing a love for them and a habit of referring the works of nature to their Great Creator" (*Familiar Lectures,* 1860, 252).

The more her approach diverged from professionalizing botany, the more strident her rhetoric. In botany, the professional issue crystallized specifically over Linnaeus, his artificial system, and the idea that identification and classification were in themselves the aims of botanical science. Asa Gray, professor of botany at Harvard and later Darwin's most prominent advocate in the United States, whose 1836 botany textbook directly competed with Phelps's, attacked her book from the first on the grounds of its amateurism. He presented his textbook in no small measure as the production of the true scientist versus the mere popularizer. (And, from the first, his book overtook hers as the biggest seller, although Phelps's remained close behind until it went out of print. Only these two texts had any longevity.) Gray granted Linnaean taxonomy its uses—every science had to name its objects of study, and Latin binomials were "universal" (because any Western scientist could employ them) and efficient. But he argued that the taxonomy, disclosing nothing about what plants were really like, could not advance the subject and might well impede scientific progress (Dupree, 52).

If Asa Gray presented his alternative to Linnaeus in the general terms of professional versus popular knowledge, he also stood for an alternative systematics that he and others designated the "natural" system. Negatively, he argued that the Linnaean system was neither easy to learn nor reliable in application. For one thing, to memorize the entire ungainly Latinate apparatus was impossible, so that one had always to rely on books (of varying quality) for identification. For another, the question of what to do with any flower that deviated from the ideal norm, as most real flowers in fact did, could be answered only by decreeing it a new species. The natural system was thus an easier tool than the Linnaean, because "the botanist who merely counted stamens was helpless when those parts were missing, or when, as is often the case, their number varied from species to species within a genus, or even among individuals"; but ultimately Gray meant for his natural system to serve ends that went much "deeper than mere ease of collecting" (Gray cited in Dupree, 52–53).

The debate was on. Gray's rejection of "ease of collecting" suggests that for him popularity could never be a measure for scientific knowledge, perhaps even that he liked the idea of pursuing a profession whose material was too difficult for the general public. Professionalism, as Burton Bledstein has pointed out, requires cordoning off an area of expertise and regulating access to it. But the professional always has something that the public needs or at least is made to want. It was not clear what professional botanists could offer the public, and the public responded accordingly. As Elizabeth Keeney puts it, "The cutting edge of professional botany turned away from the natural history of plants" to plant biology, "a program with little room for amateur involvement. This was not simply a case of professionals cutting amateurs out of the action; amateurs generally found the New Botany unappealing" (133).

Phelps had no doubt that this development was a disaster, and from the point of view of her motives—to discipline unruly femininity and attract a wide public to science—she was right. Although later editions of her botany textbook appended a (brief) section on the emerging natural system, they did so grudgingly, accompanying the discussion with a polemic on the superiority of Linnaean terminology for ordinary people. The 1860 edition complains that the natural system is too complex, requires too much prior knowledge to work pedagogically, and uses Linnaeus anyway for making its initial identifications.

The artificial system, she grants, is "not the whole of Botany, but it is the key to the natural method," a necessary "stepping-stone" to more advanced botanical study (*Familiar Lectures* 1860, 232). The preface to the 1860 edition also laments that "attempts to break up the old landmarks of the science of Botany, and to present it in an entirely new form, tend to repel from its pursuit many of its devoted friends, and to discourage beginners, by offering at the commencement nothing which the mind can regard with pleasure" (3). Use of the natural system at the outset of botanical study, she claims, has "rendered Botany far less popular than formerly; and has, in a degree, excluded it from many schools where it was once a favorite study" (299).

The "natural" system used Linnaean taxonomy for names but rejected as pointless and superficial the system's grouping of plants according to the number of pistils and stamens. Gray's system, like most nineteenth-century natural systems, depended on the perceived overall shape—the general morphology—of the total plant (as it looked like other plants or not, and as its different parts related to each other) as a means for grouping species into higher orders. The concern, in pre-Darwinian days, was motivated by the desire to chart the plenitude of a fixed creation; the argument was that what the plant looked like, in toto, had to be close to what it naturally, essentially, really was. As the natural system gained cachet among scientists, Phelps saw that it could easily lead to the search for essence, a search that she believed not only to be divinely forbidden, but also to be profoundly unscientific in Baconian terms. It was more mystified and metaphysical, more subjective, more intuitive, and finally no more demonstrably natural than the forthright artifice of Linnaeus. That some twenty different competing "natural systems" developed between 1825 and 1845 (Daniels, 113) suggests that there was nothing really "natural" about them; the fact that DNA investigations are today strikingly redefining the systematic basis of any natural classification tends to the same judgment.[7]

In time, Phelps extended her critique out beyond the protected space of her textbooks. She addressed professional scientists, composing for example several papers for meetings of the AAAS in which she reminded scientists how dependent they were on a well-disposed public, and how their enterprise required a pipeline for recruiting future generations of scientists. As the situation, in her view, continued to deteriorate, she became more outspoken. Two late essays approach the issue from different directions but arrive at the same point. "Popular Botany" says the natural system has put botany "in danger of becoming as little understood out of the sphere of learned professors, as it was in the early part of the nineteenth century. . . . We would have all persons, in every condition, learn what they can, upon all branches of useful knowledge. Especially would we rescue the flowers, with which God has beautified and diversified the earth, from the rigid grasp of the uncompromising botanist, who would forbid all study of plants, but in that particular direction which he deems most strictly scientific" (*Reviews and Essays*, 238–239). She memorializes Amos Eaton to contrast the modern professional as a backslider:

> Shall we . . . go back to the practice of the dark ages, when knowledge was confined to the cloister, or the schools of the learned? [Eaton] informed miscellaneous audiences, and the students of schools in which he lectured, that there was such a science; and, by teaching the simple analysis of Linnaeus, enkindled an enthusiasm for the study of plants. Interest in botanical excursions gave a new impulse to the love of nature—the languid pulse of the morbid student was quickened—and the pallid cheek became flushed with the healthful exercise and agreeable excitement incident to such exploring expeditions. Plants assumed a new importance when every weed was known to have its flower, and appropriate name and place in botanical classification. Admitting that, among these young students,

few ever became distinguished botanists; that, when they had collected plants, and arranged them in their herbaria, they stopped short
in their investigations . . . shall we refuse to learn anything of the objects around us, because we cannot know everything respecting them?
(257–258)

In her "Essay on Popular Science," Phelps argues that self-interest
should lead professionals to encourage amateurism, and she insists—not without a degree of pathos—on the validity of her own, now apparently outdated,
mission:

[As] there has been an enlargement of the knowledge of the laws
which govern the vegetable kingdom among the few who devote
themselves to the study of the science, there has been a loss of enthusiasm for botanical pursuits among students in our schools and
colleges; this is to be deprecated. . . . As an humble laborer in the
field of education, with no claims to originality or discoveries, the
author of this paper has sought to illustrate and simplify the discoveries and systems of others; so as to interest and enlighten those
minds which, perchance, had never conceived the idea of scientific
relations, and which had heretofore regarded science as dry and re-
pulsive. (285)

Thus, what scientists interpreted as progress, Phelps interpreted as regression. If the difficulties and remoteness of the new science were likely to
put the woman popularizer out of business, they were also likely to increase
the public disaffection that her work had forestalled. To abandon Linnaeus
symbolized for her the abandonment of the entire interlocking enterprise that
had enabled her to proselytize on behalf of the sciences in the first place,
and through which proselytizing she had carved out a particular place for
women—and a unique place for herself—in antebellum public culture.

Phelps's views on all subjects remained remarkably constant throughout her career of more than fifty years. The science she learned and popularized in the 1820s and 1830s was the science she stayed with. She updated
her textbooks, but she found the dramatic changes in the structure and content of the sciences after the Civil War alarming. This is not only because
relearning everything she thought she knew was too daunting for a woman
now in her seventies, or even because the sciences were getting increasingly
arcane, but also because paradigm shifts in the sciences introduced an element of instability in scientific knowledge that did not comport with the ideas

of system and regularity that had drawn her to science in the first place. In a paper of 1869 she complained that "we no longer have any light, caloric, electricity, or magnetism; all are resolved into *force, vibration, etc.*," and she confessed "to a love of established principles" (*Reviews and Essays*, 296). As the theories of science increasingly countered human common sense as she understood it, science's ability to help people master or apprehend the world diminished. She thought science was increasingly encouraging "hallucination" (Bolzau, 449).

Inevitably, perhaps, she rejected Darwin. (The fact that Asa Gray was the most vocal U.S. advocate of Darwin may have had something to do with this.) In pre-Darwinian decades when various so-called "developmental" theories were already much in the air, she insisted that "we have no reason to suppose that any new species of animals or vegetables have been produced since the creation" (*Familiar Lectures,* 1836, 126). She dismissed evolution theory as unproven and argued that Darwin's *Descent of Man* (which caught the attention of the public far more than *Origin of Species*) degraded humankind by denying its unique status in creation: "Let us honor Darwin for all the good he has done in search of truth," she wrote in a paper of 1874, "but may no member [of the AAAS] ever be found willing to sell his birth-right, as a child of God, created by Him in His own image, for a miserable mess of *potage*, 'evolved from a primordial cell'" (Bolzau, 449–450).

It is not at all surprising that Phelps was nostalgic for a golden age of popular science to which she had made substantial contributions. It is perhaps somewhat surprising, however, that she had nothing at all to say about the tentative opening of scientific careers to women after 1870. Indeed, all of her many opinions about the New Woman were negative. To the distress and, then, the scorn of suffragists, she joined and even became corresponding secretary of the Woman's Anti-Suffrage Association in Washington, D.C.

Often in a career, someone who has worked to expand the boundaries comes to think that where she drew the line is where the line has to stay. Phelps's work accepted, indeed required, a gender-typed division of labor between two kinds of professionals. Insofar as her career had partitioned the work of science between always male producers and often female transmitters and consumers, insofar as she thought professional science was rejecting its necessary popular base, at the end of her career she could see doors only closing, not opening.

CHAPTER 3

Sarah Hale and the Circulation of Science

*F*rom the 1830s through the 1870s, Sarah Hale was probably the best known, most respected, and most influential woman of letters in the United States. During her forty-year tenure as editor of *Godey's Lady's Book*, she built the journal into the nation's most widely read women's magazine, with an estimated 150,000 subscribers in 1861 (Chielens, 145). It is of considerable cultural significance, therefore, that Hale persistently advocated science study for women, constantly instructed her women readers in the benefits science was bringing to them, and regularly published scientific material in the *Lady's Book*[1] as well as its predecessor, the *Ladies' Magazine*.[2]

Critics hostile to sentimentalism, and convinced in advance that women's magazines exist to waste women's time and money, have long distorted Hale's achievements and the character of the *Lady's Book*. A few earlier critics made the case for taking Hale and the magazine she stood for seriously—Ruth Finley argued that Hale's understanding of the popular mind made her more effective than radical feminists of the day in bringing lasting benefits to women's lives; Isabelle Entrikkin pointed out how much nonfiction the *Lady's Book* carried. But as late as 1983 Louis Banner dismissed the journal as a "fashion magazine" and censured its supposed idealization of insipid, passive femininity (19). In 1986, well after the emergence of second-wave feminist criticism, a historian of periodicals flippantly (and inaccurately) described the *Lady's Book* as running "the gamut from clothing to hair styles, from music to domestic economy, from mawkish, moralistic fiction to doubly mawkish, moralistic poetry" (Chielens, 144).

But the reality is that Hale cared far more about how women thought than about how they looked. It is true the *Lady's Book* published an elegantly engraved, hand-colored fashion plate every month (these are now collector's items). It is also true that Hale used her power as editor to circulate the idea of a separate women's sphere. But, far from associating that sphere with confinement to the home space, and far from idealizing female inanity, Hale urged women to work actively and in public for all the social causes that comported with and advanced their gender interests.[3] Throughout her life she sought to identify such causes, and among the many she endorsed, women's education always came first. A New Englander by birth, she had imbibed the region's faith in literacy; she had studied some science with her brother, and after her marriage, she and her husband together read botany, mineralogy, and geology systematically (Finley, 35–36). These experiences convinced her that good men neither feared nor scorned women of intellect who desired an education. To the contrary, it strengthened the bonds between the sexes.

In 1859, in an untitled editorial column, she recalled for readers that her favorite girlhood studies had been—in order—the natural sciences, French, and composition; she advised these same readers to read history, biography, and natural science (*Lady's Book* 58:80). She accepted the proposition that the scientific mind was the highest expression of human intellect. She urged women to study science both to show that their mental capacities equalled men's and to attain the intellectual heights for themselves. Moreover, her own emergence from impoverished seamstress to social eminence through literary work made the economic advantages of education for women quite clear. From the beginning to the end of her career—and despite many theoretical and tactical permutations as her sense of the essentially feminine altered, and as she became personally more devout—Hale consistently publicized an ideal of the educated woman, with science at the center of her learning.[4]

Hale began her editorial work under the aegis of firm Enlightenment principles, writing in 1828 (in a *Ladies' Magazine* essay on women's education in Spain) that "though nature has bestowed a different, and peculiar organization upon our bodies, she has made no difference in our minds; our souls she has not made an inferior species, nor has she impressed the stamp of degradation upon our talents. On the contrary, I am persuaded that, if women had, in all times and ages, enjoyed, equally with men, the advantages of instruction, we should have exceeded them in the productions of genius" ("Female Education in Spain," 529).

I have alluded in chapter 1 to her enumerations of scientific courses in women's schools, and to her argument that women should read about science rather than what were deemed gender-appropriate belletristic and moralistic works. The radical force of her argument makes it worth repeating: "The disparity (*inferiority*, as men, perhaps rightly, call it) which is observable between the minds of the sexes, is perpetuated (if not wholly induced) by the almost exclusive attention of women in her mental pursuits to subjects of taste, sentiment, and devotion"; "the best and most sure means of permanently elevating the female mind" requires learning the sciences ("Science and Sentiment," 273).

In decades marked by scientific and technological optimism, when the telegraph, railroad, rotary press, and other major innovations were thoroughly transforming the texture of life in the United States, and when the market revolution was bringing new products and comforts to ordinary Americans at an unprecedented rate, Hale worked to show women how good all these changes were for them. She claimed, indeed, that women were technology's main beneficiaries. They were the ones freed from the onerous labor of making cloth, soap, candles, and other home manufactures; they were the ones who could now go out and buy these items from among an array of more attractive (and better-made, she always insisted) goods. That fewer women were manual laborers and more were genteel consumers did not, to her, signify a loss of autonomy or agency. On the contrary, it was an unambiguous cause for celebration. Even women who worked as mill operatives or domestic servants were better off, in her view, than they had been in earlier times, for now they worked with such contrivances as mechanical looms, sewing machines, reliable cooking stoves, and spigot faucets. Hale wanted women to realize that every one of these devices testified to the historical progress in which they themselves were profoundly implicated. Because these changes improved women's lives, she also wanted women to understand the principles behind them and recognize the role science was playing in their lives. Thus, she expounded and advocated both theoretical science, to improve women's minds, and technology, to improve their material circumstances.[5] At some level, these two projects merged, because she understood that women could develop their intellects and spirits only when technology had freed up their time from endless soul-numbing, body-taxing drudgery.

Across the decades Hale advanced many other women-and-science arguments. Learning and demonstrating scientific knowledge would strengthen women's minds, impress men with female mental capacity, make life more interesting and enjoyable, make women more attractive social companions (compensating for the inevitable loss of physical beauty over time), increase appreciation for nature's orderliness and God's goodness demonstrated therein, help women carry out their allotted tasks more effectively—including instruction of the young—and help them contest skepticism in an informed, effective manner.

By the 1850s, however, a heightened sense of national crisis had led her to focus on women's redemptive spirituality rather than on the reasoning capacities she had stressed earlier in her career. She had never imagined that women might become original scientific geniuses, but now she argued (scientifically!) that women were constitutionally unsuited for scientific originality. They compensated for this lack, she claimed, by spiritual superiority. But even as she made this move, she became less interested in learned women whose display of scientific knowledge demonstrated their powerful intellects, and more interested in women who actively used their knowledge of science to better their conditions and those of other women. She was a national leader in the 1850s campaign to give women the scientific training necessary for them to practice as licensed physicians. After the Civil War she seconded Catharine Beecher's efforts (see chapter 4) in favor of establishing a women's scientific track in college, where sciences were to be taught, learned, and applied by women, for women, on behalf of women's specific roles and needs. This advocacy of careers for women in medicine and domestic science invented applied science professions for women in ways that the flexible boundaries of Hale's women's sphere could easily accommodate.

*H*ale did a small amount of original science writing herself, including for example a three-part series on plant physiology in the *Ladies' Magazine* beginning in February 1832. Titled "A Page from the Book of Nature," the series shows how scientific knowledge brings depth to ordinary observation rather than, as romantic ideology would have it, stripping the natural world of its mystique. Take, for example, a tree:

> We see, in the centre of the trunk and of every branch, a slender column of pith; around it we see a cylinder of heartwood; next comes alburnum, or new wood. This wood abounds with minute longitudinal veins for the passage of the sap, which we observe is passing up, on the principles of capillary attraction, till a portion of it reaches the extremity of every leaf. The leaves are furnished with small pores for transpiration. (February 1832, 71)

More typically, however, she compiled scientific notes from a variety of sources, called attention to women's scientific achievements whenever she found them, and cited scientific books by women and ran extracts from them.

To help those without access to formal schooling learn what she thought women ought to learn, she published a wide range of scientific essays and notes. The *Lady's Book* uses science for much of its filler: in the first year of Hale's editorship, for example, the filler includes a list of the alkaline and neutral substances in the earth, observations about the chemistry of ripening fruit, the optics of color perception, the acoustics of sound in water, how magnets work, how ores are smelted, and much more. Numerous ambitious, illustrated scientific features—on the steam engine, calico dying, chemistry experiments for youth, vegetable physiology, Alexander von Humboldt's invention of physical geography, mechanical drawing, uses of the microscope—might lead a reader to think this was a popular science journal, not a ladies' magazine. But blurring this distinction is exactly Hale's intent. The *Lady's Book* was a journal of popular science precisely because it was a women's magazine.

Each month the *Ladies' Magazine* and the *Lady's Book* reviewed or noticed new books. In some months science books—especially textbooks and books for children—made up most of the notices. Mentioned in the *Ladies' Magazine* are such titles as *The Child's Botany; New Theory of Earth; Trimmer's Natural History; History of Botany; Scientific Tracts; Conversations on Vegetable Physiology; Natural History of Insects; The Naturalist; The Culture of Silk; Natural History of Quadrupeds; First Book in Astronomy; Knowledge for the People, or, the Plain Why and Because; The Eye; The Connection of the Physical Sciences; Comstock's Physiology;* and *Lamarck's Genera of Shells.* Among books noticed in the *Lady's Book* are *Practical Organic Chemistry, Incentive to the Cultivation of the Science of Geology, Textbook of Chemistry for the Use of Schools and Colleges, Elements of Analytic Geometry and of the Differential and Integral Calculus, A Treatise on the History and Management of Ornamental and Domestic Poultry, Theory of Pneumatology,* and *The Theory of Light.* A list of recommended reading in the *Ladies' Magazine* for October 1835 included twenty-five science books. Already in 1831 Hale was using the term *domestic science* and arguing that all women's traditional tasks could—and should—be reconstructed in scientific terms: "It is a sad waste to put fuel under a boiling pot," she wrote in her *Ladies' New Book of Cookery.* "There is a degree of heat in water called the boiling-point; and all the coals or wood in the world cannot make water hotter in an open vessel; *it can but boil*" (79).

Though she advocated botanical study for women, Hale saw it more as an avocation than a central academic subject. She played down Almira Phelps's taxonomical approach in favor of something more holistic but not, on that account, less scientific. "In recommending the study of botany," she wrote in the "Editor's Table" June 1838, "we mean not to encourage such a smattering of it as is confined to its 'technical terms.' We have heard persons discourse largely on the science, whose acquaintance with it extended no farther than to 'the *stamen, calyx* and *petal*'" (*Lady's Book* 16:284). She used botany to introduce entomology, writing in the "Literary Notices" of the *Ladies' Magazine* for August 1832 that "as insects are always the attendants or lovers of flowers, ladies who study Botany would find it advantageous to obtain some knowledge of Entomology likewise, if it were only to save themselves from being frightened at bugs and spiders" (8:384). She published her own flora for children in 1833, *Flora's Interpreter: or, The American Book of Flowers and Sentiments,* which sold well enough to be revised and reissued several times. Designed, as she put it in her own brief notice of the work, "to attract the attention of the young to the interesting and improving study of Botany" (*Ladies' Magazine* 6:331), it was playful and relatively unsystematic. Her popular cookbook, in contrast, addressed an adult audience of anxious homemakers. *Ladies' New Book of Cookery* organized an enormous repertory of recipes, helping to negotiate the cultural transition from cooking as a traditional activity transmitted orally from woman to woman, to cooking as a solitary print-dependent and standardized practice. Even more significantly, perhaps, the book connected cooking to food chemistry and physiology, citing scientific facts from works by the German organic chemist Justus Liebig and the Scottish physiologist Andrew Combe. Hale wants women to understand "the philosophy of Cookery" because "woman, to be qualified for the duty which Nature has assigned her, that of promoting the health, happiness and improvement of her species, must understand the natural laws of the human constitution" (ix).

*I*n the early 1850s Hale began to emphasize both the limits of science and women's unfitness for doing original science. Her new scheme, set out most fully in her huge biographical compendium, the *Woman's Record* of 1852 (second edition, 1855), connected the earth-focused character of science, its philosophic materialism, to the limitations of the male mind. It allocated to women's differently constituted mentality the task of guiding the world on the last leg of its journey toward moral perfection. An emphasis on female spirituality was by now quite culturally conventional; but for Hale, insofar as it seemingly rejected the Enlightenment rationality on which she had based her career, it looks like something new, not to mention an intellectual regression. The question why she endorsed an image of woman as man's spiritual partner rather than his mental equal at this point has many likely answers, ranging from the need to sell magazines to the (correct) perception that reason had done little to stem the rising tide of sectional discord. As early as her 1827 novel *Northwood*, Hale had fretted over the diverging values of white northerners and white southerners; she could conceive of no disaster worse than the breakup of the Union. Whatever might prevent that event demanded all her energies, and apparently she began to believe, or at least to hope, that spiritual power might do the job.

The important point here is that despite the shift in ideological emphasis, Hale did not abandon her belief in science. She even explained the mental difference between women and men in scientific terms. The introduction to *Woman's Record* argues for woman's gender-specific spiritual role in history on the basis of physiological sexual difference:

> Philosophy has become clear-sighted to the importance of physical and mental improvement; new discoveries in science are rife on every side, each one designed to aid man in his appointed task of subduing the earth; but who has found out the way to attain that moral power which only can enable him to govern his own spirit, and thus fit him to rule in righteousness and peace over the world he is conquering? (xxxv)

"Man" here means the male, whose province is the earth. Woman has another task, in support of which Hale offers a theory of female intellect based on a unique blending of the Bible with science. Eve, she says, the last (hence, heretically, the best) work of creation, is Adam's isomer:

> She was made "a help meet for him" in Paradise; and that he there needed her help shows that he was not perfect while standing alone. She must have been nearer perfection than he in those qualities which were to "help" him. She had not his strength of body or his capacity of understanding to grasp the things of earth; she could not help him in his task of subduing the world; she must, therefore, have been above him in her intuitive knowledge of heavenly things. (xxxvii)

To this exegesis Hale adds a scientific footnote: "Chemically tested, their bodily elements were similar; like diamond from carbon, woman had been formed from man; yet the refining process which increased her beauty and purity did not alter this elemental identity; and hence they were one in the flesh" (xxxvii). Making mind an attribute of brain, reasoning from the empirical observation that women scientists are exceedingly rare—not one of the women in *Woman's Record* "has ever made herself famous by great discoveries in physical science, or by any wonderful invention" (xlvi)—she argues that "woman has very little of that kind of genius termed mechanical or inventive" (xxxvii).

This gender difference, she says, cannot be attributed to women's inferior education, because badly educated men have "studied out and made curious inventions of mechanical skill; women never." Thus—still demonstrating her own logical abilities—Hale proposes that "the difference between the constructive genius of man and woman is the result of an organic difference in the operations of their minds. That she reasons intuitively, or by inspiration, while he must plod through a regular sequence of logical arguments, is admitted by all writers on mental philosophy; but there is another difference, which has not been noticed. Woman never applies her intuitive reasoning to mechanical pursuits. It is the world of life, not of things, which she inhabits" (xlvi).

This explanation answers Hale's need to find an attribute in women equal to the challenges of modernity, which in this formulation demands the guiding hand of a less material sensibility than the mechanically minded male. As she explains in her sketch of Mary Wollstonecraft, "To bring about the true Christian civilization, which only can improve the condition of our sex, the men must become more like women, and the women more like angels" (*Woman's Record,* 328).

This description represents women's moral and spiritual power as a real force, an "imponderable" like gravity, electricity, magnetism, and heat—powers whose effects are manifest even though they, themselves, elude the grasp of human measuring apparatus. In short, Hale describes women as literally—not sentimentally—more ethereal, more constituted of ether, than men. No crank theory, the idea of the ether pervaded popular and scientific thought until Einstein did his calculations without it.[6] Mary Somerville's explanation of the force in her *On the Connexion of the Physical Sciences* encapsulates the belief: Electricity "is generally supposed to be an ethereal fluid in the highest state of elasticity surrounding every particle of matter; and as the earth and the atmosphere are replete with it in a latent state, there is every reason to believe that it is unbounded, filling the regions of space" (11). Later Somerville observes that "there are strong reasons for believing that not only the molecular forces which unite the particles of material bodies depend on the electric fluid, but that even gravitation itself, which binds world to world and sun to sun, can no longer be regarded as an ultimate principle, but the residual portion of a far more powerful force generated by that energetic agent which pervades creation" (111).

If the ether is an everyday scientific concept, so also is its association with women, as for example when Nathaniel Hawthorne in *The House of the Seven Gables* describes Phoebe as an ethereal creature who seems rather to float than walk, or Margaret Fuller admits to believing that women are more electrical by nature than men. These are not metaphors but scientific speculation, and Hale's argument is that since women are organically more ethereal than men, they are also more spiritual. She might be borrowing directly from Somerville when she explains in *Woman's Record* that feminine influence, though "hidden from the public eye," is fundamental.

> The most mighty agent in the material world is least known. The sun, brilliant and powerful, gives light and heat to our planetary system . . . but the mightier influence of gravitation, which binds Orion and the Pleiades with our planet, controls the universe, and reaches—perchance—to the throne of God; who has seen gravitation, or can estimate its power? (xlv)

Hale's analysis of the four women scientists she is able to find in the entire historical record, though highly celebratory, makes clear that none is a creative scientist of the first rank; indeed only two are even practicing scientists. She points out (rightly) that the astronomers Caroline Herschel and Maria Mitchell—her two practitioners—learned their science by helping a man— Herschel her brother, Mitchell her father (*Woman's Record*, 354, 744). She says Caroline Herschel died "crowned with the glory which woman's genius may gain, working in the way Divine Providence appointed her,—as the helper of man" (354).[7]

The other two scientific women in Hale's account—Jane Marcet and Mary Somerville—were science writers, a profession of which Hale of course heartily approved. She reminds readers that Marcet's chemistry made the subject popular in the United States and England "by presenting the leading facts of this science so plainly illustrated as to be within the reach of ordinary minds" (732). And although she calls Somerville "the most learned lady of the age" and the "glory of her sex throughout the world" (789), she points equally to Somerville's "womanly virtues" and makes it clear that Somerville possessed "great scientific knowledge," not scientific originality.[8] Quoting from Somerville's dedication of her *Connexion* to Queen Victoria, which expresses her hope of making "the laws by which the material world is governed more familiar to my countrywomen" (789–790), Hale says that nothing "more charmingly illustrates the true moral elevation of feminine character than this" (790).

Hale also spun Somerville to her own purposes when she wrote that Somerville had

> done more by her writings to Christianize the Sciences than any living author; nor do we recollect one, except it be Sir Isaac Newton, among departed philosophers, who has approached her standard of sublime speculations on the visible creation united with childlike faith in the Divine Creator. Physical science will, henceforth, have a religious power; for, though the mind of man is not sufficiently in harmony with moral goodness to make such an advance as Mrs. Somerville has done, no more than Peter and John could *see* the angel at the tomb of the Saviour, yet, when they heard from the women that Christ was risen and followed in faith, the revelation of the truth was made clear to the reason of the apostles. (789–790)

Hale's gender-specific organic theory is also displayed, although less elaborately, in the *Lady's Book*, as for example in the January 1851 "Editor's Table," where Hale asserted that "the true woman cannot work with materials of earth, build up cities, mould marble forms, or discover new mechanical inventions to aid physical improvement" (January 1852, 65).

But, at precisely the same time that *Woman's Record* made its chemical argument for women's spirituality, the quantity and quality of science and technology material in the *Lady's Book* increased strikingly. In September 1850 a long essay by Henry Tuckerman on Alexander von Humboldt described the science of physical geography he had founded and placed his achievement within a survey of the history of science. The lead essay in April 1852, by J.D., "James Watt, Improver of the Steam Engine," featured technical diagrams explained in technical language: "The first vessel, P, being emptied of its air, the cock was again opened, when the force of steam from the boilers pressed upon the surface of the water with an elastic quality like air, still increasing in elasticity till it counterpoised or exceeded the weight of water ascending in the pipe S, out of which the water was immediately discharged when it had once reached the top" (44:245).

In June 1852 Hale ran the first installment of an illustrated series by C. T. Hinckley called "Everyday Actualities" that canvassed such new technologies as bleaching, calico printing, typesetting and publishing, stone-cutting and quarrying, artesian wells, enamels and enameling, manufacture of gas and gas fixtures, construction of pianos, paper making, shipyards, food preservation, lapidary work, and diamonds. Each article described mechanical processes and connected them to an academic science: chemistry for bleaching, geology for artesian wells; organic chemistry for food preservation; mineralogy for diamonds.

The May 1852 issue saw the first of a series of essays on vegetable physiology by Harlan Coultas, a professor of botany in Philadelphia who contributed many essays during this decade. The series covered wildflowers, mosses, ferns, trees; the structure, processes, and geographical distribution of plants; plant fertilization; nutrition; and hybridizing. The May 1853 *Lady's Book* introduced a monthly column, anonymously authored, "Chemistry for Youth" (a reminder of the importance of the journal for women as mothers as well as individuals), which covered crystals, heat, light, combustion, elective affinities, and other topics. The January 1854 issue initiated two series: an anonymously authored technical course in drawing accompanied by precise mathematical illustrations, which transformed the traditional female accomplishment into an exact science; and a series by D. W. Belisle called "Celestial Phenomena," which described "the most interesting and visible astronomical features of the month" (48:60).

The June and July 1854 *Lady's Book* carried an anonymous two-part essay, "Physical Training," about human physiology: "Each moment of our lives, chemical changes and interchanges are going on between the atoms, throughout every portion of our frames" (48:526). The November 1854 issue began a long-running illustrated column, "Parlor Amusements," describing experiments to be performed at home and explaining the physics or chemistry behind them. September 1856 saw the first of three *Lady's Book* essays on conchology; in June 1857 the magazine started a column on aquariums, explaining marine biology and describing diverse fish; and the September 1859 issue carried an essay on the "Butterfly Vivarium" (59:310–312). These are only some of the science features. In choosing her science writers, Hale bankrolled in part the profession of scientific popularizer and helped give it her own slant, since the writers she sponsored shared her views.

Several series often ran in the same issue, along with occasional essays on optics, astronomy, geology, scientific instruments (the microscope, telescope, telegraph, barometer, thermometer), mineralogy, and subfields of natural history. At the back of the book Hale continued to recommend scientific publications and to publicize women's schools that taught science. In

April 1860 she noticed Darwin's *Origin of Species* without fanfare: "The student of natural history will find a thousand matters of interest in the pages of this volume" ("Review," 60:373). She mentioned books by Thomas Huxley, as well as other titles relevant to evolutionary theory, in the same neutral manner.

Ongoing columns of household hints applied science to activities like cleaning, cooking, and home doctoring. The "Editor's Table" for May 1854 announces that "it would be very useful and conducive to the health and happiness of families, if the mothers of families, and women in general, were familiar with the principal doctrines of anatomy, physiology, and pathology, so as to understand, to some degree, the organizations, functions, and diseases of the human system" (46:463). The first of "Fifteen Rules for the Preservation of Health" (October 1860) is: "Pure atmospheric air is composed of nitrogen, oxygen, and a very small proportion of carbonic acid gas. Air once breathed has lost the chief part of its oxygen, and acquired a proportionate increase of carbonic acid gas; therefore, health requires that we breathe the same air only once" (63:364). A regular column, "Sick Room and Nursery," gave way to one called "Practical Hints on the Domestic Management of the Sick-room," which in turn gave way to a "Health Department"—each more clearly organized as scientific than its predecessor.

During this period, scientific allusions and analogies became routine in the magazine's stories and poetry. "The Brown Canvas Bag," by Kate Seton, a story about treasure hunting, has passages like: "'I have discovered a variety of mica about a mile from here,' said he, and he showed her some distinct prismatic crystals implanted on feldspar and shooting into quartz" (41:224). In January 1853, a poem by Rufus Waples titled "The Electricity of the Heart" uses science for its metaphor and also implies that people were learning science from the magazines. The poem's conceit is in its title—no electricity equals that of the heart:

> Learn by scientific rule
> Wonders never taught in school
> Telegraph the country over;
> New effects of heat discover;
> On astronomic journey stray;
> And trace the comet's gilded way;
> Discover planets in the sky
> With thy telescopic eye;
> Swift as a sunbeam upward run,

And measure spots upon the sun;
Study the wonders of the age
In ev'ry periodic page. (46:71)

Thus, even as she explained women's lack of scientific creativity in organic, scientific terms and gave women a compensatory spirituality, Hale continued to argue for the importance of their knowing science and worked to help women acquire it. The dominant message in the *Lady's Book* in the 1850s and 1860s expressed her mixed belief that however central women's spirituality to their historical destiny, women also needed the intellectual ballast that scientific knowledge could give them.

Moreover, during the 1850s Hale began aggressively to argue for the right, indeed the necessity, of women training as physicians to serve other women. This enterprise involved publicizing women who were becoming doctors, advocating the establishment of women's medical colleges (she was particularly active on behalf of the Female Medical College of Pennsylvania, in Philadelphia, which graduated its first class of eight women in March 1852), and even arguing for the propriety of women studying in men's medical colleges in locations where women's schools did not yet exist. Hale broached the topic in *Woman's Record* through her sketch of Elizabeth Blackwell, next to Mary Somerville the living woman she seems most to have admired.

Blackwell's successful effort to matriculate in a medical school made her the first licensed woman physician in the United States (see chapter 10). Hale uses her biography in *Woman's Record* to argue passionately that medical training for women, far from an impropriety, is biblically and rationally sanctioned because women who are exposed—literally—to the hands and eyes of male doctors are involuntary "sufferers and subjects of medical indelicacy" (585). "Is it not repugnant to reason, as well as shocking to delicacy, that men should act the part of *midwives*? Who believes that woman could not acquire all the requisite physiological and medical knowledge?" (585).

Hale opened her campaign for women doctors in the March 1852 issue of the *Lady's Book*, which carried an "Appeal to American Christians on Behalf of the Ladies' Medical Missionary Society." This article asserts "the propriety of admitting young women to the study of medicine, and qualifying them to become physicians for their own sex and for children" (44:185). In presenting the scientifically trained woman doctor as necessary for preserving female delicacy—she considered it especially shocking that the advance of civilization had actually eliminated women midwives—Hale was using her social position as national arbiter of female propriety on behalf of what might have been seen as a striking departure from gender norms. She did not, however, want women to return to midwifery, which she associated with ignorance and superstition. Through medicine she found a way to demand access to a level of scientific training for women higher than anything else current in her culture.

> Let the good and learned physicians of Philadelphia open Schools for training female medical students, and permit any lady who pays the matriculation fee of five dollars to attend one course of lectures, and their halls would be crowded. The study of medicine belongs to woman's department of knowledge; its practice is in harmony with the duties of mother and nurse, which she must fulfil. It is not going out of her sphere to prescribe for the sick; she must do this by the fireside, the bedside, in the "inner chamber," where her true place is. It is man who is there out of his sphere. (44:187)

In the "Editor's Table" the following month Hale praised the sculptor Harriet Hosmer for successfully studying "the science of anatomy" in preparation for her work, which shows "the superiority of the female mind in the study of *anatomy*, thus pointing to woman's true profession in the sciences, viz., the medical. In this science, females will excel wherever they are permitted to enter on the study" (44:293). In January 1853 the "Editor's Table" regretted that few women had yet "entered the arena—where their greatest honors as public benefactors are yet to be won—of medical science" (46:80). In John Wilson, a Philadelphia physician, Hale found a health columnist who shared her views. He argued in "Health Department" in January 1862 that women should be admitted to men's medical colleges because this would save the cost of building new schools, because "orthodox" education would be assured, and because women at such colleges would be mentored by male doctors just as men were (64:94). In October 1862 he wrote that although (of course) women physicians would treat only women and children, their education had to include all branches of medicine, including "Anatomy, Physiology, Medical Chemistry, Materia Medica and Therapeutics" as well as "Midwifery, and Diseases Peculiar to Women" (65:402).

   Hale's campaign for women physicians annexed scientific training to women's sphere on the grounds of female modesty as well as on the grounds that nursing the sick had always been part of women's home duties. From this beginning she expanded alliances between women and the sciences by making other household regimes scientific. "The Science of Cooking Meat" in November 1868 explains how substances like albumen and gelatin make up different parts of various meats, and advises women that cooking meat properly requires knowledge of such matters (77:445). A January 1873 essay called "Turning an Honest Penny" says:

> There is nothing undignified in knowing how to cook according to science. Quite the contrary. Inferior cookery is, if you like, undignified, because ignorant; but that kind of preparation of food which includes real scientific knowledge as well as clever manipulation does not rank below the healing art, of which women are now so eager to be counted professors. (86:50)

What Hale had already called "Domestic Science" as far back as the *Ladies' Magazine* became her final undertaking on behalf of women and the sciences, conducted with characteristic energy despite her advanced age. While the domestic science or home economics curriculum for college women was not established until after the Civil War, the presumption that women should learn the sciences in connection with everyday duties had obviously figured powerfully in Hale's antebellum work. But once higher education was made available to women, this became an important curricular issue. Hale had influentially supported Matthew Vassar's venture into women's higher education, but she frequently argued with the outcome. She insisted effectively that the institution's name be altered from Vassar Female College to, simply, Vassar College. She complained less effectively that only one professor was a woman. And she quarreled with the abstractness and irrelevance to women of the school's curriculum.

In an "Editor's Table" critique in 1870 Hale objects to the school's preference for astronomy over chemistry. "Vassar College, it is understood, was established for the excellent purpose of giving to young ladies an education equal to that received by young men at the best universities. The mistake is in considering that this education, to be equal, must be similar to that which young men receive"; why, she asks, are Vassar women learning astronomy, good only for navigation, rather than chemistry, "the most important science of all," one that "well deserves to be called the queen of studies," the "true household science—which, in its different branches of organic and inorganic chemistry, illustrates every department and appliance of our daily life, the food we eat, the clothes we wear, the houses we build, our medicines, our farms, our gardens" (80:349).

The trajectory of Catharine Beecher's career as an educator, which I take up in chapter 4, fused women's sphere even more emphatically than Hale did with an education in applied science. For both women, conceptualizing the home as laboratory constructed all women as professional scientists; simultaneously, gaining women's admission to real laboratories on the basis of the useful work they might do for domesticity opened a new women's career.

In the "Editor's Table" for January 1872 Hale prints one of her own poems, "To American Science," wherein she enacts the woman's role as spiritual monitor of scientific endeavor (while also demonstrating the requisite knowledge to do this work effectively):

> Thou hast harnessed the lightning,
>   And saddled the sea:
> Now bridle the winds—
>   In service for thee,
> Then read, on the rainbow,
>   What beauty is worth,
> While using its colors
>   To fertilize earth. . . .
> God's steps through the ocean
>   What eye can discern?
> The trained soul of Science
>   His pathways must learn.
> Do fires in the centre
>   Hot rivers call forth,
> Lest frosts from Pole Circles
>   Should desolate earth? . . .
> O Science, be loyal!
>   No "substance" save Faith,
> On all that men hope for,
>   Can help them in death.
> Bow down to the Highest;
>   Hold fast to true thought;
> And on thy white banner
>   Write: "What Hath God Wrought!" (84:93)

She follows the poem with a meditation on technology and women's creativity:

> The mechanical inventions and appliances by which the world is to be subdued take up a larger and larger place in our thoughts. The discoveries of science bear fruit to the service of man. We need not go over the list so often cited, but we remark how many of these wonderful appliances are adapted for the comfort and convenience of women. The sewing machine, the washing machine, the cooking stove . . . how forlorn would a woman be deprived of these!
>
> Yet, in the making of these, she has no share. The earth has been made fruitful, subdued, and embellished by man alone. . . . Nor is there the slightest indication, either in Nature or in Revelation, that the work was intended for women. (83:93)

Hale's Enlightenment assumption that observation of natural phenomena would lead inevitably to piety has disappeared; she no longer believes that scientific rationalism conducts one automatically to spiritual insight. Spiritual minds are needed for spiritual perceptions. But, occasionally, even in these late days, hints of the Enlightenment surface along with clear indications that Hale was keeping up with scientific developments. In January 1876 an "Editor's Table" essay on the mothers of scientists criticizes Francis Galton's compendium of scientific biographies, advancing a full-scale nurture argument against Galton's claim that women were naturally unscientific (this is how Galton interpreted the statistic that celebrated scientists were three times more likely to have been encouraged in science by their fathers than by their mothers). "Most of the eminent scientific men whose biographies Mr. Galton has investigated are over fifty years of age. Their mothers, therefore, were educated in the early part of this century," she points out, a period when "no woman could have been educated in science"; matching argument for argument she claims that the fact that a quarter of these men were supported by their mothers proves "the natural proclivity of women to scientific studies is much greater than that of men." "Mr. Galton," she winds up, "has formed a particular notion of the feminine character, which has led him to an over-hasty inference from the facts which he has collected" (92:90).

Columns in 1876 quote from public lectures about the depths of the sea, the extent of space, discoveries in chemistry. In September 1877 Hale muses that science shows simplicity to be a dream; we have gone beyond the knowledge that the imagined four elements actually consist of "carbon, oxygen, hydrogen, and nitrogen" to realize that "in all probability these elements are themselves compound, and that the only limit to our search after simplicity is the imperfection of our blowpipes and our microscopes" (95: 258–259).

In December 1877 Hale, approaching the age of ninety, said farewell to her readers and her profession. In a retrospective "Fifty Years of My Life" she says her main object in the *Ladies' Magazine* had been to promote the education of her own sex; and that when she moved to the *Lady's Book,* her "efforts for the education of women were continued with increased interest." Arguing like Phelps for her own cultural importance, she suggests "that some part of the great change which has come over our educational system is due to my constant presentment to the claims of woman as a teacher." With the public schools for boys and girls now mainly taught by women, and private schools for girls almost entirely under women's control, "the verdict of public opinion is, that our children are better taught than in former times, and that woman, as an instructress, is in her rightful place" (95:522–523). Regarding the shifting rationale or context, Hale had consistently striven to make sure that part of women's equipment for their "rightful place" would be plenty of science.

CHAPTER 4

Catharine Esther Beecher and the Sciences of Home

Catharine Esther Beecher (1800–1878), oldest daughter of Lyman Beecher, sister to other famous Beechers, shared the family commitment to uplifting and educating the public.[1] She published on topics ranging from theology to moral philosophy to arithmetic to calisthenics to women's health to corruption in the churches. Like so many other activist women of her generation, she found her special niche in women's educational reform. But she was best known for her two substantial books of domestic advice, the 1841 *Treatise on Domestic Economy* (reprinted seventeen times) and its extensive 1869 revision, *The American Woman's Home; or, Principles of Domestic Science*.[2]

The first of these books established Beecher as "a national authority"—perhaps *the* national authority—on the "well-being of the American home" (Sklar, 151). The *Treatise* stood out from the higgledy-piggledy norm in the increasingly crowded field of domestic advice books because of its rational organization, its managerial approach to housekeeping, and the causal, scientific explanations that accompanied its prescriptives. Within a few years of publication, the *Treatise* had made Beecher, literally, a household name.

From the perspective afforded by these two books, it is of the utmost importance to recognize that Beecher conceptualized women's home duties as the basis of a new profession in which science was applied to the tasks at hand. She was not the first to use the term *domestic science*, but more than any other writer she was responsible for popularizing the phrase among its target audience of girls and women. She did this because she believed profoundly that if new scientific knowledge and technologies were applied to the home, the quality of American life would be radically transformed for the better. Homemaking could not have been a science in earlier times because the relevant knowledge did not exist, but the times had changed. Nor was there any need, in simpler times, for homemaking to have been scientific; but now, "the increase of civilization and its elegancies and conveniences have greatly increased the need of scientific training for mothers and house-keepers, who, never having been thus instructed themselves, are not qualified to train their daughters" (*Woman Suffrage*, 134–135).[3]

Just the "one item of selecting and superintending the management of stoves and furnaces, demands much scientific study and practical instruction" (*Woman Suffrage*, 134); and this example could be multiplied many times. Beecher insisted that woman's allotted work in the nineteenth century was just as home centered as it had always been, but that modern homes required modern women to run them. Moreover, the home changed again between 1841 and 1869, thanks largely to technological advance. Although Beecher saw the products of technology as improvements, she also thought they needed to be understood if they were to be used advantageously.

Those who learned to manage effectively the new world of domestic goods and knowledges ought, in her view, to be considered true professionals. I am not talking here about construing the woman teacher of women's subjects as a professional, which Beecher also did, but rather about the woman at home who, in common parlance, was not a professional. (Calling her a homemaker today instead of a housewife recognizes the issue but also avoids it.) In the nineteenth-century context of an ever more widely disseminated ideal of prestigious professionalism, women at home were losing out. Indeed, over the course of the century as the bourgeois genteel woman figured ever more prominently in national demographics, she was defined increasingly as a woman who did not work because she did not need to. That she worked—and that her work deserved professional recognition and status—were key tenets in Beecher's advocacy of domesticity. In yoking the two terms *science* and *professional*, she carried out a project that was as much conservative, in the literal sense, as it was progressive. And this is what Beecher meant it to be.[4]

Beecher convinced herself that once homemaking was reconceptualized as applied science, and once the applied scientist at home was recognized as a scientific professional—even though she was a woman—then women would gladly stay at home, because they would enjoy the social respect that everybody aimed for and because the work itself would be challenging, interesting, and satisfying. Social leaders, she argued, should not "entice" woman "into new professions, and those as yet exclusively held by men," but "aim rather to retain her in her most appropriate sphere, by rendering it so attractive and honorable, that she can not improve her condition by forsaking it" (*Letters to the People*, 189).[5]

One needs to concede at the outset that Beecher never faced some crucial facts: that this work at home was unpaid, and that it isolated the woman from her peers in a fashion not typical of other professions, at least before the era of computer networking. In certain fundamental ways, that is to say, it was not structured like any other profession. Nor, of course, did Beecher ever imagine her applied scientist as the creator of new knowledge or products. Her project was, perhaps, based less on the fear that women would be "enticed" out of the home space than on her certainty that genteel women were not likely to encounter any reasonable alternative to homemaking in the foreseeable future. Like many early national ideologues, she believed that a stable middle class was the backbone of a republic, defending simultaneously against the threats of working-class agitation and upper-class extravagance. The potential benefit to the nation in the huge increase of middle-class people would be no benefit at all if middle-class women strayed from their duties. She meant to reconcile such women to, and improve their productivity in, their inevitable but also progressive role in the polity. Of course, Beecher's optimism never allowed her to contemplate the possibility that women's work, whatever it might be, would always be less socially prestigious than men's work. (Is it a coincidence that the U.S. State Department, according to a front-page story in the *New York Times* for September 5, 2000, lost cachet as a place to work at just the moment when a woman became secretary of state?)

Approached from the angle of her scientific rather than her professionalizing agenda, Beecher's vigorous advocacy of domesticity for women might at first seem incompatible with her endorsement of science. But it should be clear by now that none of the women advocates of science, however they linked science with the womanly, saw it as a threat to womanhood rightly understood. On the contrary, they believed it contributed in various ways to women's highest development. Beecher ascribed women's traditionally inferior status to men, in every social rank, to the culture's lack of "a just appreciation of woman's profession" as homemaker, at the same time arguing, perhaps surprisingly, that the women were bad housekeepers; she attributed their ineptness to women's lack of "such a liberal and practical training" for household duties "as men secure for their most honored professions" (*Woman Suffrage*, 20). Professionalism was her answer to social disrespect for housework; science was her answer to the shoddiness of housework that warranted disrespect. Not only the culture, but the women themselves, did not value or understand their calling.

Beecher argued that Enlightenment rhetoric praising the universality of the classical curriculum obscured the fact that men had always been educated for vocations, not for leisured civility. "Most universities of Europe and of this country were founded to educate the clergy. Next came the training of those who administer laws, and then of those who cure the sick. These are named the *liberal professions*, because society has most liberally provided for the scientific training of those who perform these duties" (128). She never stopped complaining about the uselessness of literary and abstract science studies for women, and the unfairness of a system that celebrated one and scorned the other: "Let the young women of this Nation find that Domestic Economy is placed, in schools, on an equal or superior ground to Chemistry, Philosophy, and Mathematics, and they will blush to be found ignorant of its first principles, as much as they will to hesitate respecting the laws of gravity, or the composition of the atmosphere" (*Treatise*, 46).

Beecher therefore by no means meant to undervalue women's intellects in arguing for gender-specific education. She wanted women to receive gender-specific education because this was exactly what men received. This would mean a different education, even in scientific terms, because education was always meant to channel people toward their culturally ascribed work; to give women the precise equivalent of a man's education meant giving them an equivalent level of training to men's, for women's vocation.

> Do not young ladies learn, from books, how to make hydrogen and oxygen? Do they not have pictures of furnaces, alembics, and the various utensils employed in *cooking* the chemical agents? Do they not learn to understand and to do many as difficult operations as any that belong to housekeeping? All these things are studied, explained, and recited in classes, when everyone knows that little practical use can ever be made of this knowledge. Why, then, should not that science and art, which a woman is to practise during her whole life, be studied and recited? (44)

But if she tested every subject by its use value, she nevertheless constantly made science her authority, scientific expertise her measure of truth. It might not be an exaggeration to say that she anticipated, reflected, and helped further the general shift of cultural prestige from religion to science. (This goal would comport well with her theological struggle against the Calvinism in which she had been reared.) She instructed her readers in the basics of such relevant sciences as chemistry, physics, and—above all—physiology and anatomy. She constantly sought out new scientific and technological information that might be useful to intelligent homemakers. And at the end of the century, the women scientists (mostly chemists) who invented the field of home economics looked back to her and memorialized her as their inspiration.[6] This group inherited the dilemmas she failed to resolve and ultimately did no better than she—arguably they did worse—at advancing a "separate but equal" professional agenda. But their aims, like hers, were to carve out a space for women in which they might apply science to women's traditional work in a professional manner.

*I*n directing her energies toward public activism on women's issues, Beecher took a well-established route. The school she founded with her sister Mary in 1823, incorporated as the Hartford Female Seminary in 1827, was favorably publicized by Sarah Hale. In its early days, Beecher and her sister did almost all the teaching themselves. Course preparation was a formidable task, because along with history, composition, and arithmetic, the school's three-year curriculum included science instruction in botany, mineralogy, geology, natural history, geography, geometry, astronomy, chemistry, and natural philosophy (Harveson, 47–48).

Hartford Female Seminary offered so many subjects because the Beecher sisters assumed, in true Enlightenment fashion, that "there is in mind no distinction of sex, and that much that passes for natural talent is mainly the result of culture," from which it followed that women should be educated like men (*Educational Reminiscences*, 14). Beecher never abandoned this Enlightenment belief that minds are not sexed. What changed radically was her idea of what conclusions and recommendations ought to be drawn from this fact. In the Beecher family, she recalled, intellectual endowments had no relation to gender. Her mother and aunts loved science. They discussed Lavoisier's new discoveries with "enthusiastic interest" and tested them with experiments "in the kitchen and study. Aunt Esther was deeply interested in medical science, and probably had read medical works as extensively as most physicians of that day" (*Woman Suffrage*, 128). Beecher remembered how her mother "with no aid but a small encyclopedia, performed some remarkable mathematical calculations where my father was helpless"; indeed, she insisted that "by the sciences studied in one small encyclopedia and two or three other scientific books, my mother was, if not superior, fully equal to my father in mental power and culture" (67–68).

Given that her father was "imaginative, impulsive, and averse to hard study," while her mother was "calm and self-possessed"—given that he actually "seemed, by natural organization, to have what one usually deemed the natural traits of a woman, while my mother had some of those which often are claimed to be the distinctive attributes of man" (*Reminiscences*, 15–16)— Beecher never believed for an instant in innate gender differences of mind. She became the advocate of a gender-specific curriculum not because she thought women were incapable of learning men's subjects, but because she saw no point in their doing so. "The discussion of the question of the equality of the sexes, in intellectual capacity, seems both frivolous and useless, not only because it can never be decided, but because there would be no possible advantage in the decision" (*Treatise*, 142).

At her Hartford school, Beecher noted, many students were working themselves into nervous collapses. Tutoring herself at night and teaching what she had learned the next day, she herself broke down from overwork. She came to believe eventually that she had permanently ruined her health at this time. (A lifetime of sampling diverse medical therapies provided the basis for many of her publications on health.) Resigning from her school in 1831— Hartford Female Seminary continued to flourish for many years after she left it—she devoted the rest of her career to an entirely different model of women's schooling from Hartford's. But again, she did this not because she doubted women's mental capacities in comparison to men's. Men too broke down under the weight of their studies.

She attributed the nervous illnesses at Hartford specifically to an erroneous understanding of life's basic physicality—to ignorance of relevant scientific facts about human beings. The sciences she was learning and teaching had no bearing on experience. Breakdown taught her, she later said, that minds were housed in material brains; minds, although not necessarily sexed, were necessarily embodied. The idea that mind had no sex too often led to the idea that mind had no body; women who, thinking they would become less physical in proportion as they became more mental, studied themselves into hysteria, were making a lethal mistake. Beecher thus posed and answered the question how women should be educated from the standpoint of one who had tried the Enlightenment agenda and found it lacking. "How came the Author to write such a book?" she asked in the preface to the *Treatise*—and answered: because "she has herself suffered from the want of such knowledge, in early life; because others, under her care, have suffered from her ignorance" (xxi). In her own case, she explained, the school curriculum with its "constantly increasing demand for more studies, and decreasing value and respect for do-mestic pursuits and duties," ultimately "exhausted the nervous fountain, and my profession as a school teacher was ended" (*Woman Suffrage,* 20–21).

Beecher's phrase "nervous fountain" here follows the teachings of con-temporary physiology, according to which a fluid manufactured in the physical brain, from nutriment furnished by the blood as the outcome of digestion, circulates through the nerves and carries impulses from the brain to the rest of the body. Like every other aspect of the living body, this fluid is continually depleted and reconstituted. Without adequate fuel and fire, the brain cannot make the nervous fluid. Hence, nervous breakdowns are material, prevent-able diseases. "The first cause of mental disease and suffering," says the *Trea-tise* unsentimentally, "is not unfrequently the want of a supply of duly oxygenized blood" (187).

Preserving and enhancing woman's health in school and after therefore became central to her program, leading to an emphasis on physical educa-tion in school and regular exercise at home. Beecher is signally responsible for the introduction of physiology and calisthenics into girls' schools in the 1840s; she popularized the work of Dio (Dionysius) Lewis, who pioneered calisthenics in the United States. For, although she thought mental disease and suffering were not specific to women, she also saw that men had much more opportunity to exercise outdoors and thus to replenish their supply of duly oxygenated blood. Especially as the rising standard of living produced a genteel urbanized class of home-bound, idle women, their nervous diseases increased.

In this one respect, Beecher was indeed nostalgic for an earlier era of what she imagined as robustly physical women. *Home* (in a passage written by Stowe) invoked the "strong, hardy, cheerful girls, that used to grow up in country places, and made the bright neat, New-England kitchens of old times—the girls that could wash, iron, brew, bake, harness a horse and drive him, no less than braid straw, embroider, draw, paint, and read innumerable books" in contrast to the "fragile, easily-fatigued, languid girls of a modern age, drilled in book-learning, ignorant of common things" (317–318). Inso-far as women were schooled in cramped and unventilated quarters, and fur-ther immobilized indoors for hours of study, education made their lives materially worse.

If women are to be educated in the information and skills that will lit-erally keep them and their families alive, then Beecher's distress over the cur-rency of the "pernicious and mistaken idea, that the duties which tax a woman's mind are petty, trivial, or unworthy of the highest grade of intellect and moral worth" becomes quite understandable. Every woman, she continued, "should imbibe, from early youth, the impression, that she is training for the discharge of the most important, the most difficult, the most sacred and interesting duties that can possibly employ the highest intellect. She ought to feel that her station and responsibilities, in the great drama of life, are second to none" (*Treatise*, 144).

*B*eecher assumes that women's work requires knowledge of the sciences and technologies of human bodies and the physical spaces on which they depend, which reach out from the home to other physical spaces—the school, the church—and beyond these to the cosmos, which is the source of the air, light, heat, and nutriment required by bodies for survival. One might characterize Beecher, although the term is anachronistic for her time, as a *domestic ecologist*. She sees the physical body in constant interaction with the material world that surrounds it.

A reader who associates women's sphere with female ethereality, or spirituality, or moral superiority to the male, may be startled by Beecher's lengthy, detailed (and illustrated) discussions of how to choose and use the best stoves or furnaces or water closets. Yes, the mother is a teacher of her children, but her main pedagogical work involves instilling principles of order and decorum among her charges. The home Beecher gives advice about is a physical container that should be constructed and maintained according to the needs of those who dwell within, needs that are only to be understood through science. Of course the home she has in mind is a Christian home; but she sees no use in worrying about the residents' doctrines if noxious vapors are poisoning them. Systematic and informed attentiveness to the body's material needs—above all on behalf of robust physical health—was what Beecher defined as women's work. Her usual approach is bluntly mechanistic.

The *Treatise on Domestic Economy* strove to communicate its science in accessible language and through a rational organization, making the subject "a *branch of study* and not miscellaneous activities," defining it "as a science and not a series of mere handicrafts or technical activities" (Marjorie Brown, 188). Her book differed markedly from the heterogeneous advice manuals of the day, precisely because these manuals did not conceive of their material as scientific. Only Beecher wrote in this vein: "Before attempting to give any specific directions on the subject of this chapter, a short sketch of the construction of the human frame will be given, with a notice of some of the general principles, on which specific rules in regard to health are based. This description will be arranged under the general head of Bones, Muscles,

Nerves, Blood-Vessels, Organs of Digestion and Respiration, and the Skin" (*Treatise*, 48).[7]

Beecher segues from a polemical introduction to American women's particular responsibilities and challenges—like Hale, she thinks American women are destined "to be made effectual in the regeneration of the earth" (14)—to her real subject in the chapter called "On the Care of Health." This chapter outlines human physiology with the help of nine illustrations of the skeleton and internal organs. The next six chapters, on food, drink, clothing, cleanliness, early rising, and exercise, develop from and refer back to the physiology, chemistry, and physics of bodily needs that she has set forth at the beginning. One chapter on family relations is sandwiched between these chapters and others on the construction of houses, on heating, and on lighting. The family is thus inserted between the physical casings of bodies and houses. Beyond home are schools, churches, and workplaces, all of which Beecher judges, in the light of physiology and anatomy, as inadequate, if not downright dangerous, to the bodies they enclose.

Beecher's segment on family relations displays the mother as household manager and, as such, first the preserver of family health and physical well-being, next the instiller of system, order, and decorum. These, to Beecher, are necessary for the efficiency that is basic for doing one's work. Efficiency, the watchword of developing technocracy, is thus installed in tandem with the ongoing industrialization of the Northeast and sited in the home rather than the factory. For Beecher, efficiency is at once a new virtue and the updating of a very old one—the New England woman's gift of "faculty."

This rational, practical, knowledgeable, updated New England mother is also a teacher; she encourages her children's curiosity, gladly answers their questions, and constantly leans on and thereby indoctrinates her children in the authority of science. The *Treatise* contains hundreds of locutions like: "it is found, by experiments" (71); "in such cases, experiment, alone, can decide" (79); "for a similar reason" (82); "it may be set down as an unchangeable rule of physiology that" (85); "the experiments of physiologists all prove" (87); "the experiments of medical men have established the fact, that"; "extensive investigations have been made in France"; "this proves" (94); "it is a universal law of physiology, that" (108); "experiments, repeatedly made by chemists" (211). Beecher describes many scientific experiments, gives the results of others, names scientists, and explicates their findings. Maternal readers are thus connected to—affiliated with—science as its instructed consumers and advocates.

Beecher's physiology of bodies needing good air, good food, uncon-

stricting dress, and physical activity authorizes a move to physics and chemistry—physics for such concerns as air currents and the mechanics of efficient versus inefficient household devices; chemistry for combustion, the
composition of air, principles of sound diet, and appropriate cooking. Many
sciences converge on the human body to form a unified interdisciplinary field
of knowledge—physiology and anatomy, chemistry, physics, botany (in its
applied form of horticulture), natural history (in its applied form of animal
husbandry), geology and mineralogy (soils and fuels), and astronomy (heat
from the sun's rays)—in her academic program of women's sciences. The issue
for her is not which science is learned, but why it is learned and how it is
learned:

> A problem in arithmetic or geometry is far more interesting, and
> therefore more quickening to the intellect, when it is directly applied
> to some useful, practical purpose. Thus a woman who is daily cal-
> culating her butcher's and grocer's accounts, or trading in stores, is
> cultivating her intellect as much or more than she would by study-
> ing arithmetic in college or school without any end but to escape
> reproof or marks of imperfection. . . . Thus in kitchen affairs, domes-
> tic chemistry, though on a small scale, is constantly studied and prac-
> tically applied. Again in the care of infants and the sick, the discipline
> of the physiologist and the physician are united. (*Woman Suffrage*,
> 125–126)

*T*he *American Woman's Home* markedly adjusts the *Treatise* for a more advanced technological age. Its revisions speak to some major changes in household economies and women's work therein over the twenty-nine years since
the first publication of the *Treatise*. Yet, the much greater amount of scientific material, a good deal of it apparently quite current (the preface correctly
says that although the book should be considered a revision of the *Treatise*,
"a great portion of it is entirely new, embodying the latest results of science"
[15]), is placed within a much more nostalgic frame, in which self-sustaining
rural communities are described as the ideal but impossible cultural form.
Beecher is now suggesting much more overtly what she only implied in the
Treatise—that modern science is the route through which the best aspects of
an imagined, lost New England can be preserved and transmitted to the future.

Scientific advances dictate alterations in content, in phrasing, in organization. A new first chapter on "A Christian Family," far more pietistic than
anything in the *Treatise,* quickly abandons Christian ideology to view the

family as a working, not a worshiping, unit.[8] Thus she reverts to questions of material home construction, the "house contrived for the express purpose of enabling every member of a family to labor with the hands for the common good, and by modes at once healthful, economical, and tasteful." Wise women "will aim to secure a house so planned that it will provide in the best manner for health, industry, and economy, those cardinal requisites of domestic success" (24). Chapter 3, "A Healthful House," shifts to analyzing the relation between a building and the way it does or does not maintain the body.

The now overwhelming focus on heating, ventilation, and other air-centered concerns enlarges the earlier book's interaction between the physical body and its physical container, giving a whole chapter to "Scientific Domestic Ventilation" and another to "Stoves, Furnaces, and Chimneys." A much expanded course in physiology is scattered and iterated throughout the text rather than contained in one chapter; up-to-date explanations are provided for eating (digestive and breathing organs), dressing (bone structure), and bathing (skin structure). Chapters on family relations, including those with servants, continue to emphasize order and system. Chapter 35, "Earth Closets," brings the book back with a thud to the materiality it has never really abandoned: "The earth-closet is an invention which relieves the most disagreeable item in domestic labor, and prevents the disagreeable and unhealthful effluvium which is almost inevitable in all family residences" (403). Chapter 36, "Warming and Ventilation," returns to Beecher's great obsession with breathable air, an obsession that causes her repeatedly to remind people that they are part of, and dependent on, the physical world they inhabit.

As in the *Treatise*, Beecher hammers incessantly at the idea that the home space within which people eat, sleep, and breathe often kills them because the women in charge of home do not understand or apply the sciences of life. Subheads for Chapter 3 make the point: "Household murder—Poisoning and starvation the inevitable result of bad air in public halls and private homes—Good air as needful as good food—Structure and operations of the lungs and their capillaries and air-cells—How people in a confined room will [make] use of the oxygen of its air and overload it with refuse carbonic acid—Starvation of the living body deprived of oxygen" (ii).

Along with expanded physics and chemistry and updated natural history, Beecher now includes the galaxies (astronomy) and the earth's interior (geology). That "the earth is heated by radiation from the sun," that "air is not warmed by the passage of the sun's heat through it but by convection from the earth," speaks directly to the management of furnaces (79). Among the more than doubled number of illustrations in the new text are pictures of the microscope, an instrument absent from the *Treatise*; whereas the word "cell" did not show up in the *Treatise*, the *Home* uses the concept frequently and illustrates the cell structure of several different organs. Chapter 36 gestures toward the germ theory of disease, though it does not use the word:

> There are some recent scientific discoveries that relate to impure air which may properly be introduced here. It is shown by the microscope that *fermentation* is a process which generates extremely minute plants. . . . The microscope has also revealed the fact that, in certain diseases, these microscopic plants are generated in the blood and other fluids of the body. . . . And, what is very curious, each of these peculiar diseases generates diverse kinds of plants. . . . It is now regarded as probable that most of these diseases are generated by the microscopic plants which float in an impure or miasmatic atmosphere, and are taken into the blood by breathing. (421–422)

The reference to fermentation suggests familiarity with the work of Pasteur. Because the germ theory was only developed in the 1860s and 1870s and did not achieve wide circulation before the late 1870s (Tomes, 184), it seems clear that Beecher was keeping in touch with new scientific developments.

Finally, the terms *science* and *scientific* appear much more often in this book than in its predecessor, on almost every page and in a range of contexts. "This important duty of a Christian woman is one that demands more science, care, and attention than almost any other" (*Home*, 58); "the evils resulting from the substitution of stoves instead of the open fireplace, have led scientific and benevolent men to contrive various modes of supplying pure air" (58); "every woman should be taught the scientific principles in regard to heat, and then their application (66); "we shall give a brief outline of some of the leading scientific principles" (66); "modern science has proved" (141); "we are now prepared to consider the great principles of science" (142); "true cleanliness of person involves the scientific treatment of the skin" (150). If the *Treatise* had suggested that science was on the horizon of women's interests but ought to be central, *Home* now evokes science so familiarly and frequently as to suggest that Beecher addressed an audience fully indoctrinated in a scientific ideology.

𝓑eecher designed her *Treatise* and *American Woman's Home* as all-purpose books, useful for home and school alike. She assumed that a traditional apprenticeship system of girls to their mothers, who had informally apprenticed with their mothers, and so on, either no longer existed or, if it did, ought to be superseded. New kinds of information demanded new delivery systems and new teachers. From the start, she tried to find ways of training teachers to teach domestic subjects. She spent years of her life and invested much of her royalties establishing schools that would produce the teachers she thought women needed.

This enterprise fared far less well than her textbooks, in some part because she was a difficult person to work with, but in larger part because the curricular thrust in the elite girls' schools was overwhelmingly to teach subjects taught to men. The *Treatise* was adopted by the Massachusetts School Library System in 1842, but there is little sign that domestic science, or domestic economy, became regular fixtures in any of the prestigious women's schools, or indeed in the women's schools more generally (Woody, 415, 431, 441). Mary Lyon's Mount Holyoke academy required its pupils to do housework; but Mount Holyoke was designed for women from the agricultural and artisan classes, not the bourgeoisie; and even here, there was no formal study of the domestic arts (see chapter 9). Indeed, this was both an intellectual and a class issue; there was no avoiding the association of homemaking with physical labor and the downgrading of physical labor that accompanied rising social status. However much Beecher might argue to the contrary, her program looked retrograde to those who saw education as a way to amass or preserve the cultural capital of a literary as opposed to a manual education.

Still, Beecher's gender views attained some postbellum prominence as the advent of higher education for women opened so many new opportunities. All at once a plethora of postsecondary institutions for women emerged: single-sex liberal arts colleges in the East, coeducational land-grant colleges in the Midwest devoted to agriculture and technology, normal schools everywhere preparing women to teach in the hugely expanded field of public secondary education. Beecher directed her postbellum energies especially toward the colleges. Here the final battle for domesticity as a scientific subject was to be waged and, at least in Beecher's version of it—although well after her death—lost.

Beecher's late work redirected complaints over women's overly abstract education from the academies to the liberal arts colleges, where "young women are taught to draw mathematical diagrams and to solve astronomical problems; but few, if any of them are taught to solve the problem of a house constructed to secure pure and moist air by day and night for all its inmates" (*Home*, 58). She revived her contrast between understanding scientific principles in relation to tasks and learning them in a vacuum. While recognizing what makes a good stove is useful and "will cultivate the intellect quite as much as the abstract reasonings of Algebra and Geometry," the ability to solve problems in geometry is a skill for which young women "never have any practical use" (*Home*, 69–70). Beecher objected to the educational model set by Vassar, "the most conspicuous of the so-called colleges of women," whose curriculum was "very nearly the same as that of Yale and Cambridge, and nothing withdrawn or added with reference to the preparations of woman for her distinctive profession as housekeeper, mother, nurse, and chief educator of infancy and childhood" (*Reminiscences*, 184).

The year after the *American Woman's Home* appeared, she entered the field of college education by revising this book into a textbook for college use called, simply, *Principles of Domestic Science*, again with Stowe listed as coauthor. The text addresses not only the students who will go home better prepared to run their households, but also their teachers who, it is now hoped, are being recognized as professors of domestic science. She proposes specifically that professorships should be endowed in the colleges for this purpose. She justifies this new profession on two grounds.

First is the huge influx of immigrants needing domestic education:

> We are now entering upon a great and hazardous experiment, on which the prosperity and even the existence of our country depends. The nations of Europe and Asia have but begun that immense flood of emigration that is coming by millions; a large portion to enter our kitchens and schools. And the housekeepers and school-teachers of our country are to become missionaries, not to foreign lands, but to the heathen thronging to our homes and our schools. Oh! what glorious and yet fearful responsibilities rest on all of our profession! (*Principles*, 366–367)

Next is the large number of redundant women created by the Civil War who need employment. To turn these procreatively superfluous women into teachers of domesticity to immigrants demands another level of teacher, the teacher of teachers, the professor of education. "As the general rule every true woman would prefer to be a wife, mother, and housekeeper, could her ideal be fully met. But in multitudes of cases this can never be, and so, every women should prepare herself not only for the ordinary duties of the family state, but also for some profession to secure an *independent* livelihood" (*Reminiscences*, 201).

It is an ingenious move to yoke the supposedly needy immigrant population to the redundant genteel women, to place the most talented superfluous women as a higher level of pedagogue, the class of professoriat dedicated to a scientific and prestigious curriculum. *Principles of Domestic Science* hopes that "the department of practical life which hitherto has been, and must generally be, woman's favorite, peculiar and chosen one, might receive the honor of professorships, lectures, and scientific treatment, in the same manner as those branches which fit men for practical life" (357), adjusting Beecher's argument of 1841 to the postbellum condition:

> Were there employments for women honored as matters of science, as are the professions of men; were institutions provided to train women in both the science and practice of domestic economy, domestic chemistry, and domestic hygiene, as men are trained in agricultural chemistry, political economy, and the healing art; were there endowments providing a home and salary for women to train their own sex in its distinctive duties, such as the professors of college gain—immediately a liberal profession would be created for women, far more suitable and attractive than the professions of men. (359)

This new version of Beecher's argument against classical and abstract scientific education, her call for women's scientific professorships, well suited the early home economics agenda, which similarly looked outward at a needy population and inward toward the prestige of professional women. Beecher's writings became a kind of foundation for the discipline. The New England chemist Ellen Swallow Richards, who specialized in "Sanitary Engineering," the chemistry of pure food and especially of water, also organized the field of home economics "almost single-handedly" in the 1890s (Rossiter, *Struggles and Strategies*, 68). Ironically, perhaps, she had matriculated at Vassar, Beecher's "so-called" woman's college; but she selected Beecher as the field's foremother.[9] Her disciplinary rationales followed Beecher: "We cannot go back to any example in the past. Educated women must mark out a new plan for themselves. Our girls must be taught to recognize the profession of housekeeping as one of the highest" (*Food Materials*, 10).

Like Beecher, Richards tried unsuccessfully to install a home economics curriculum rather than a literary or abstract scientific one in the elite eastern women's colleges. It was in the Midwestern land-grant colleges, with their foundational technological emphasis, that home economics took hold. In the *American Woman's Home* and the *Principles of Domestic Science* Beecher had already recognized that the applied and technological emphasis of the land grant colleges would be more congenial to a home economics curriculum than the new colleges in the old eastern states. "The care of a house, the conduct of a home, the care of health, and the management of children and servants, are just as worthy of scientific treatment and scientific professors and lectureships as the care of farms, the conduct of manures and crops, and the raising of stock," she wrote—clear allusions to the agricultural and mechanical emphases of the land-grant schools. Then she went on to propose an equivalent "course of instruction on domestic philosophy and chemistry" for women, including

> first, the Chemistry of Cooking; next, Caloric or Heat in relation to domestic life, which would embrace all the principles of warming houses, of constructing furnaces, stoves, grates, and cooking-ranges, chimneys, and other heat-making and carrying arrangements; lastly, domestic Hydraulics, or the philosophical application of water to domestic uses and purposes, including all about wells, pipes, boilers, faucets. (*Home*, 355–356)

Like Beecher, early theorizers of home economics saw classical education as inherently male because, whatever was said about it, it was directed toward male vocations. Like her, they thought all applied science was gendered. And like her, they preferred applied science to theoretical science for general education. Richards's student Isabel Bevier—also a chemist and a New Englander—led the way as the second president of the Home Economics Association and as a professor at the University of Illinois.[10]

Bevier exulted over "how much coeducation and the technical schools have meant in the development of the education of women" and how these schools showed "that the industrial spirit was a mighty factor in education, that courses in applied science and applied art would have a place in the school programs, and that a knowledge of the classics was no longer the only measuring unit for educational standards" (Bevier and Usher, 13). Bevier also dismissed "much of women's early work in chemistry" as "a more or less indefinite playing with test tubes in which one of three results was expected—a beautiful color, a bad odor, or an explosion"; in contrast, in the land-grant schools a woman would quickly discover that "her brother took chemistry and bacteriology, not because some one had told him that it ought to form a part of a liberal education, but because he expected to use this knowledge later in his work with soil or in the dairy"; borrowing Beecher's example, she said women had realized "that the laws of heat could be illustrated by the kitchen range quite as adequately as by the steam engine" (14).

Another later home economics text, proselytizing for the field, also specified the felt gender bias of typical science instruction:

> It is only within comparatively recent times that any effort has been made to apply the same laws of heat and energy and chemical reaction to the fields in which they have the greatest application for women. The charge that women are not interested in science and do not grasp its principles, do not in fact have scientific minds, is due rather to the fact that in the past these principles have been taught through phenomena that do not come into the life and knowledge of women, than that women have any less ability for comprehending the truths of the subjects. (Cooley, 73)

Richards herself wrote that "the mechanical setting of life has become an important factor and this new impulse which is showing itself so clearly today for the modified construction and operation of the family home is the final crown or seal of the conquest of the last stronghold of conservatism, the home-keeper. Tomorrow, if not today, the woman who is to be really mistress of her house must be an engineer, so far as to be able to understand the use of machines" (quoted in Hunt, 289–290).

These critiques expose the covert gendering of allegedly universal science while installing gender openly at the level of application. This was exactly what Beecher had worked for, accepting and celebrating the gendered division of labor and turning to science as a partner for women's work equally with men's. Beecher's expectations for women teachers prefigured the home economists' expectation that women scientists would be implementers of gender-specific applications of science rather than participators in the creation of the science that was to be applied.

The ideological conflict over women's proper sphere at the heart of home economics did not disappear and was greatly complicated by the drift of the field away from natural science toward social science, psychology, and a frivolous consumerism. Women became professors of home economics before they became professors in other fields, but where women scientists over the long run were concerned, this "now seems to have hurt them as much as it helped" (Rossiter, *Struggles and Strategies*, 65). Separate but equal never produced equal prestige or salary; homemaking never became a profession. Wisely, Richards never surrendered her position as professor of sanitary engineering to accept a professorship of home economics.

Vast changes around the turn of the nineteenth into the twentieth century introduced for women many new professions centered on the frank program of "Americanizing" an immigrant population. Putting aside the political implications of cultural superiority and legitimate surveillance involved in these professions (of which the teaching of American literature is certainly one!), this idea of domestic science increasingly positioned the homemaker as a passive recipient of expert knowledge. In a 1900 article in the *Woman's Journal* Richards opines, Beecher-like, that "women, as a whole, have not become imbued with the scientific spirit of the age. They still cling to tradition. They defy natural law." Then she swerves crucially from Beecher's view. It is not, she continues, "a profound knowledge of any one or a dozen sciences which women need, so much as an attitude of mind which leads them to a suspension of judgment on new subjects, and to that interest in the present progress of science which causes them to call in the help of the expert" (quoted in Hunt, 290–291).

Burton Bledstein has shown how the postbellum elaboration of a professional culture of experts demanded and produced a complementary but dependent, hence inferior, culture of nonexperts. If not by definition, then by default, the female population was shunted into the nonexpert position. A belief in the interactive equality of affiliative audience with professional scientist was lost. Beecher, sensitive as she was to the increasing status of the professional ideal, clearly believed that women would not be satisfied if they were pushed to the cultural margins as mere onlookers or spectators. She imagined the female citizenry as recipient, but also as practitioner. This theorized reciprocity became less and less realizable in the postbellum era, as the home economists themselves recognized. There is a parallel here to the situation Almira Phelps deplored in postbellum botany: Ordinary people—women in particular—were being excluded from the practices and knowledges of science because these practices and knowledges had become far more specialized and mathematically demanding than their educations could accommodate.

In effect, Beecher's attempt to turn domestic women into scientific experts simply failed. But her attempt to help women move into scientific professionalism as professors of domestic economy gained momentum. In a kind of spiraling sequence, however, the emergence of a culture of specially female scientific professions (and, after the turn of the century, of social scientific professions) further disempowered women at home; the end that Beecher had in view—making home a space of satisfaction and productivity for women—failed altogether to be realized. Moreover, the funneling of professional women scientists into departments of home economics cut them off in numerous ways from scientific achievement and recognition.

Beecher never objected in principle to women's becoming scientists in the male sense of the term. But she restricted the actualization of this principle to exceptional women. A passage (in fact by Stowe) in *Home* grants that "every woman has rights as a human being which belong to no sex, and it ought to be as freely conceded to her as if she were a man," but then it limits these rights where science is concerned. If one is a born astronomer like Mary Somerville, then—but only then—"let not the technical rules of womanhood be thrown in the way of her free use of her powers"; for it is thoroughly absurd "to make the education of woman anti-domestic" in the foolish belief that all women were potentially Somervilles (*Home*, 316–317).

CHAPTER 5

Susan Fenimore Cooper and Ladies' Science

Susan Fenimore Cooper's *Rural Hours* (1850) showed how scientific knowledge contributed to an ideal of gracious country living for women.[1] The book's anonymous publication "by a Lady"—at a time when anonymous authorship had gone out of style—quaintly made the point that the author's name mattered less than her class affiliation.[2] The book is shaped as a journal kept almost daily throughout a year, beginning and ending in spring. It merges accounts of excursions in the Cooperstown environs with associated material pieced together from a huge array of print sources, most of them scientific.

Modern editors of *Rural Hours* describe the book as "a dynamic interplay of science and literary nature writing" (xi). Lawrence Buell calls Cooper a "literary bioregionalist" with an "encyclopedic passion for bringing bibliographical resources to bear" on her "native township" (406). Both descriptions point to Cooper's interleaving of the literary, the scientific, and the sheerly descriptive; but in confining the focus to Cooperstown ("literary bioregionalism") they overlook the way in which Cooper's use of scientific texts remakes the township as an item in a global survey, with the result that excursions in Cooperstown become a gateway to the world. Bibliographic allusions place the native township on a map that, in turn, is clearly shown to be the product of reading in the library. *Rural Hours* signals its intertextual intentions as early as the second entry (March 7), when the sighting of a loon introduces observations by Charles Lucien Bonaparte (probably from his 1838 *Comparative List of the Birds of Europe and North America*) about loons in the Alps and Apennines (4–5).

The reason for elevating nature into textuality involves, one might surmise, Susan Cooper's practical awareness that country life was rather dreaded than welcomed by genteel women. As an acute natural observer and inveterate reader, Cooper presents a way of being in the rural world that shows other elite women how to make rural life—in Sarah Ripley's phrase cited in chapter 1—"supportable," and quite specifically supportable to "fine ladies" (Goodwin, "Botanic Mania," 20). As Cooper says in a late footnote, the book, written "by a learner only," is offered "to those whose interest in rural subjects has been awakened" as "a sort of rustic primer, which may lead them, if they choose, to something higher" (330).

Behind Ripley's comment, and behind Cooper's book as well, one senses the writers' awareness that "ladies" usually hated rural life because it was boring and boorish. Cooper wants to change that perception, in part by changing the character of rural life itself. She writes in her introduction to *The Rhyme and Reason of Country Life* that she wants to contribute, and help other women contribute, to the "national progress" toward "country life in its better form" (31, 30). By "better form" she means a country life suitable for, and reflective of, genteel cultivation. Where Sarah Hale or Almira Phelps urged science on women as a means to attain and demonstrate their rationality, Cooper urges it on them as a way to attain and demonstrate that they had class.

This work on behalf of rational rural gentility had particular relevance to the decades when the appurtenances of leisured country life increasingly became signifiers of class status. Thanks to such emerging social markers as summer homes, weekend retreats, landscaped grounds, gentlemen's farming, recreational hunting, and scenic tourism, a group of urbanites with newly disposable income were being enticed back to a countryside whose poverty perhaps they or their parents had fled.[3] There had of course been from classical times a tradition of literary pastoral countering urban corruption with ideals of rural simplicity; but practically speaking, the harsh conditions of early national rural life did not support facile associations between the country and cultivated leisure.

There are many ways to account for the increasing reconstitution, in antebellum America, of vacant country real estate as adult playgrounds; the point is that people who well knew the harshness and sordidness of country life needed to be coaxed back to nature by learning to see it differently. It was no accident that the vogue for natural history in England and the United States arose just as access to country life became a status marker in both nations.[4] This coincidence may also help account for the success of *Rural Hours*, which was both fully aware of changing times and specifically directed toward women readers. The purpose of Cooper's work is to model country life as a constant intellectual, civilized, rational pleasure and therefore to show ladies a rational, civilized way of being ladylike. Country ladies demonstrate their class by reconstituting their rustic surroundings through a combination of literary and scientific knowledge.

In earlier chapters I have alluded to the function of school geography as a protoscience. The geographical approach to terrain in *Rural Hours* would not seem unfamiliar to readers, nor would its journal-like structure, which they would have encountered in the many biography-memoir hybrids published in the nineteenth century. The book obviously synthesizes these forms, along with models drawn from English writing about rural life.[5] Yet, the immediate inspiration for *Rural Hours* was probably the example of the well-known traveler and inventor of the science of physical geography (arguably, the construer of geography itself as a science), Alexander von Humboldt.[6] The first two volumes of Humboldt's magisterial and immensely popular multivolume *Cosmos* appeared in English in 1848, just when Cooper began her own project. Their publication led to the reissue of some of his earlier travel writings; the 1840s had also been the great decade of U.S. scientific exploration, including the Fremont land expedition and the Wilkes naval expedition.

Although *Rural Hours* does not resemble *Cosmos* in form, Humboldt's excitement about the huge world out there waiting to be catalogued, every individual item of which had some (perhaps as yet unknown) relation to the whole, could easily motivate a project whose aim is less to catalogue the locale accurately than to perceive its relation to the global. To be sure, Humboldt really traveled to all the places he wrote about, while in *Rural Hours* Cooper does her voyaging beyond Cooperstown through print resources. But this is exactly the point of *Rural Hours*; it shows how the judicious use of print resources allows country ladies to experience their surroundings as a cosmopolitan adventure.[7] *Rural Hours* may thus be thought of as a book of travels in which the use of scientific texts turns the local into the global while making travel a textual affair. Cooper shows repeatedly that even local terrain is unintelligible without the text-based interpretation. There is simply no recognizing the plant or bird one has sighted without consulting a guidebook; among diverse printed sources, none serve her purposes better than scientific works of natural history.

Because Cooper thinks that knowing where one is in the world requires textual knowledge rather than intuition, she collapses the distinction between reality and textuality just as she blurs the boundary between real and arm-chair travel. This is not to say that *Rural Hours* has no grounding in the real world. According to David Jones, the modern editor of the 1887 revision, her botanical identifications are of a caliber that "perhaps only a trained bota-nist can fully appreciate" (xxx). Yet, to the extent that the book is an instructed record of observations, it necessarily calls on texts. Anything but the artless, spontaneous record of walks and drives it sometimes pretends to be, *Rural Hours* thoughtfully refracts the notes on which it is based, which may have been recorded initially to be the basis for a book.[8]

Entries in Cooper's virtual journal vary from brief descriptions of the day's weather to extended set pieces, essays sometimes running to six thou-sand words or more. The connection between these essays and the day's out-ing is sometimes quite tenuous, suggesting that they might have been written independently of their position in the book. When bad weather precludes ex-cursions, especially in winter, Cooper chooses sometimes to describe what she sees outside the window, sometimes to concentrate entirely on summa-rizing and commenting on books. Some of her many topics are botanical and ornithological identifications, the habitats of undomesticated flora and fauna, agriculture, horticulture, sylvaculture, milling, mining, political economy, rural technologies, local architecture, hunting, fishing, folkways, holidays, and bib-lical exegesis. Among her print sources are books of natural history, includ-ing the official surveys of New York State and some of the New England states; journal, pamphlet, and newspaper items; statistical reports; geogra-phies; scientific travels; histories; and the Bible.

As she connects the terrain with the library, Cooper emerges as an ex-emplar of female rationality and decorous piety whose combination of sci-entific amateurism with Christian orthodoxy would not have been out of place twenty-five years earlier than the actual publication year of *Rural Hours*. No Transcendental intuitionist, she believes in the biblical God of Christian Rev-elation, who has authored nature but is not resident in it. As a devout Epis-copalian, she derived orthodox homilies from natural observation; these, scattered here and there in *Rural Hours*, are arguably the book's weakest seg-ments. She writes for example on May 16: "At hours like these, the immea-surable goodness, the infinite wisdom of our Heavenly Father, are displayed in so great a degree of condescending tenderness to unworthy, sinful man, as must appear quite incomprehensible—entirely incredible to reason alone— were it not for the recollection of the mercies of past years, the positive proofs of experience" (45).

If the whole book read like this, there would be little reason to open it now. But the persona also represents a contemporary revision of the English amateur scientist and gentleman perambulator, a sort of nationalized, feminized, and updated Gilbert White. Cooper writes in *The Rhyme and Reason of Country Life* that it is the union of Christianity with a "general diffusion of a high degree of civilization which has led us to a more deeply felt appreciation of the works of the creation," such that "the verse of the fields—the rural hymn,—becomes the last form of song, instead of being the first" (27, 29).[9]

As she construes country living as an opportunity for women readers to develop themselves as genteel ladies, she hopes to disrupt the traditional association of women *with* physical nature by showing them how to think *about* physical nature, so as to perform themselves as intellectual beings. This is a common motif among all advocates of a scientific education for women. But Cooper nuances the work of the previous generation of scientific affiliates, who argued that women should be proficient in science to demonstrate their possession of reason, by proposing that possession of scientific knowledge also testifies to their possession of class.[10]

There is much in *Rural Hours* about the shortcomings of uneducated folk; that Cooper is no rustic boor is something she is at pains to clarify, less perhaps because of any insecurity she might feel than because of the likely insecurities of her readers. She approaches country people themselves less as conservators of useful local knowledge than as a population in need of instruction. She often asks for the whereabouts of a plant she is seeking, or for the name of a plant she has found, only to encounter entrenched ignorance:

> It is really surprising how little the country people know on such subjects. Farmers and their wives, who have lived a long life in the fields, can tell you nothing on these matters. The men are even at fault among the trees on their own farms, if these are at all out of the common way; and as for the smaller native plants, they know less about them than Buck or Brindle, their own oxen. . . . The women have some little acquaintance with herbs and simples, but even in such cases they frequently make strange mistakes; they also are attracted by the wild flowers; they gather them, perhaps, but they cannot name them. (83)

In the context of pervasive rustic ignorance, Cooper's emphasis on right naming has obvious class implications. Her chief strategy in every botanical excursion in *Rural Hours*—to see what is there at a particular point in the calendrical year, to identify and interpret it according to the best authorities—

is something other than the desire to know nature as it really is. It is rather to know nature as the educated, enlightened, and well-bred know it. Whether she goes in quest of a particular natural object or takes what she finds, her proceedings always require names. The knowledge of the natural world she desires already translates the natural world into taxonomy. The concept of the "same" plant implies a standard. One cannot assert, or know, that the "same" plant is being differently named in different places or that "different" plants are getting the same name in different places without a stable point of reference. This stable point can only be imposed, top down, by scientific botany. The marsh marigold, for example, is a "handsome" flower called cowslip by the "country people"—"though different entirely from the true plant of that name" (30). She wants the name to be "true" to the "true" plant because she wants to integrate the particular with the general, the local with the global, under the sign of an Enlightenment universal science that is chiefly concerned to identity discrete species correctly so as to compile a comprehensive planetary inventory of the creation.[11]

But if, on the one hand, Cooper installs a distinction between herself and the rural population, or more generally between herself and those who needed to earn their own livings, she also installs one between herself and the sciences on which she relies to elevate herself above country and working people. She says her book, written "by a learner only," makes "no claim whatever to scientific knowledge" (3). In calling herself a learner only, she may be distancing herself from the financially needy women textbook writers whom she might otherwise seem to resemble. At any rate, she portrays herself as sitting gratefully at the feet of such notable natural historians as James Ellsworth De Kay (330), or "Professor S. F. Baird, Major Le Conte, and Mr. M. A. Curtis," who are thanked for personal help in her edition of Knapp (20). De Kay compiled the zoology and ichthyology volumes of the New York State natural history survey; the zoologist Spencer Baird helped amass the Smithsonian's natural history collections; John Eatton Le Conte, an army topographical engineer, produced an elegant North American lepidoptera; Moses Curtis was a botanist and ornithologist. All these men were family friends.

Yet her admiration for these experts is carefully balanced by a recognition that their professional work needs translation to suit the needs of amateurs in the country. Except for a few self-conscious Linnaean footnotes, she uses vernacular names, because they are attractive and accessible, and therefore (for an audience that must be persuaded to her project rather than commanded) useful. Although in many ways as eager as Almira Phelps to conscript women for science and use science for disciplinary purposes, for her audience the pedagogical stance of a Phelps or Catharine Beecher would be counterproductive. She chooses to present herself as a student for whom continuing with her science is a refined intellectual entertainment. Science merges with esthetics; Cooper suggests even that Linnaean taxonomy as such is merely the arbitrary nomenclature of scientists rather than anything inherent in the species or genus. She has, of course, no smidgen of a constructionist attitude toward scientific professionalism; it is simply that her old-style Natural Theology maintained that in relation to the mind of God, all systems of human naming are necessarily artificial.

Because names are artifices, even though they are necessary, Cooper feels free to use those best suited to her purposes, which are to make nature scientific and make science attractive to an esthetically sensitive group of genteel women. The best choice for this group is the English vernacular. She rejects Native American names with considerable vehemence as unpronounceable and, of course, ungenteel. The combined plainness and picturesqueness of English vernacular names are esthetically pleasing; using them at once makes clear that the user has no professional scientific pretensions and is of English descent. The focus on the esthetic comports with the Natural Theology idea that God's goodness and wisdom are evident in his making nature beautiful, which gives people pleasure and prepares them to admire it as evidence of the divine government of the cosmos. All this is at stake in one of the book's set pieces (June 23), which complains specifically about Latinate botanical nomenclature:

> What has a dead language to do on every-day occasions with the living blossoms of the hour? Why should a strange tongue sputter its uncouth, compound syllables upon the simple weeds by the wayside? If these hard words were confined to science and big books, one would not quarrel with the roughest and most pompous of them all; but this is so far from being the case, that the evil is spreading over all the woods and meadows, until it actually perverts our common speech. (83)

The rationale for common names asserts itself soon after this passage: "If we wish those who come after us to take a natural, unaffected pleasure in flowers, we should have names for the blossoms that mothers and nurses can teach children before they are 'in Botany'" (87).

Because she wants to make her subject attractive, Cooper is interested in esthetics. But because attractiveness has its use, esthetics is more than a luxury. Taking pleasure in rural scenery, and pointing to the beauties that have caused that pleasure, become elements of a rationalized, systematized approach to surroundings. Cooper may well have thought of esthetics itself as a nascent science. Several discourses already recognized as scientific—notably optics and acoustics, divisions of natural philosophy, or physics—involved reciprocal interactions between human perceptual apparatus (eye and ear) and environment. Drawing and painting were both increasingly defined as professional, teachable skills requiring systematic knowledge of geometry (for drawing), chemistry (for pigments and solvents in painting), and physics (for understanding color and light and the optics of perception). Cooper's *Elinor Wyllys,* which features a character who wants to be an artist, contains several discussions about the optics and chemistry of painting light.

"Taste," too, had been a major target of Enlightenment efforts to systematize esthetic response. Cooper's language of "pleasing effect" throughout *Rural Hours* assumes the existence of universally accepted standards that can be transmitted, as for example through Andrew Jackson Downing's bestselling treatise on landscape architecture. Working from Edmund Burke and other theorizers of the sublime and picturesque, along with the work of English landscapers like John Loudon, Downing—a close associate of the Cooper family whom Cooper cites—describes taste as an inalienable, objective attribute of natural objects, from which position his prescriptions for constructing and appreciating country surroundings were made to seem entirely objective.[12]

In between the beginning and end of scientific perception, for both of which Cooper require a stabilized name, she connects named objects in a scientific web of other names. Even the most apparently unmediated entry turns out on closer examination to be thoroughly, adroitly comparative. Take trees, for example. Before the end of May (the journal begins on March 4) she has identified local varieties of alder, ash, aspen, bass-wood, beech, birch, butternut, chestnut, elm, hemlock ("Some of the hemlocks have a much closer and more compressed upright growth than those commonly met with; so that one is almost tempted to believe there are two distinct varieties" [51]), hickory, locust ("always the last to open its leaves" [50]), maple, oak, pine (we have "but one pine," she will write later on, "though that one is the chief of its family; the noble white pine" [129]), poplar (but not "the great northern or balsam poplar," which "is found at Niagara and on Lake Champlain, but the farmers about here seem to know nothing of it" [43]), spruce, sumac, tamarack (an easy find, since "there are many planted in the village, and in summer they are a very pleasant tree, though inferior to the European larch" [30]), walnut, and golden willow ("the weeping willow is not seen here, our winters are too severe for it" [31]).

Cooper's method of authenticating her identifications follows guidebook convention; it notes the distinctive features of the species, that is, the features that differentiate it. Accordingly she must inform readers about a great deal that she does *not* see: not the great northern or balsam poplar, not the European larch, not the weeping willow. She also explains why she knows some things to be what they are rather than something else—for example, because local winters are too severe for weeping willows, the willow one sees is another kind. Sighting meadowlarks on July 30, she writes that "climate seems to affect them but little, for they reach from the tropics to 53° north latitude, and they are resident birds in the lower countries of our own State" (136)—information with no basis in anything that Cooper could actually have seen. In the course of observing and identifying a total of approximately fifty species of local birds, Cooper describes a much larger number of species. One bird leads to another—the sight of a white-bellied swallow (the tree swallow) invites discussion of other kinds of swallows: the bank swallow, "entirely a stranger here, though found on the banks of lakes and rivers at no great distance; we have seen them, indeed, in large flocks among the sand-hills near the Susquehannah, just beyond the southern borders of the county" (36); the cliff swallow, "also a stranger here," the first pair of which only appeared in New York State in 1824 (37). Blue jays lead to "another kind of jay—the Canada jay—sometimes seen in this State" (193); a pair of golden-winged woodpeckers to other woodpeckers—"we frequently see the downy woodpecker, and the hairy woodpecker, in the village" as well as the "handsome red-head, one of the migratory woodpeckers" now "much more rare in our neighborhood than it used to be" and the pileated woodpecker, "said to have been occasionally seen here of late years; but we have never observed it ourselves" (187).

Two paragraphs about naturalized weeds name sixty-six of the "most common," which are "now choking up all our way-sides" (64–65)—a remark suggesting to a rapid reader that she saw and recognized this astonishing number of species during just a few walks. Closer attention suggests however that she is simply summarizing material from a systematic botany: "others still might be added to the list" (65). When she says that "the shepherd's-purse, with others, is common in China, on the most eastern coast of Asia" and "the gimson weed, or Datura, is an Abyssinian plant, and the Nicandra came from

Peru" (65), she is not really describing the weed in her own locale. She has abstracted it from the immediate place and reconstructed it as a datum in the global picture. Although she calls "foreign" weeds "troublesome," "noxious," an "evil" requiring "patient care and toil" to keep within bounds, making it "the chief labor of the month to wage war upon their tribe," there is no sign that she recognizes why foreign weeds might easily overcome the indigenous. Her interpretation of the fact is strictly theological: "These noxious plants have come unbidden to us, with the grains and grasses of the Old World, the evil with the good, as usual in this world of probation. . . . The useful plants produce a tenfold blessing upon the labor of man, but the weed is also there, ever accompanying his steps, to teach him a lesson of humility" (66).[13]

The passage makes conventional use of natural phenomenon to construct a Christian homily (what Buell calls "homiletic naturism" [402]). If, however, Cooper sermonizes from natural history, so too does she attempt to understand the Bible itself as a scientific document. Just as she wants to get the name right for local plants, she wants to get the names right for biblical references to flora and fauna. The entry for May 1 contains a long discussion of the likely species of willow referred to in Psalm 137: "When we read of those willows of Babylon, in whose shade the children of Israel sat down and wept, thousands of years ago, we naturally think of the weeping willow which we all know to be an Asiatic tree. But the other day, while reading an observation of a celebrated Eastern traveller, the idea suggested itself, that this common impression might possibly be erroneous" (31). (Readers who "naturally" think of the weeping willow when they read Psalm 137 because they "all know" it to be an Asiatic tree comprise an ideally educated audience.) Now, having been provoked by Sir Robert Ker Porter's reference to the gray ozier willows of Palestine, she consults "several" travel books and finds no reference in any of them to the weeping willow. "The assertion, that it is the tree of the Psalmist is universally made, but we have never yet seen a full and complete account of the grounds for this opinion; and, so far as we can discover, no such statement has yet been published" (32).

This passage makes it once again abundantly clear how much *Rural Hours* is about translating nature into information through which it can be intellectually and instrumentally known. In winter, when bad weather keeps her housebound and few species are to be observed through the window, Cooper often works up descriptive lists of birds and animals that she has never seen but that have been spotted in the region (the parakeet! the ibis!). Winter is also the time to write at length about the great mammals who have disappeared from the region. The social value of all these facts for Cooper is their transformation of rural life into an intellectual text, which makes the provincial into a cosmopolitan and translates bleak days into mental festivals.

*T*he seasonal approach in *Rural Hours* is itself another sign of Cooper's belief that nature requires translation and abstraction to be comprehensible. She recognizes that, while the seasons are facts of nature independent of the human, they are apprehended in human, that is, instrumental terms by human beings. Being able to predict and prepare for seasonal change in whatever climate one resides is the basic fact of human survival and hence of human history. The sciences of natural history recognized this fact; all official surveys were inventories of resources for present or future exploitation. Natural historians frequently referred to Linnaeus's recommendation that farmers should chart natural growth for agricultural purposes. In Howitt's *Book of the Seasons*, Linnaeus is quoted as saying that every farmer should "diligently mark the time of budding, leafing, and flowering of different plants" and "also put down the days on which his respective grains were sown" so that, "by comparing these two tables for a number of years, he will be enabled to form an exact calendar for his spring corn" (101–102).

Samuel Deane's well-known and often reissued *New England Farmer*, which from its first appearance in 1797 was calling for an Enlightened—experimental—rather than traditional approach to farming, urged "naturalists" to chart blossoming along with leafing on a local level. Because vegetation "is not equally forward, in each degree of latitude," they should list

> a considerable number of trees and shrubs, which are common, and near at hand; carefully watch their appearances, and minute the times of the first opening of their leaves, and also of their blossoming. . . . When these accounts are obtained, let trials be made by sowing a certain kind of seed before, at, and after the foliation, or the flowering, of some particular plant, and the produce compared. Let accurate experiments of this kind be yearly repeated, with all the most useful spring plants; by this, in a few years, complete kalendars may be obtained for every degree of latitude in this country. The consequence will be, that the farmer will be able infallibly to read the true times of sowing, by casting his eye upon the trees and shrubs that are about him. (236–237)

Deane wants similar "kalendars" of weather, winds, and "state of the atmosphere" made for "every climate in this country" (486).

The purpose here is not to know nature in the Thoreauvian sense (although Thoreau also prided himself in *Walden* for making the earth say beans instead of grass and in his late journals aspired to compile just such calendars, which he even spelled with a *k*), but to enable humans to use the earth for their own sustenance. Susan Cooper believed that this connection of people to the earth was divinely ordained, and therefore, as Johnson and Patterson observe, that it "is consistent with God's will" that "humans convert the wilderness into a land that is shaped and cultivated" (xix).

> The hand of man generally improves a landscape. The earth has been given to him, and his presence in Eden is natural; he gives life and spirit to the garden. Where there is something amiss in the scene, it is when there is some evident want of judgment, or good sense, or perhaps some proof of selfish avarice, or wastefulness, as when a country is stripped of its wood to fill the pockets or fill the fires of one generation. ("Dissolving View," 82)

Because Cooper thought the earth had been given to humankind, she also thought the human presence could always be discerned on it. She likes to make the landscape reveal its human history.[14] For example, in *Rural Hours* for June 27: "While observing, this afternoon, the smooth fields about us, it was easy, within the few miles of country in sight at the moment, to pick out parcels of land in widely different conditions, and we amused ourselves by following upon the hill-sides the steps of the husbandman, from the first rude clearing, through every successive stage of tillage, all within range of the eye at the same instant" (89).

A habit of superimposing landscapes for purposes of topographical history is especially visible in Cooper's essay "A Dissolving View," published in an 1852 anthology about American scenery, *The Home Book of the Picturesque*. The essay culminates with an overlaying of "merrie England" on a prospect of Cooperstown as she observes it from a nearby height. Wooden bridge, courthouse, seven taverns, a dozen stores, churches, and a hundred houses disappear; the town "dwindles to a mere hamlet" with "low, picturesque thatched cottages," an old church, a tavern, "two or three small, quiet-looking shops," and a stone bridge. Surrounding hills are "shorn of wood," hedges divide the fields and line the roads, there are country houses, a castle, a former convent, and no fewer than nine similar hamlets in view (91–92). The "same" topography cannot be the "same" when it has a different human history; scenery always represents and reflects national character, national history, and the national economy.[15]

The significance of human history for the landscape is so compelling to Cooper that in "Dissolving View" she even takes issue with Louis Agassiz's claim that America is, geologically speaking, an old land compared to Europe (thereby disclosing, of course, that she was up to date on her Agassiz). "He tells us that in many particulars our vegetation, our animal life, belong to an older period than those of the eastern hemisphere"; but "without doubting this theory"—of course one does not openly challenge an expert!—"still there are many peculiarities which give to this country an air of youth beyond what is observed in the East. There are many parts of Europe, of Asia, of Africa, which have an old, worn-out, exhausted appearance; sterile mountains, unwooded moors, barren deserts and plains" (90).

Here Cooper is not talking about the cultural superiority of the United States, or even its political promise; she is talking about deforestation and depletion of resources. Her concerns are land use and overuse—concerns that have led Johnson and Patterson among others to identify her as proto-environmentalist. Far more important than the picturesqueness of the stone bridge in this English picture is the fact that it, like the other structures described, is made of stone. The hills shorn of wood mark a historical point in the economic development of a society when wood is no longer available, a point exactly and dangerously coincident with increased population. In Cooperstown, by contrast, all the structures are wooden, and there are plenty of trees around. That England is an "old" country and the United States a "new" one, in human terms, is written in the amount of forested land.

But Cooperstown is in process, just like any other place on the globe. The English story is destined to become the American story as well. Today, Cooper writes in *Rural Hours* (July 28), a person fond of the forest, "by picking his way, and following a winding course, may yet travel a long mile over a shady path, such as the red man loved." Already it takes work and imagination to fantasize the locale as wholly forested; "another half century may find the country bleak and bare." This phrasing suggests regret, and there is some of that; but she also describes deforestation as a "wonderful change" (128), having awakened a land that "lay slumbering in the twilight of the forest. Wild dreams made up its half-conscious existence" (127). In the context of Cooper's drive to intellectualize, phrases like "slumbering" and "half-conscious" are negatives. Understanding the productive capacity of the earth and exploiting it are positive goods; misuse of the earth, always possible, is understood not in terms of nature itself as an absolute good, but in terms of exhausting a resource that the human population depends on.

Insofar as human consumption of the earth's products marks the end point of Cooper's rationale for understanding nature in scientific terms, the market enters her account. For example, in *Rural Hours* a long section on maple sugar (April 1) begins with two socioeconomic facts: "Fresh maple sugar offered for sale to-day; it is seldom brought to market early as this" (13). From this starting point Cooper moves to a full description of rural sugar-making technology: "A hole is first bored into the trunk, from one to three feet from the ground"; a small trough is inserted, "usually made of a branch of alder or sumach, which is sharpened at one end and the pith taken out for two or three inches"; the sap drips into buckets, "a regular article of manufacture in the country," made of pine "or at times of bass-wood," and selling "at twenty cents a piece" (14). That local maple sugar is mainly produced for farm use—not for village sale—is explained as the market outcome of cane sugar's being "produced so easily, and so cheap, from the West Indies and the southern part of our own country, that there is little motive for making that of the maple an article of commerce. Maple sugar sells in the village this year for nine cents a pound, and good Havana for six cents" (15–16). At the end of her discussion, Cooper abandons the village food mart for the global intellectual mart, via the natural history and geography that always returns her to print; "Many other trees are tapped for their juices in different parts of the world. . . . They prepare from the sap of the Palm of Chili, a syrup of the consistency of honey, using it as an article of food. In Northern Europe, the birch sap is made into a drink which they call birch-wine. . . . In the Crimea, the Tartars regularly make sugar from the fine walnut-trees on the shores of the Black Sea. So says Dr. Clarke in his Travels." The entry ends with statistics offered for no apparent reason other than that statistics are good to know: "According to the last general Census, the whole amount of maple sugar made during one year in this county, with a population of 49,658, was 351,748 pounds, or nearly eight pounds to each individual. The whole amount of sugar made in the State, was 10,048,109 pounds" (16).

In the longest set piece in the book, about disappearing forests (July 28, 125–135), Cooper channels trees through pietistic, esthetic, and moral discourses before settling into the blended statistical, scientific, and commercial approaches that fundamentally characterize *Rural Hours*. "What a noble gift to man are the forests!" she begins, romantically enough; but practicality enters immediately: "What a debt of gratitude and admiration we owe for their utility and their beauty!" (125). She thanks the Creator; expatiates Bryant-like on the mingled signs of life and death in the forest; invokes a formulaic prehistory of vanished Indians. Then her inventory begins: "Perhaps two-fifths of the woods in our neighborhood are evergreens, chiefly pine and hemlock. . . . Neither the yellow, the pitch, nor the red pine is known here. . . . The oak of several varieties, white, black, the scarlet, and the red; the beech, the chestnut; black and white ashes; the lime or bass-wood; the white and the slippery elms; the common aspen, the large-leaved aspen; the downy-leaved poplar, and the balm of Gilead poplar; the white, the yellow, and the black birches, are all very common" (129).

After several paragraphs like this she starts to lament—not however over lost trees as an environmentalist might expect, but over rustic ignorance:

> One would think that by this time, when the forest has fallen in all the valleys—when the hills are becoming more bare every day—when timber and fuel are rising in prices, and new uses are found for even indifferent woods—some forethought and care in this respect would be natural in people laying claim to common sense. . . . Our people seldom remember that the forests, while they provide food and shelter to the wildest savage tribes, make up a large amount of the wealth of the most civilized nations. . . . Our fields are divided by wooden fences; wooden bridges cross our rivers; our village streets and highways are being paved with wood; the engines that carry us on our way by land and by water are fed with wood; the rural dwellings without and within, their walls, their floors, stairways, and roofs are almost wholly of wood; and in this neighborhood the fires that burn on our household hearths are entirely the gift of the living forest. (132–133)

True to her class, Cooper blames this waste on "the people" and suggests that those with long-term investments in land—owners as opposed to tenants—are more apt to conceive of trees as a renewable market crop as well as in "an intellectual and in a moral sense" (133). These things go together. "There is also something in the care of trees which rises above the common labors of husbandry, and speaks of a generous mind" (134). Only when the entire population becomes highly civilized—and "time is a very essential element, absolutely indispensable, indeed, in true civilization"—will ordinary farmers recognize that "a large shady tree in a door-yard is much more desirable than the most expensive mahogany and velvet sofa in the parlor" (133). Interchanging the tree with furniture, equating the esthetic with the civilized, attaching a literal cash value to the esthetic (and hence to the civilized), Cooper fuses esthetics and cash: "How easy it would be to improve most of the farms in the country by a little attention to the woods and trees, improving their appearance, and adding to their market value at the same time!" (134).

Many passages in *Rural Hours* show appreciation of country ways, but at best these are graciously patronizing or amusedly nostalgic. Cooper's distinction between herself and the country folk allows her to consider them as though they too are part of nature, are objects for her imperial gaze. One of the most extended set pieces in the book (July 3) describes a visit to a farm where the interconnections between old-fashioned virtues and agricultural practices are exhibited. Cooper assures her perhaps skeptical readers that one "who goes to enjoy and not to criticise, will find enough to please him about any common farm, provided the goodman be sober and industrious, the housewife be neat and thrifty" (96). "We went into her little buttery; here the bright tin pans were standing full of rich milk; everything was thoroughly scoured, beautifully fresh, and neat" (97). An encounter with local schoolchildren whose clothes are neatly patched (October 31) produces a celebration of the patch as evidence of old-fashioned prudence, simplicity, good sense, class awareness, and industry; it shows that the wearer is "not ashamed of honest poverty, and does not seek to parade under false colors," and it is "honorable to that man or woman to whom Providence has appointed the trial of poverty" (226).

As she thinks about how these patched children are being educated, she produces a deeply conservative critique of contemporary U.S. pedagogy for encouraging self-expression ("impulse") rather than "restraint," which ought to be "more especially the moral point in education." Where instruction in restraint is absent, she writes, "discipline and self-denial are wanting, with all the strength they give to integrity, and honor, and true self-respect, with all the decencies of good manners which they infuse into our daily habits" (228). Cooper need not say directly, indeed must not say directly since that would be indecorous, what is nevertheless redundantly clear in her self-presentation: that she herself exemplifies the outcome of an education in restraint, and that the scientific languages through which she mediates her encounters with nature exemplify the constant disciplining of her intellect.

To sum up: For Cooper the highest form of human relation to the created world is devotional, but *Rural Hours* is only occasionally a devotional book. It is a secular work privileging natural science above other forms of knowledge as a way to connect with one's surroundings and connect one's surroundings to the information web that is reconstituting human understanding. The book elaborates and updates a republican ideal of a lady's life that detaches her from idleness, frivolity, and extravagance and turns her into an industrious worker on behalf of developing her own intellectuality through acquisition of information, thereby raising the civilized tone of rural society. Cooper's special work for the sciences is to show that they are the epitome of socially desirable knowledge, and thereby to translate them into items for genteel consumption. As I have been showing, the Enlightenment goal of construing women as mental beings took on special force when connected to science. Cooper clarifies what might always have been the class implications of this argument by making the lady who does science in amateur fashion into the highest development of the human female. Raising the social tone by assimilating science into the lady's repertoire becomes Cooper's special mission and gives the lady herself a mission as she comes to occupy the amateur position vacated by male professionals.

As she successively revised *Rural Hours* to keep it cogent in a changing world, Cooper interestingly shifts the balance between nature and science. In her preface to the lightly revised 1868 version of *Rural Hours*, Cooper alludes to changes in rural life brought about by the telegraph, gaslight, and railroad. These have made some of the work she had done to connect Cooperstown to the wider world superfluous. The country, if distant from the city, was no longer isolated from it. Concurrently, primitive rurality begins to assume a nostalgic charm. Despite the inroads of modernity, she assures readers, we still "may be as rustic as we please. The hills, and the woods, and the lake, may still afford us true delight" (xxvii). In 1850, in contrast, she had aimed to move the rustic world into the modern age.

The revision of 1887 is far more drastic. Removing her preface of 1868, Cooper also deletes about a quarter of the 1850 text. Deletions include entries that merely mention the weather, all biblical exegesis, dated criticism of local practices, obsolete statistics, global natural history, and, in fact, most of the scientific materials. The residual book contains little more than accounts of the excursions, so that the descriptions of natural phenomena appear much less mediated and contextualized than they had in 1850. Now, too, the book is published as Cooper's, not as an anonymous lady's.

It would appear that the lady herself, and her mission as well, have become obsolete in the late nineteenth century. With no lady in the title, and no criticism of the locals for their ignorance, *Rural Hours* is far more egalitarian in 1887 than it had been in 1850. The disappearance of the science is related, of course, to the vanished lady, because its role had been predicated on representing a specific kind of gentility.

By this point, too, the wilderness ethos had become far more powerful in American thinking about nature after the Civil War, as the West was "opened" and the idea of national parks as preserves of pristine nature took hold. The wilderness myth produced a corresponding form of imaginative nature writing, the one we know today—a form idealizing unmediated communion with an imagined untouched nature, a nature lacking human history and detached from the scientific understanding that humans had imposed on it.[16]

Without its panoply of scientific references, *Rural Hours* in 1887 looks much more like this newer sort of nature writing than did Cooper's book of 1850. From this angle one might call the 1887 *Rural Hours* a gesture of disaffiliation from science. Although Cooper would never go so far as to construct her natural world as a form of anti-science, or claim that Cooperstown was wilderness, or blame science and technology for the distresses of modernity, the late version of the book clearly intimates that one ought to approach local flora and fauna not for their value as natural history or global inventory, but as items useful for imagining a wilderness that exists, perhaps, somewhere else. Because she is no longer writing as a midcentury lady, Cooper has abandoned her science.

CHAPTER 6

Elizabeth Cary Agassiz and Heroic Science

*I*n 1850 Elizabeth Cabot Cary of Boston married the Swiss-born scientist Louis Agassiz, whose immigration to the United States four years earlier had given the nation its first bona fide scientific celebrity. She raised the three adolescent children of Louis's first marriage (his first wife, from whom he was separated, died in 1849). She managed the family finances, even founding and administering an elite girls' school in their home for eight years to meet expenses. Over time, she fed and housed dozens of her husband's colleagues and assistants. She also learned his science, developed an elegant literary style, and by the early 1860s had became his amanuensis, interpreter, publicist, ghostwriter, and apologist.[1]

Elizabeth Agassiz was one among hundreds of nineteenth-century women for whom science was a family matter; the majority of working scientists in England, France, and the United States probably received some amount of scientific help from wives, daughters, and sisters who prepared and catalogued specimens, took notes, handled correspondence, organized field trips, prepared and checked manuscripts, and carried out myriad other necessary tasks.[2] But Elizabeth Agassiz turned this conventional affiliation into a literary profession more successfully and systematically than anyone else.[3] Her labor, undertaken in commitment to a particular scientist, promoted science more generally in the culture by circulating the figure of her husband as a paradigm of what a scientist ought to be. Whether the picture she painted corresponded to the real man was beside the point. The numerous Agassiz Clubs founded after the Civil War for local study of natural history, in which his name was perpetuated, owe perhaps as much to her publicity as to the work of the man she publicized.

Unlike at least some women associated with professional scientists, Elizabeth Agassiz made none of the discoveries attributed to and claimed by the men. She never assisted her husband in the physical work of field or laboratory. She adopted the stance of appreciative onlooker, what Christoph Irmscher has called "a position of graceful innocence" (250). But this strategic position only partly masked her energetic work on Louis's behalf. In a memorial composed shortly after her death, Thomas Wentworth Higginson described her in action through a typical anecdote of people trying vainly to understand one of Louis's scientific drawings. Just as they would be about to give up "in utter hopelessness," she would "glide up behind them and say sweetly, 'Oh, I think I am lucky to be able to explain that one drawing, for I happened to be near by when the professor was explaining it yesterday. I think it represents, etc.' till both the inquirers felt forever armed with knowledge especially when supplied from the lips of a lovely woman" (Paton, 58).

In twenty-five years of science writing, as well as in person, Elizabeth Cary Agassiz performed this disappearing act, either effacing her own contribution or pointedly contrasting it to Louis's achievements as the product of a weaker feminine versus stronger masculine intellect. Implicitly and explicitly, minimizing her contributions to his public reputation, she represented herself as a devotee of beauty and Louis as a rational, scientific male. More precisely, she depicted herself as a lover of beautiful surfaces and a seeker after esthetic impressions, compared to Louis as a believer in the beauty of underlying, objectively real structure. Moreover, she showed that uncovering and explaining underlying structure was the scientist's allotted task and one that demanded far more rigor and intelligence than the esthete's pursuit of pleasure.

Identifying esthetic enjoyment of surface as natural to both women and the less educated, while ceding the abstract perception of structure to men, Elizabeth made women lesser creatures than men on the Enlightenment ladder, where reason is the highest human attribute. Still, she finds that women's natural possession of an esthetic sensibility allows them to do the necessary, derivative work of belletristic scientific writing. Like Susan Cooper, she addresses an audience of leisured women (but unlike Cooper, of men as well) rather than students. Her work, however, is no less necessary than that of professional pedagogues. Her work, like theirs, leaves scientific men free to devote their stronger rational powers to the production of original science. What

Almira Phelps had written in the 1830s remained true for Elizabeth Agassiz even fifty years later: Women could not hope to add discoveries of their own to science but should consider it a privilege to be "permitted to share" in its "sublime discoveries," and to "feast on the banquet of knowledge, prepared by others" (Phelps, *Fireside*, 185).

There is no sign that Elizabeth had any interest in science before she met Louis. Her home studies centered on the old-time female accomplishments of music, drawing, and languages. But from the time she founded the Agassiz school in 1855 (which featured Louis's lectures as its main attraction),[4] and continuing to the end of her husband's life, she attended most of his lectures, took copious notes, and shaped them into the compositions that formed the basis of "much of what he published" (Hawkins, 22). Among these, at least twenty-one lecture-based popular articles in the *Atlantic Monthly* were written entirely by her and later revised by her for three books: *Methods of Study in Natural History* (1863), *Geological Sketches* (1866), and *Geological Sketches, Second Series*, appearing in 1875 after Louis's death.

Under her own name Elizabeth brought out two natural history books about radiates—an introductory text for young children and an adult guide to the New England seacoast—citing Louis or his son Alexander as the sources for all the facts and strenuously insisting on her own amateur status.[5] She accompanied Louis on several of his late expeditions and validated his professional work—along with her own amateurism—by becoming an accomplished travel writer, whose work included three *Atlantic Monthly* articles ("A Dredging Excursion in the Gulf Stream," "In the Straits of Magellan," and "A Cruise Through the Gallapagos") and a big book about the so-called Thayer expedition to Brazil. Although *A Journey in Brazil* was published as a collaboration and is usually catalogued under Louis's name, in fact she was its principal author, as everybody in their social circle knew and as Louis himself readily acknowledged in the footnotes and addenda that he provided (e.g., *Journey*, 495).

Finally, after Louis's death in 1873, Elizabeth worked for years on a substantial biography of her husband, *Louis Agassiz: His Life and Correspondence*, which was published in 1885. It became at once the main source of information on his life and ideas and remains so to this day; Agassiz's biographer Edward Lurie depends on it for much of his material. Directly in the *Life* and *A Journey in Brazil*, and indirectly in her ghostwritten essays, Elizabeth portrayed her husband as a lofty thinker, a man of pure science, a pure man of science (Irmscher, 251; Bergmann, "Widows").

In fact, by the time of his death, Louis's obdurate anti-Darwinism and retrograde insistence that humans were several species, not one, had substantially eroded his reputation among professional scientists. Elizabeth worked to enshrine him in public opinion, to help him regain some of the professional respect he had lost, by representing him as an incarnation of the highest scientific ideals. She even argued that the unpopularity of his findings in the scientific community made his perseverance particularly admirable. Showing the scientist at work as well as explaining his ideas, Elizabeth Agassiz accomplished what few other scientific popularizers had even attempted. Science in action, as she depicted it, was a narrative of exciting discovery in which the scientist's winning humanity was displayed equally with his fierce brilliance and his heroic tenacity.

After Louis's death Elizabeth moved in with his widowed son Alexander, who had become a prominent marine biologist in his own right as well as an extremely successful mining consultant. Alexander carried forward his father's dream at Harvard of establishing a museum of comparative zoology. But although she read much of Alexander's work in progress and talked science with him, she did not write for him. Drawn by the combination of her social status and her husband's reputation into the cause of women's education, she supported the founding of Radcliffe College and became its first president in 1894. Ever diplomatic and conciliatory, in her public speeches she opposed coeducation. She did not object to the installation of science courses in the Radcliffe curriculum—she even singled out the work of assistant in astronomical laboratories as a new career path for women—but she never imagined the new college as a training ground for women scientists. Her presidential writings, strategically launched from a nineteenth-century domestic perspective, reassure audiences on the brink of a new millennium that "the largest liberty of instruction cannot in itself impair true womanhood" but will only "enlarge and ennoble, the life of the home" (Paton, 363).

*B*ecause the science that Elizabeth popularized was her husband's, a quick survey of Louis's career seems in order.[6] Louis Agassiz came to the United States from Switzerland in 1846 with an international scientific reputation in zoology, geology, paleontology, and embryology, sciences that he worked hard to interrelate. His 1840 *Etude sur les Glaciers* conceptualized the Ice Age; his massive study of fossil fishes (1843–1844) was definitive for its time; he proposed that embryo development was key to species identification and argued for the embryonic capitulation of species hierarchy. Arriving in the United States to give lectures at the Lowell Institute in Boston, he remained as Professor of Natural History at Harvard, where he devoted immense energy to establishing a teaching museum of comparative zoology that would house examples of every animal species. This museum continues to exist.

He also lectured widely, attracting audiences far beyond the norm in an era when science talks were among the most popular offerings on the lecture circuit. All accounts make him out to have been a charismatic teacher and a spellbinding lecturer. For U.S. scientists, his decision to stay in the states was a coup; no native-born scientist had anything like his reputation. Louis's struggles in Europe to master science despite poverty and lack of social status—he came from poor rural folk—made him especially receptive to the project of disseminating scientific knowledge widely across the general population—both to create public patronage in the absence of aristocratic support, and to open the field to merit. Scientists hoped that he would help win public support for underfunded science. (Some of his professional enemies claimed that he was interested in funding only his own science, however.)

For Louis Agassiz, understanding the principles according to which species might be truly differentiated was the primary goal of natural history. To do this required the finding and classifying of every created organism (past and present) in a system exactly correspondent to God's design. Taxonomy for him was therefore the science's end as well as its beginning. He believed that creation itself could not be the object of scientific study. As the instant actualization of divine thought through divine power, creation was beyond human apprehension. Scientists could recover the structure of God's mind and understand God's thought, but scientific understanding to him could never lead to the creation of a living organism. He found this view incompatible with pre-Darwinian developmental or transmutation theories of species flux, with their focus on origins—that is, on the moment and method of creation. From his view it followed that each species had been created once and for all, at which time God had placed it in its designated spot on the globe. Now and then the Deity wiped out all species with a global catastrophe and replenished the earth with new species, thus creating the fossil record. Because the scientist had been given the privilege of discovering and describing creation's plenitude and its history as well, Agassiz thought frankly that men like himself were the most advanced representatives of humanity. Because science (he imagined) was a Western invention, he placed the Caucasian species at the top of the human taxonomical tree.

Pre-Darwinian and Darwinian evolution threatened this blend of Enlightenment Natural Theology and romantic *Naturphilosophie*. In 1857, two years before the publication of *On the Origin of Species*, he launched a preemptive strike, a book-length "Essay on Classification," which insisted that creation was fixed and that "developmental" arguments were flawed. He chose Georges Cuvier's four-part zoology (vertebrates, mollusks, articulates, and radiates), among competing taxonomies, as closest to God's plan, and he also argued vigorously that all other taxonomic systems were based on false deductions from the evidence. The classification essay explained that each of the four types elaborated an entirely different structure through numerous variations that could be hierarchically ranked according to their complexity. Over time he insisted that every new species identified—and according to Lurie, he was driven to "discover" many species that were, in fact, varieties—confirmed the fixity of God's plan.

The publication of *On the Origin of Species* led Agassiz to focus all his research on work designed to disprove Darwin.[7] In the preface to *Methods of Study in Natural History,* the first volume of Elizabeth's *Atlantic* articles, Louis is made to say that his chief motive for printing his public lectures is to circulate the concept of species fixity—to marshal, one might say, educated public opinion against the emerging scientific consensus. The preface calls the essays an "earnest protest of the transmutation theory, revived of late with so much ability, and so generally received" (iii).

In her 1885 biography, which appeared well after Darwin had carried the day at least in the United States, Elizabeth insisted in her own voice that a theological anti-Darwinism had dominated Louis's thought for many years:

> The coincidence between the geological succession, the embryonic development, the zoological gradation, and the geographical distribution of animals in the past and the present, rested, according to his belief, upon an intellectual coherence and not upon a material connection. So, also, the variability, as well as the constancy, of organized beings, at once so plastic and so inflexible, seemed to him controlled by something more than the mechanism of self-adjusting forces. In this conviction he remained unshaken all his life, although the development theory came up for discussion under so many various aspects during that time. His views are now in the descending scale; but to give them less than their real prominence here would be to deprive his scientific career of its true basis. Belief in a Creator was the keynote of his study of nature. (371–372)

But by 1885, Elizabeth Agassiz was also ready to concede—what Louis could not—that species fixity was not a necessary inference from his own discoveries:

"Except for the frequent allusion to a creative thought or plan, this introduction to the Fishes of the Old Red might seem to be written by an advocate of the development theory rather than by its most determined opponent, so much does it deal with laws of the organic world, now used in support of evolution" (*Life*, 371).

These words do not so much define her own views as they attempt to salvage what can be retained from Louis's enterprise insofar as that enterprise can properly be called scientific. For Louis had extended his zoological idea of species fixity to human beings, arguing on the basis of morphological differences—differences in perceived shapes—that the human "races," so obviously different to the eye and situated around the globe among such markedly different flora and fauna, could not be considered members of a single species. It followed from this reasoning, as he saw it, that just as no true admixture of species was possible, neither was any true mixing of humans. The everywhere visible counterevidence to this conclusion produced such remarkable unscientific and manifestly false allegations as the claim that mulattos were infertile and infirm. As Irmscher points out, Louis Agassiz claims alternatively that different human species cannot intermix, and that they ought not to (270).

This argument functioned to combat the threat of miscegenation, and ultimately to support social ideas of firm racial segregation. Although Louis Agassiz was not proslavery, his views clearly bolstered the proslavery position; even though many orthodox southerners maintained the biblical position that all humans derived from a single act of creation, they were hard put to offer a scientific explanation of subsequent "racial" differentiation. As Stephen Jay Gould has eloquently shown in *The Mismeasure of Man*, Louis Agassiz's advocacy of human polygenesis verged on the pathological, so much that it might have preceded his theories of species fixity rather than the other way around. Despite the obvious scientific shortcomings of this part of his program, Elizabeth wrote it into Louis's legacy at a time when she might easily have left it out: "It was Agassiz's declared belief that man had sprung not from a common stock, but from various centres"; "His special zoological studies were too engrossing to allow him to follow this line of investigation closely, but it was never absent from his view of the animal kingdom as a whole" (*Life*, 496–497).

Although Linda Bergmann has argued ("Widows") that Elizabeth comes across in the *Journey* as much more flexible and tolerant than Louis, so that the "voices of husband and wife" are not "perfectly melded" ("Elizabeth,"

189), that book to my eyes unselfconsciously and unvaryingly deploys a vernacular version of his taxonomy. As Irmscher points out, it is the spectacle of what she viewed as the "enfeebled character of the population" of mixed bloods in northern Brazil that leads her in the *Journey* to rehearse Louis's theories about the "detriments of racial mixing" (270). For another example, she pigeonholes a promising servant "who, by her appearance, had a mixture of Indian and black blood in her veins." To be sure, she assesses this servant favorably, because she "seems to have the intelligence of the Indian with the greater pliability of the negro" (224)—but there is no missing the chauvinistic racialism at work here. And in the *Life,* she gratuitously drags in large segments of an extended 1863 correspondence between Louis and the abolitionist Samuel Howe on the "relation between the black and white races," pointedly associating Louis's position with science and Howe's with sentimental philanthropy (591–617).

In this correspondence Louis looks forward to the "prospect of universal emancipation" but does so less from a philanthropic point of view than "because hereafter the physiologist and ethnographer may discuss the question of the races and advocate a discriminating policy regarding them, without seeming to support legal inequality" (603). Although he says that obviously it cannot yet be known what black people may ultimately achieve, he also says that all existing evidence shows them to be less capable than whites for the work of "fostering human progress and advancing civilization, especially in the various spheres of intellectual and moral activity" (603). In other words, black people will never be scientists. It seems unlikely to me that Elizabeth would have brought this material into her narrative so prominently if she thought including it would seriously damage her husband's posthumous reputation or if she seriously disagreed with it. Her own background, after all, was "Cotton Whig," not "Conscience Whig." She suggests obliquely but unmistakably that Louis's views, which according to her he heroically maintained in spite of the sentimental counterposition on human equality, will eventually carry the day.

Elizabeth's service as her husband's publicist and ghostwriter required her to create a scientific voice for him, an esthetic, pedagogical voice for herself, and texts that both voices might cohabit comfortably. She trained herself to this work by writing popular science texts of her own. In 1859, about a year before she began work on Louis's essays, she published a juvenile textbook titled *Actaea: A First Lesson in Natural History. Actaea* is the Latin word for coastal lands, but the book is not a study of an ecosystem; rather it describes the classification of radiates by looking especially at those species who inhabit the tidal pools around Nahant where the Cary clan vacationed.[8]

The book is constructed along the conventional lines of a home-use textbook for children. It is not a Marcet-like dialog, but a series of letters from Elizabeth to her two (real) nieces, Lisa and Connie. The book—structured by Louis's taxonomy into chapters on sea anemones and corals, coral reefs, hydroids and jellyfish, starfish and sea urchins—works mainly on the surface and talks "familiarly" to children: "I hope that the Sea-Anemone has interested you so much, that you will like to hear about some other animals of the same kind, which live also in the sea, and of which I have a strange and wonderful story to tell you" (15). At the conclusion, she apologetically names her subjects as polyps, acelephs, and echinoderms: "This is the end of my stories about Radiates, dear Lisa and Connie, and I hope you will forgive this little bit of science and the hard names at the close" (81).

As is conventional in this genre, the exposition pretends to respond to the children's "Now, Aunt Lizzie, tell us a story" by telling "true stories, and not about little boys and girls, but about animals" (7). It assures them that "If you knew a little more about" animals in the tidal pools around Nahant, they "would interest you quite as much as the little fishes you liked to see swimming about in your Aquarium last summer" (8). The narrator brings her young readers into the text actively and imaginatively through narrative and a focus on the senses:

> It will be rather slippery on the wet sea-weed, but we shall not mind one or two tumbles, if we find what we are seeking. . . . We will not be deceived by his uninviting looks. We will take him up very softly, parting him gently with our fingers from the rock, for he is very tender and adheres closely to his resting place; and when we have him safely at the house, we will put him in a glass bowl with some sea-weed and a few stones that he may, if possible, believe himself to be still at home in his puddle. (8–9)

Perhaps drawing on the pestolozzian perspective that she would have encountered in her year at Elizabeth Peabody's school, perhaps working from Louis Agassiz's own well-known insistence on close observation as the basis for any true natural science (his tag line, "Study nature, not books," was much repeated), the text links tactile details ("you must imagine them light-colored, and soft and delicate as the down on a feather" [10]) with functional explanations suited to the life experience of children ("Pretty and soft though they are, you will hardly believe that they have attached to them an instrument which is as dangerous and deadly to all the little animals which the Sea-Anemone likes for its food, as the claws of your pussy are to a mouse" [10]). The introduction of taxonomy at the conclusion invites children to see this "first lesson" as the beginning of the climb toward the ideal beauty of abstract classification represented by the scientific understanding.

Six years later, with Alexander's help, Elizabeth published a more grown-up, more comprehensive, version of *Actaea*. Called *Seaside Studies in Natural History*, the book attempts to present its facts "in such a connection, with reference to principles of science and to classification, as will give it in some sort the character of a manual of Natural History, in the hope of making it useful not only to the general reader, but also to teachers and to persons desirous of obtaining a more intimate knowledge of the subjects discussed in it" (v).

Taxonomy comes first in this more advanced format; the book is dedicated to Louis, "whose principles of classification have been the main guide in its preparation" (n.p.). Species are arranged within orders, each is described, and the whole is preceded by a description of the radiates as a group. The book features taxonomy in Louis Agassiz's terms—not as a necessary but arbitrary set of conventions but as the preliminary to understanding the real structure of the natural world. But interrelation does not mean interfusion or even interdependence; rather it means the theme and variations by which different species represent increasingly complex versions of a single idea, each of them manifesting an expression of God's mind, and all of them amounting to divine plenitude.

Seaside Studies continues to rely on the narrative form and concrete, dramatic description that propelled *Actaea*, though Connie and Lisa have disappeared as audience surrogates. In place of the passage cited earlier, we now read that "the curious in such matters will be well rewarded, even at the risk of wet feet and a slippery scramble over rocks covered with damp sea-weed, by a glimpse into their crowded abodes. Such a grotto is to be found on the rocks of East Point at Nahant. It can only be reached at low tide, and then one is obliged to creep on hands and knees to its entrance" (9).

If explanations of animal function are much expanded in *Seaside Studies*, so too is the quantity of esthetic writing: "When the sun strikes through from the opposite extremity of this grotto, which is open at both ends, lighting up its living mosaic work, and showing the play of the soft fringes wherever the animals are open, it would be difficult to find any artificial grotto to compare with it in beauty" (9). An interpolated, independent essay called "mode of catching jelly-fishes" narrates the search as a quest to find beauty.

At night when phosphorescence creates numerous picturesque effects, the esthetic pleasure comprises exactly that which Elizabeth herself would come to define as "feminine" but which, in this context, is also to be understood as "popular"—the precondition, accompaniment, and goal of all writing about science designed for nonspecialist audiences.

> Our dirty, torn old net is suddenly turned to a web of gold, and as we lift it from the water heavy rolls of molten metal seem to flow down its sides and collect in a glowing mass at the bottom. The truth is, the Jelly-fishes, so sparkling and brilliant in the sunshine, have a still lovelier light of their own at night. . . . Wherever the larger Aureliae and Zygodactylae float to the surface, they bring with them a dim spreading halo of light, the smaller Ctenophorae become little shining spheres, while a thousand lesser creatures add their tiny lamps to the illumination of the ocean; for this so-called phosphorescence of the seas is by no means due to the Jelly-fishes alone, but is also produced by many other animals differing in the color as well as the intensity of their light. (88–89)

Like *Actaea*, *Seaside Studies* responds esthetically to the dissection and microscopic examination of sea creatures as much as to panoramic spectacles of phosphorescence. The net transformed by thousands of shining creatures is also ending their lives. Elizabeth does not oppose the esthetic to the scientific as womanly reverence for the earth versus masculine exploitation of it. True, the spectator sport of esthetic appreciation does not actually do the deed; but it depends on it. Moreover, as purveyor of her husband's taxonomic system, Elizabeth is not a namer of natural phenomena, not what Norwood calls her—an "Eve in the act of naming and ranking the flowers, fruits, spiders, jellyfish, hummingbirds, and horned toads of the New World" (24).

Yet it seems right to say, as Norwood implies, that if one stopped with the esthetic surface, then the woman's way of relating to the natural world would indeed be foundationally antiscientific and antimale. At least Elizabeth implies something like this herself, when she writes privately of having to combat her own feminine inclinations to do justice to her husband's science. In an 1862 letter to her sister, composed as she was just starting the *Atlantic Monthly* essays, she delights in her sister's praise because

> every now and then I am seized with doubts and fears about the articles by Agassiz, and I like to be propped up with a friendly word about them. . . . About this last May article I was especially anxious.

> You know the coral reefs are very attractive to me, and perhaps I
> have not understood any of his investigations better than those upon
> the Florida reefs; but I am conscious that what is beautiful and pic-
> turesque in his studies interest me more than what is purely scien-
> tific, and sometimes I am afraid that in my appreciation of that side
> of the subject I shall weaken his thought and give it a rather femi-
> nine character. It grows every month more fascinating to me to write
> them, and I hope we shall make another arrangement with Ticknor
> and Fields next year. (Paton, 66)

But if this is a woman's way of apprehending nature, it is more precisely the
way of a genteel, refined woman who has mastered the rhetoric of esthetics.
And one cannot help but notice how Elizabeth, identifying her cultivated,
esthetic response to the natural world as essentially feminine, also characterizes it as weak. Esthetics becomes a way to relate to nature without understanding it. Thus, to Elizabeth, men are scientific because they have greater
mental strength than women, not because they have less spiritual capacity.
She puts her own weaker, feminine abilities to good use by serving manly
science.

Louis Agassiz, fluent from childhood in French and German, quickly developed a spoken and written English style. It is not possible to assert either
that he made no contributions to Elizabeth's ghostwritten pieces, or that any
writing alleged to be wholly his writing was in fact so. As collaborators, the
two produced a web that cannot be fully untangled. Yet, the *Atlantic* articles,
purportedly Louis's but known to be hers, differ markedly from his lecturing
style as described by auditors, as well as from his more technical essays, to
which she is not known to have contributed.

For example, in a reminiscence of Agassiz published in the *Atlantic
Monthly* for February 1874, Theodore Lyman describes the very lectures that
the *Atlantic Monthly* articles purportedly transcribed. He refers to Louis's
fondness for technical terminology and proposes that the vaunted clarity of
his lectures was actually the construct of friendly audiences moved by "the
power of his enthusiasm." Agassiz, he says, would often

> plunge among difficult matters of structure and morphology, where
> only technical language could be used. Then it was curious to watch
> the faces of the thousand people who sat listening to him, and see
> their expression of struggling perplexity, as the great professor, with
> ever-increasing rapidity of thought and word, went on through nucle-

ated cells, vibratile cilia, and epithelium. All the while the audience tried hard to understand, and listened with unflagging interest till the firm ground of every-day facts was reached again. (226)

Elizabeth's lectures, published under his name, use technical language very sparingly and almost always with definitions and applications that make the terminology accessible.

James Russell Lowell's verse elegy for Louis, published in the *Atlantic Monthly* for May 1874, affectionately recalls his friend's frequent lapses from English: "Not seldom, as the undeadened fibre stirred / Of noble friendships knit beyond the sea, / German or French thrust by the lagging word" (593). More acidly, William James satirized Louis's accents and syntax in an 1865 letter (James was part of the team that went to Brazil): "Look out, sir, dat I take not your skin!" he is made to say (Feinstein, 171). Elizabeth's Louis in contrast is lexically fluent, syntactically correct, and—of course—accent free. And when she republished the essays in book form, she revised them further for smoothness and elegant simplicity.

Yet again, Agassiz's colleague Jules Marcou complained in his own biography of the man that Louis's professional lectures were too much like popular performances to be good science. He says they were sententious, punctuated by inappropriate pauses for applause, "too theatrical," more like "addresses than ordinary expositions of scientific questions" (97–98). Yet Elizabeth's essays, presumably representing just such popular performances, lack theatricality and declamatory periodicity.

Comparing passages from the *Contributions* and *Methods*, taking Louis as author of the former and Elizabeth of the latter, one immediately sees striking stylistic differences. It is not that Louis was writing for professionals and Elizabeth for laypeople: Louis wrote in the preface that he expected to see the book "read by operatives, by fishermen, by farmers, quite as extensively as by the students in our colleges, or by the learned professions" (*Contributions*, 1:x). Evidently, therefore, his idea of the popular involves a declamatory, hortatory, periodic style of the sort that Elizabeth never used. For example, his exegesis typically involves a series of confrontational rhetorical questions; Elizabeth's never does. Louis:

Did not nations speak, understand, and write Greek, Latin, German, and Sanscrit, before it was even suspected that these languages and so many others, were kindred? Did not painters produce wonders with colors before the nature of light was understood? Had not men been thinking about themselves and the world before logic and metaphysics were taught in schools? Why, then, should not observers of nature have appreciated rightly the relationship between animals or plants before getting a scientific clue to the classifications they were led to adopt as practical? (*Contributions*, 1:137–138).

Elizabeth:

> We do the thing before we understand why we do it: speech precedes grammar, reason precedes logic; and so a division of animals into groups, upon an instinctive perception of their differences, has preceded all our scientific creeds and theories. (*Methods*, 31)

Louis's descriptive sentences are longer and more complex than Elizabeth's, his diction more elevated. Elizabeth, but not Louis, exclaims about the wonder, beauty, delicacy, and elegance of natural objects; she uses metaphors that are both everyday and esthetic—she compares a sea anemone's body to fringed and folded curtains, to a vaulted roof, to flounces. Where Louis's descriptions are governed by an abstract protocol—proceeding from top to bottom, outside to inside, left to right—hers usually relay the perceptions of a situated observer who is often written into the text. It is possible that his reputation for pedagogical clarity was the creation not only of a friendly audience, but also of a friendly ghostwriter.

The so-called Thayer expedition to Brazil, named for its financial backer, took Louis, Elizabeth, and a team of research assistants to the Amazon (they called it the Amazons) in 1865–1866. Nathaniel Thayer, a rich amateur, rejected evolutionary theory and admired Agassiz. The chief theoretic aim of the expedition was to amass data about Amazon zoology in support of the anti-Darwinian position. The practical goal was to acquire as many specimens as possible for the museum. A third purpose was to investigate Brazilian geology.

Apparently the expedition contributed neither to zoology nor to geology. Louis insisted that he found evidence of glaciation in Brazil, but his claim was never accepted in scientific circles. The species he discovered neither invalidated nor validated Darwin's theory of origins; they could have equally been put there by God or evolved there. Many specimens were mishandled in preparation; many barrels shipped to Cambridge were never even unpacked during Louis's life. The accounts of massive faunal destruction are chilling to read today. Yet Elizabeth never expressed any doubt about the expedition's purposes, methods, or results, writing glowingly in the *Journey* that "without self-glorification" Louis found it "impossible not to be gratified when the experience of later years confirms the premonitions of youth, and shows them to have been not mere guesses, but founded upon an insight into the true relations of things" (233–234).

The decision to publish the account as a popular travel book authored chiefly by Elizabeth has puzzled later biographers. Lurie says it "received little attention from professional scientists, except when they registered amazement" over its geological claims about glaciation (357). But nontechnical, popular accounts of scientific journeys were quite common. Often, such a published account would precede the technical scientific reports; it could be produced far more quickly and for taxpayer-supported expeditions would assure the public that the expedition had not wasted public moneys. In at least one crucial case, a woman had participated centrally in writing the popular narrative—this is the account of the Fremont expedition, thought by many scholars of U.S. history to have launched the mania for western settlement in the 1840s. It had been authored in large part by Jesse Benton Fremont. In her case as in Elizabeth's and others, reviews freely conceded that women often had the popular touch that men lacked.

Fremont's narrative, however, made no mention of Jesse's participation in the writing process, while *Journey in Brazil* was published as a jointly authored book and frankly acknowledged to be Elizabeth's work except when she claims to be quoting Louis directly or when Louis chimes in with an initialed footnote. The result is recognizably a woman's travel book more than a scientific account, discussing domestic arrangements, furniture, cookery, interactions among women, and women's life stories.[9] But the prominent space given to the expedition's scientific goals and procedures produces a hybrid that Elizabeth would later call a "partly scientific, partly personal diary" (*Life*, 630).

Enfolding the scientific journey within the woman's account, the text subjects both Louis and his science to a distinctly female, although affectionate, gaze. Its general work for science (as opposed to its specific work for Louis) involves popularizing the beloved scientist as beloved and scientist both: a being at once appealingly human and awesomely divine. In conveying Louis's scientific theories, Elizabeth shows that theorizing itself—the assimilation of facts into provisional generalizations that are progressively refined to correspond more and more exactly to the empirical record— incarnates the desire that, far more than any particular theory, is the highest expression of humanity and the true meaning of science. "The end of man, his aim, his glory," Louis says in one of the reported shipboard lectures, "is the knowledge of the truth" (*Journey*, 96).

The narrative contrasts Elizabeth's leisurely, even languorous engagement with one picturesque and interesting episode after another, against Louis's focused quest that begins on shipboard with daily lectures to his assistants and is forwarded by the continual plot question: Will the expedition achieve its goals? This contrast marks a gender difference, allowing Elizabeth clearly to differentiate her woman's openness to serendipitous delight from his manly drive to prove a theory. Rather than making his science attractive by interlarding it with an appreciative but possibly inappropriate estheticism, she is able here to run the esthetic and the scientific on parallel tracks, making the text attractive overall by feminine appreciation of natural wonders while protecting science from undue feminization.

The scientist himself, however, is always one of the objects offered up for esthetic appreciation, so that in the long run his project is encompassed by hers: "A rough sea to-day, notwithstanding which we had our lecture as usual, though I must say, that, owing to the lurching of the ship, the lecturer pitched about more than was consistent with the dignity of science. Mr. Agassiz returned to the subject of embryology, urging upon his assistants the importance of collecting materials for this object as a means of obtaining an insight into the deeper relations between animals" (20). Clearly, this is writing about Louis in a way that Louis himself could not have written, but it is written for his benefit:

> He has improvised a laboratory in a large empty room over a warehouse in the Rua Direita. . . . Here in one corner the ornithologists, Mr. Dexter and Mr. Allen, have their bench,—a rough board propped on two casks, the seat an empty keg; in another, Mr. Anthony, with an apparatus of much the same kind, pores over his shells; a dissecting-table of like carpentry occupies a conspicuous position; and in the midst the Professor may generally be seen sitting on a barrel, for chairs there are none, assorting or examining specimens, or going from bench to bench to see how the work progresses. (59)

A strategy openly distinguishing masculine from feminine styles of appreciation gives Elizabeth the freedom to be as esthetic as she pleases: "The sun went down in purple and gold, and, after its departure, sent back a glow that crimsoned the clouds almost to the zenith, dying off to paler rose tints on the edges, while heavy masses of gray vapor, just beginning to be silvered by the moon, swept up from the south" (15); "I am passing a few quiet days here, learning to be more familiar with the scenery of a region very justly called one of the most picturesque on the borders of the Amazons" (362).

The contrast in modes is sharpest when the two approaches are juxtaposed. As he busily networks with people who might help his inquiries, she enjoys the social life and opportunities for people gazing. He says, "Our work must be to study the facts, to see, among other things, of what these hills are built, whether of rock or of loose materials. No one has told us anything as yet of their geological constitution" (17); she says, "To-day we have seen numbers of flying-fish from the deck, and were astonished at the grace and beauty of their motion" (17). In one seaport town they go together to the fish market, he daily to acquire specimens, she now and then "for the pleasure of seeing the fresh loads of oranges, flowers, and vegetables, and of watching the picturesque negro groups selling their wares or sitting about in knots to gossip" (82). A walk in the tropical forest inspires her to say for herself that "it is not merely the difference of the vegetation, but the impenetrability of the mass here that makes the density, darkness, and solemnity of the woods so impressive"; and for him that "this walk in the forest was important" because he "made out one of those laws of growth which unite the past and the present" (109).

The couple sent copies of the newly published book as Christmas presents to many friends. These, in responding, demonstrated their knowledge of the work's true authorship. Longfellow rephrased Buffon: "Le style c'est la femme" (Paton, 110). Holmes gushed: "So exquisitely are your labors blended, that as with the Mermaiden of ancient poets, it is hard to say where the woman leaves off and the fish begins"; Emerson wrote of his pleasure that Elizabeth had been "the angel of woman in Brazil" (Lurie, 357).

𝓔lizabeth's massive biographical narrative, *Louis Agassiz: His Life and Correspondence*, incorporated many primary sources, especially extracts from his published writings and big chunks of correspondence sent to and received by him. This sort of "memoir," as it was called, compiled by a relative or close friend, was standard in the American nineteenth century. Despite claims to accuracy, the primary materials were always heavily edited, a reality that everybody understood. Especially in New England, such memoirs were often written about clergymen, featuring the subject's self-sacrificing devotion to God's truth. Often these memoirs were written by the deceased men's wives or daughters.

Elizabeth effectively redirected the genre's familiar sacrificial trope toward the situation of a scientist, synthesizing correspondence (much of it translated by her from French or German), life narrative, and scientific exposition. She merged the typical celebration of a life devoted to spiritual things with a narrative of the intrepid voyager and explorer: in the Alps, in Brazil, across continents. Thus she produced the familiar composite image of the scientist as a hero in both the terrestrial and intellectual realms, an image much loved, not surprisingly, by scientists themselves.

For Elizabeth to do this work was to rescue her husband from the detritus of his scientific theories as well as the shortcomings of his character by making him a pure scientist. When, after the book appeared, others who had known him complained about the accuracy of the depiction, they had to concede that her work was appropriately womanly and wifely. Nor did they dispute her ideal of the scientist. Rather, they questioned whether Louis aptly represented the ideal. Thus, whatever her ultimate success as a portraitist of her husband, she succeeded handily in portraying science as a thrilling, demanding, exotic, taxing, heroic voyage toward ideality. She made research into an adventure and presented scientific discoveries and theories as events in a life of both mental and physical action.

Elizabeth had to immerse herself in Louis's correspondence and publications, correspond with his friends and colleagues, and learn enough French and German to read and translate his letters and scientific papers. Writing this biography demanded, as had the *Journey*, that she comprehend and convey the essence of his scientific work, including the early material on which his reputation as a serious scientist had been based. In this book her grasp of his science is spacious and sure, and her ability to expound it accessibly is impressive. Here, for example, is her summary of his findings on fossil fishes:

> The most novel results comprised in this work were: first, the remodelling of the classification of the whole type of fishes, fossil and living, and especially the separation of the Ganoids from all other fishes, under the rank of a distinct order; second, the recognition of those combinations of reptilian and birdlike characters in the earlier geological fishes, which led the author to call them prophetic types; and third, his discovery of an analogy between the embryological phases of the higher present fishes and the gradual introduction of the whole type on earth, the series in growth and the series in time revealing a certain mutual correspondence. As these comprehensive laws have thrown light upon other types of the animal kingdom

beside that of fishes, their discovery may be said to have advanced general zoology as well as ichthyology. (*Life,* 239)

Anchoring science securely in a narrative of exploration and discovery, of trials and triumphs, and motivating the science in the idealistic integrity of the seeker, she produced science as a heroic novel or an epic, with a protagonist and a plot. This is splendid publicity for an enterprise at the very moment when solitary scientific heroism, if it had ever been the reality, corresponded less and less to the reality of emerging corporate academic and industrial science. Its usefulness as an image for science went far to mitigate whatever criticism scientists might have been inclined to offer of Louis's outrageous views and his difficult personality. Thanks to his wife's work, Louis Agassiz did, indeed, become a kind of paradigmatic example of the scientist at his best.

The work of constructing her husband as a hero is visible throughout Elizabeth's book:

> The secret of his greatest power was to be found in the sympathetic, human side of his character. Out of his broad humanity grew the genial personal influence, by which he awakened the enthusiasm of his audiences for unwonted themes, inspired his students to disinterested services like his own, delighted children in the school-room, and won the cordial interest as well as the cooperation in the higher aims of science, of all classes whether rich or poor. (408)

In "Widows," Bergmann stresses the invisibility in Elizabeth's account of Louis's entrepreneurial, even mercenary, disposition, his love of show biz, his "tendency to meld the boundaries between personal and professional finances" (9), the "manipulations and maneuvers" by which he founded his museum (11). Elizabeth's "Louis Agassiz is a savant, not a showman," Bergmann observes, "and the distinction became increasingly crucial as the standards of professional science were becoming more clearly defined" (13).

The failings of Louis's character, insofar as they appear at all in the biography, are attributed to his despair over the stony indifference of the culture to the needs, not of the man, but of the science he stands for. Doing science, and especially establishing the museum, required a great deal of money: "Like all men whose ideals outrun the means of execution, he had moments of intense depression and discouragement. Some of his letters, written at this time to friends who controlled the financial policy of the Museum, are almost like a plea for life," Elizabeth wrote (*Life,* 681). At the time of the *Life*'s publication, Alexander Agassiz was trying to secure better financing for the museum than his father had been able to attain. There may well have been a fund-raising purpose behind Elizabeth's presentation of Louis Agassiz as a virtual martyr for science.

Narrative is everywhere in *Louis Agassiz: His Life and Correspondence*, as Elizabeth merges the physical adventures of the field scientist with the intellectual goals of a theorist. Problem and solution become the story's beginning and end, voyage its plot. "It is not uninteresting to follow these young minds in their search after the laws of structure and growth, dimly perceived at first, but becoming gradually clearer as they go on. The very first questions hint at the law of Phyllotaxis, then wholly unknown, though now it makes a part of the most elementary instruction in botany" (39–40); "it will be seen later how the restless aspirations of childhood, boyhood, and youth, which were, after all, only a latent love of research, crystallize into the concentrated purpose of the man" (101); "the science of conchology had heretofore been based almost wholly upon the study of the empty shells. To Agassiz this seemed superficial. Longing to know more of the relation between the animal and its outer covering, he bethought himself that the inner moulding of the shell would give at least the form of its old inhabitant" (283); "he was convinced that, as a sheet of ice has covered the northern portion of the globe, so a sheet of ice has covered also the southern portion, advancing, in both instances, far toward the equatorial regions. His observations in Europe, in North America, and in Brazil seemed here to have their closing chapter" (723). Indeed, Elizabeth presents science itself as a quest for narrative shape: "Following the same comparative method, he intended to track the footsteps of the idea as he had gathered and put together the fragments of his fossil fishes, till the scattered facts should fall into their natural order once more and tell their story from beginning to end" (288).

Selections from Louis's correspondence show his European connections and reputation; Elizabeth makes much of letters to and from Alexander von Humboldt, the culture hero we have already met. It meant a great deal to Americans that Humboldt had been an early patron of Louis's, and she quoted extensively from his letters of generous praise. She also quotes from letters in which Louis praises U.S. scientists, including James D. Dana and Asa Gray, with both of whom Louis had quarreled quite publicly. No doubt she meant to show her husband's magnanimity. Bergmann points out that this material also portrays the U.S. scientific "community" less as the shifting confederacy at once ego fissured and friendship linked that it actually was, and more as a group of "cordial but purely scientific" intellects, "held together by the pursuit of facts and the informed discussion of their significance" without regard to "personal alliances and friendships" ("Widows," 12). In other words, Elizabeth portrays the whole scientific establishment as impelled by the same ideal motives that supposedly motivated her husband. At the same time, this representation of the scientific community isolates the scientist from the social and professional networks that supported or impeded him, turning each into a solitary adventurer, a democratic individualist.

As Bergmann also notes, in contrast to the *Journey* where Elizabeth is so visible although subordinate a player, Elizabeth truly effaces herself from the narrative in the biography. A few third-person sentences comprise the whole of her self-presentation: "In the spring of 1850 Agassiz married Elizabeth Cabot Cary, daughter of Thomas Graves Cary, of Boston. This marriage confirmed his resolve to remain, at least for the present, in the United States. It connected him by the closest ties with a large family circle" (477). It connected him as well to the inner circle of well-heeled Bostonians, a point that Elizabeth does not make. Nor does she show the large family circle and the supportive network of his children and wife playing any role in his science; even though the whole of Nahant Island—where he summered and did marine research—was a family preserve, the family impact on his science is omitted. Writing the scientist out of his networks, Elizabeth affirms the idea that science was individual discovery, with the scientist the sole creator and proprietor of findings and ideas that, in fact, had been made possible by many people.

The afterlife of this memoir shows that Elizabeth's self-effacement succeeded. Lurie, for example, relies on the book heavily, praising its "perception and insight" and differentiating it from typical Victorian hagiography (422). Where Elizabeth's account differs from those of other biographers, he accepts her version. Yet he ignores Elizabeth's literary contributions to Louis's career. His index refers to her domestic life, love for Louis and his children, courtship, marriage, founding the school, traveling with Louis, and nursing him through illness—the whole array of standard feminine behavior—but apart from "work for museum" the index cites none of the professional assistance she gave her husband (431). Lurie calls Elizabeth "Lizzie." At the same time, he unwittingly accepts the heroic stance toward its subject that Elizabeth herself developed, choosing in the subtitle of his biography to describe Agassiz's as "a life in science." Thus, he accepts both her representation of Louis and of science. A feminist might deplore his erasures; but, obviously, Elizabeth herself was not a feminist. From her own perspective, her very invisibility would be evidence that she had achieved her goal. Her affiliative, ghostly work for her husband, not least in and by its self-erasure, powerfully contributed to popular ideas of what science was and how it was done.

CHAPTER 7

Testing Scientific Limits

EMMA WILLARD AND MARIA MITCHELL

$\mathcal{T}$he women of letters working for sci-
ence proposed a range of affiliative models. Positively, they wanted to appeal to the largest possible number of women; negatively, they assumed
women could never become professional scientists themselves. Recognizing
that their work required the endorsement of professionals if it was to succeed, they addressed scientists as well as women, insisting that their program,
rightly understood, posed no threat to scientific men. Reared in a culture that
accepted some degree of social hierarchy as both inevitable and necessary,
they outlined models of productively asymmetric interaction between women
and scientists even before the 1830s—students and teachers, assistants and
executives, popularizers and originators, consumers and producers.

But after the 1830s their advocacy increased in clear correlation with
the emergence of information as an enormous growth industry. Not only were
the material results of science and technology obviously transforming the texture of everyday life and requiring a population (including women) trained
in a range of new mechanical skills (weights and measures in cookery, for
example). Science and technology ministered to an information-hungry age
because they were predicated upon endless discoveries of new knowledge.
Women of letters interested in science—exactly because as women of letters
they were attuned to the burgeoning needs and opportunities of print culture—
adroitly called attention to the role their own sex might play in absorbing (or
more precisely, in purchasing) all this new material. In an ever-expanding spi-
ral, constructing women as consumers of scientific information reinforced

ideas of science as commodity and scientists as producers of intellectual as well as material goods.

Actually, scientists like Benjamin Silliman, Amos Eaton, and Edward Hitchcock had recognized the advantages of having women among their audience early on. Many men of science throughout the century—men who after all thought of themselves as the most progressive and enlightened members of society—welcomed women who shared their high views of the scientific enterprise, especially when these women ceded the role of scientist per se to men. It is not that they felt threatened and thought "affiliationists" would counter attempts by more radical women to occupy masculine ground. (In fact, radical women tended to celebrate female intuition and spirituality over rational empiricism.) Rather, these men of science saw how well their aims meshed with the initiatives of the women affiliates.

In an era when original work more and more defined the professional, only one woman—the astronomer Maria Mitchell, who on October 1, 1847, discovered a comet—was recognized for original scientific achievement. The overall number of women trying to do "real" science—that is, carry out an original scientific project under professional auspices and be known for having done it—seems to have been extremely small. No doubt women here and there, lost to the record, accomplished such work, most likely in finding and identifying local botanical and zoological species.[1] Perhaps some inventions patented by men were really women's doing.[2] But Sarah Hale—constantly on the prowl for examples of women's intellectual achievements and ready to believe that a man like Isaac Newton was the highest realization of human possibility—found no woman scientist in the nation besides Mitchell. Chances are, therefore, that the overwhelming majority of scientifically inclined American women had accommodated their interests to the affiliative positions that had been marked out for them.

Even Mitchell, the apparent exception, was ultimately to argue that original scientific work lay outside the women's sphere in this country and this century, making affiliation by far the wiser choice. Her significant innovation was to define a mode of doing science that was itself a form of affiliation; she used herself as a case in point. She explained her discovery as the outcome of practiced routine, not genius. She fully accepted the idea of the true scientist as a lone discoverer, even as she proposed that there was such a thing as ordinary science—what, following Thomas Kuhn, might be called *normal science*—that could be done by ordinary people including women like herself, providing they submitted to the requisite discipline. Her case, coupled with that of Emma Willard, who tried for some forty years to be recognized as the scientific genius she believed herself to be, are exceptions that test but do not prove the rule: Science was for women only insofar as they accepted their gender-determined secondary place in its regimen.

Willard, never admitting the least doubt over the brilliance of her scientific work, attributed her failure to win acclaim specifically to the fact of her womanhood in a culture resolutely closed to female accomplishment. It was not, she insisted, that her science was poor, but that professionals would not accept that any woman might be an original scientific genius. Rather than judging her work on its merits, she wrote, scientists will say that "she chooses a subject unsuited to her sex" (*Treatise*, vii; *Theory*, 9); that "she goes out of her sphere" (*Respiration*, 3). She believed she had overcome through her own efforts the obstacles put in her way by professionals who denied her a comprehensive scientific education because she was a woman, only to be victimized by gender discrimination in another way when professionals refused to credit her accomplishments.

Willard was partly right here; she did her work entirely outside the increasingly stringently defined professional circle (a circle designed to exclude most men along with all women) and trusted her ideas to make their way through merit (or rhetoric) alone. Mitchell's case could not have been more different. She was closely connected to the most powerful men of science of her day. Their support was crucial to the recognition she earned; in fact, speaking in professional terms, their support *was* her recognition. These men in turn used her discovery to publicize U.S. scientific achievement.

But, over the long run, little followed from this for Mitchell herself or women more generally. Not until the establishment of Vassar College (1865) did she receive a scientific appointment, and this was as a teacher of young women, not as a colleague of male scientists. At Vassar, she was more isolated from any scientific community than she had been as a moonlighting volunteer. She found her energies (familiar story) absorbed by local academic duties.

As a founding member of the Association for the Advancement of Women, Mitchell took a moderate position that reflected the melancholy realities of her own situation. She taught science to undergraduates; she publicized the scientific aptitudes of her students by contributing their astronomical observations to the *Scientific American*; she spoke about the usefulness of professional women to a big-science model. But, fully indoctrinated in scientific values and knowledgeable about the constitution of the scientific community, she was sure that women in her own time lacked both capability and opportunity—attributes that she saw as ultimately inseparable—for making major scientific discoveries. She declined to speculate on whether this was nature or nurture, writing, in a sentence whose syntactical construction is tellingly passive: "To discuss the question whether women have the capacity for original investigation in science is simply idle until equal opportunity is given them" ("Reminiscences," 908).

Emma Willard was one of the nation's most prominent public women for at least half a century, second in reputation perhaps only to Sarah Hale. Nationally celebrated as an educational reformer, a textbook writer, and a best-selling historian, she would seem to have had little need for scientific fame.[3] But she had extremely high intellectual ambitions along with extraordinary drive and unusually high self-esteem. Acutely aware that the cultural domains ceded to women had either lost status or were in the process of losing status, she wanted to locate herself indisputably among the towering intellects of her age. Inevitably, these intellects would have to be male, and inevitably, the validating achievements would have to be scientific. Girls' academies, common school reform, writing history—none of these could serve the purpose.

As a student, Willard had shown particular aptitude for mathematics. Recognizing that Enlightenment ideology had downgraded belletristic accomplishment in favor of scientific discovery, and personally inclined less toward polite letters than more strenuous forms of prose, Willard made science study a key component of the Troy curriculum from the beginning. History, of course, came first, but because it was already understood that history was especially appropriate for women to study,[4] Troy's science component set it apart from other schools and received particular notice. Troy's (and Willard's) prestige did much to encourage science study in women's schools across the country.

In the seminary's early days, when it was short-staffed, Willard ceded instruction in natural history to her sister (Almira Phelps) and taught mathematics, astronomy, natural philosophy, chemistry, and Natural Theology—a subject to which she remained devoted throughout her life—herself. She began her publishing career by contributing an appendix on ancient geography to William Woodbridge's popular school geography text of the 1820s. But her section, a compilation of dates connected to various sites on the globe, was not *scientific,* even as the term would have been understood at the time. Where the globe itself was concerned, she showed no interest in any features of terrain, even those that might have been propitious for one ancient civilization or destructive for another.

She favored teaching geography as a "comparative" subject—that is, having students memorize lists of the world's rivers from longest to shortest, mountains from highest to lowest, continents from largest to smallest, countries from most to least populous, and so on. But because most early school geographies were simply "a body of unrelated facts" (Nietz, 200) and differed little from gazetteers (Calhoun, 4), this rank ordering of information may well have better allowed students to commit facts to memory—although for the purpose of strengthening the memory itself rather than for any application of these facts.

As a history teacher Willard used maps as instructional aids. She featured maps in her textbooks, an innovation at the time that is now standard. But maps, for her, were also devices to help memory. They also allowed students to visualize expanding or contracting empires without reference to topography. An enthusiastic advocate of Manifest Destiny, she envisioned the frontier as a mathematical line moving inexorably westward across two-dimensional, empty space, testifying to the inevitable march of empire without regard to the very mountains, rivers, deserts, or prairies that students had to remember in "geography." Her disregard for biota-defining earth features reflected a highly abstract, nationalistic territorial imagination; she exhibited almost none of the Humboldtian vision of an interactive cosmos.[5]

Over her career Willard developed numerous representations to aid memory, most of them only arbitrarily connected to the subject. Her chart of the "temple of time," for example, "displayed all of history as a temple in which the national histories were paths interlaced on the floor as they reached into the holy past"; still more obscurely, "she displayed the Roman Empire as the gulf at the outlet of the Amazon River, drawing its substance from the upstream waters and past histories that flowed into it" (Calhoun, 19). Her "effort at visualizing history was too complex to be effective"; she did not repeat or develop "any one of her images within later editions of her work, nor did other writers imitate her efforts" (Calhoun, 20). If, in short, she had a talent for mathematical abstraction, she was no empiricist.

Willard's one and only, but finally life-determining, foray into original empirical science began, according to her own published accounts, in the winter of 1822, when she was attending Amos Eaton's course on chemistry while herself teaching the subject from "Mrs. Marcett's [*sic*] excellent work on that subject" (*Treatise*, 2). Walking uphill on a particularly cold day, she began to wonder how her body could produce heat. The answer came in an inspired flash. Heat was produced by combustion in the lungs; the evidence was the steam—real steam, water just over the boiling point—expelled in respiration.

Already inclined to doubt the heart's pumping power because of a comment in her favorite anatomy text (by the Scottish physician John Bell, first published in the United States in 1812, with its last U.S. edition in 1828), she concluded that the steam produced by the lungs possessed the force lacking in the heart to propel blood throughout the body (*Treatise*, 2). "The mind, excited by new and great thoughts, works with unwonted energy; and mine at once collected so many proofs, that I became perfectly convinced of the truth of the hypothesis" (*Theory*, 4).

Willard understood Baconian expectations sufficiently to feel the need of backing up her perfect conviction with experimental proof. In her school, therefore, with the help of assistants, she constructed an apparatus consisting of closed rubber tubing filled with water. A sharp blow applied to one part of the tube propelled the liquid only briefly, showing to her satisfaction that by itself the heart lacked power to keep the blood moving. (Oddly, perhaps, it seems not to have occurred to her to keep on striking the tube; but it is not her "fault" that the heart's electric pacemaker lay outside her knowledge, for anatomists were only beginning to identify electricity as the cardiac regulator.) Additional instruments built from beakers and heat sources showed steam easily doing the work that her "pump" could not. Her *Treatise* includes illustrations of the apparatus, depicting a delicate female hand striking the tubing (15).

On the basis of these experiments—one of which she thought disproved the efficacy of the heart as a blood pump, the other of which proved that steam was sufficiently powerful to move blood around the system—Willard considered her theory ready for public consumption. She was not prepared to understand that professional scientific norms increasingly demanded full-time commitment to a subject. She did not think scientists would hold her reputation as an historian and pedagog against her. Nor was she prepared to agree that immersion in female education had unfitted her to produce high-level science. Even, therefore, as she was occupied with textbooks in history and public programs for female education and teacher training, she confidently mailed her theory (in manuscript form) to a number of scientific men in the United States and overseas.

Not surprisingly, only a few responded and those who did, if they were not merely formally polite, offered criticisms of her work. Unprepared for the realities of scientific discourse, wherein every hypothesis was taken as provisional, and debate (often acrimonious) was the mode through which hypotheses were examined, Willard interpreted most criticism as hostility to the messenger's sex rather than reflective engagement with the message. She revised her theory just once, in response to an observation that—whatever her experiments with beakers might suggest—the lungs themselves were not hot enough to produce the amount of steam necessary for the work she claimed for it. She now declared that the lungs, because they were a vacuum, allowed water to become steam at a far lower temperature than in the open air. Having made her theory account for this anomaly, she saw it as practically unassailable. Thereafter all her energies went into publicizing it with an intensity that even her loyal sister Almira Phelps described ruefully as an "unfortunate mania" (*Reviews and Essays*, 314).

This theory, it is worth noting, merged the culturally powerful model of the steam engine, by which, as all recognized, the whole world was in process of being transformed, to the human body. It also merged the chemistry of combustion with the physics of phase transitions. That the human body was thereby modeled as a machine did not define her as a devotee of mechanism; to the contrary, she retained and featured the theological position that God alone could start the engine running. Everything Willard knew about the early nineteenth-century sciences of chemistry and natural philosophy, and everything she believed about divinity, converged in what looked to her like a theory of everything.

In 1846 she published, through the house of Wiley and Putnam, a book of 170 pages plus a 14–page introduction titled *Treatise on the Motive Powers which Produce the Circulation of the Blood*. It is not clear why she waited so long, but to her critics the delay meant amateurism. Her decision to use a commercial publisher rather than submit the theory to a scientific journal also told against her professionalism. The book, all things considered, received more attention than might have been expected; but responses were mostly dismissive. Indeed, Willard became a kind of example of the way science ought not to be done, and who ought not to be doing it.

Undeterred, during the second cholera outbreak of 1849 Willard saw how her theory might be applied to cure this horrible disease. Inspired by this new rationale, she published a sixty-four-page pamphlet, *Respiration, and Its Effects, More Especially in Relation to Asiatic Cholera, and Other Sinking Diseases*.[6] *Respiration* posited that cholera was caused by an accumulation of cold air in the lungs sufficient to prevent production of steam, so that the blood ceased to flow. Her therapy, which consisted in getting patients to stand upright and breathe deeply—to, as she put it, "get the bad air out of the lungs, and the good air in" (*Respiration*, 42), would of course have had no effect at all on "real" cholera; but the situation in respect to pathology was far more fluid and contested than even that of the sciences proper. The phrase "medical science" at this time was something of an oxymoron. Lacking a theory of micropathogens as disease-causing entities, medical men lumped numerous diseases now theorized as distinct under the cholera label, arriving at diagnoses via symptomatic resemblances. Obviously, nobody knew how to treat "it"; all alleged cures, Charles Rosenberg speculates, were likely due to doctors treating "persons who did not have cholera, or who had at the very worst a minor case" (65). Willard's printed accounts of cures she herself effected involved people who had fainted or otherwise suffered from shortness of breath.

There is no point in invoking a naively cultural constructionist model of scientific knowledge production to argue that Willard's theory should be put on a par with ideas about the heart as the circulator of the blood. There is, however, some point in observing that subsequent discoveries in anatomy and physiology, not to mention pathology, have long since made much of what passed for medical knowledge in the second quarter of the nineteenth century obsolete. More important to my analysis here are questions whether Willard's theory was defective in any way because, as a woman, she had not grasped or been exposed to the basis of acceptable theory building or testing; whether any aspect of its reception (or lack of reception) can be attributed to her gender; and, above all, whether her ways of publicizing it were functions of her outsider status as a woman.

That Willard had not grasped the principles of theory building seems clear, and that this was likely due to her lack of a formal scientific training in experimental situations seems probable. That these, in turn, were functions of gender is obvious. That her work was dismissed by many because a woman had authored it also seems obvious. On the other hand, in some quarters— especially in the South—it received a chivalric attention that it might not have received had its author been a man. In fact, in an era when many scientists themselves were struggling to enforce a notion of professionalism that would exclude most men along with all women, it is possible that some men of science threatened by these developments supported Willard precisely because she was so obviously *not* a professional. Whether because she was the person she was, or whether because she was a woman—but how are these to be disentangled in any particular case?—Willard interpreted all criticism of her project as unenlightened contempt for the female intellect. If contempt came from scientists, so much the worse for the profession. Her theoretical expositions often become belligerently autobiographical and defensive as they counter criticism that she finds misguided or malicious. She presents herself, even flamboyantly, as a victim of her gender. She writes: "This is not so much a subject which I chose, as one which chooses me; and if the Father of

Lights has been pleased to reveal to me from the book of his physical truth, a sentence before unread, is it for me to suppose that it is for my individual benefit? or is it for you, my reader, to turn away your ear from hearing this truth, and charge its great author with having ill-chosen his instrument to communicate it?" (*Treatise,* vii; *Theory,* 9). This kind of rhetoric is one of the traits of her scientific writing that makes it look quite unlike science writing as that genre was becoming distinguished by conventions of impersonality and objectivity.

Indeed, her published pamphlets go well beyond benign neglect of convention when they defy scientific authority to appeal directly to the people:

> Sons and daughters of the Puritans! Your fathers set the world an example of independence of mind and conscience in matters relating to the soul. They claimed the right of studying and judging for themselves in that which concerned their spiritual life and health. Suppose that you, their descendants, go one step further, and take the same course in regard to those things which concern the body, considering that the same Being who is the "Father of your Spirits" is also the "Former of your Bodies." (*Treatise,* vii–viii)

Open defiance of professional approval is a likely way to lose it; but perhaps Willard realized the game was already lost. Her tortured approaches to and retreats from professional science form a tangled web of self-abjection and self-glorification in which her female self comes foremost. Here is a telling example from *Respiration*:

> The heart, that paddle-wheel of life, cannot of itself set in motion the steam-boat of man's animal existence; and he who should deem it but the whim of an ignorant woman, that the making of a fire under the boiler would do it,—would never effect the object,—no matter how many steam-boats he had dissected,—and no matter how numerous or how sagacious his other expedients: while that ignorant woman, having learned by observation, that as the fire was, so was the boat's motion; or, having been taught by the Maker of the vessel,—she might, by the simple expedient of causing a fire to be put in the right place, do, what they could not with all their learning— set the gallant boat under head-way, full upon her course. (58–59)

Deep resentment is patent here. The toll on Willard's health and sensibilities becomes part of her scientific account, at once testifying to the martyrdom she endures and the essential femininity that makes such martyrdom particularly difficult to endure. "Spurned with contemptuous coldness" by editors, rebuffed by "learned physicians and naturalists in Europe," she even attributes her failed second marriage to the theory. "A New-York physician, of elegant and seemingly simple manners, known to me only as a popular writer on cholera in 1832, engaged to espouse my theory," and unfortunately, "I engaged to espouse him" (*Respiration*, 41).[7]

She wrote—in the scientific accounts themselves—that "rated as I am, not as a discoverer, but as one 'going out of her sphere'—a pretended Harvey in female garb, I am not assisted; but my mind, in its sensitiveness, is here chilled by a cold silence,—and there irritated by a contemptuous sneer—and I gloom in secret" (*Respiration*, 34). Yet she soldiered on, in her own view a veritable martyr: "Galileo never suffered more for science than I have done" (41).

Willard was right to worry that she would be perceived as going out of her sphere. She *was* going out of her sphere and meant to do so. Overreaching alone could demonstrate her possession of an intellect equal to the masculine; this was the upshot of a long immersion in Enlightenment theories of intellectual parity between the sexes. In 1861 she goes so far as to write that "believing that my sex stood in the way of my theory's being acknowledged, I sometimes wished that it might please God to take me out of the world" (*Theory*, 14).

On the other hand, emboldened by historical examples of scientific groundbreakers who were also rejected by the establishment, Willard elected to invoke her very exclusion as almost a proof that she was right. When Phelps asked her sister whether it made sense that she could have "discovered what physicians had not observed," Willard reportedly answered that "great discoveries had often originated with persons outside of a profession, whose powers of observation were not blunted by routine, or the habit of receiving certain doctrines as of necessity belonging to a science" (Phelps, *Reviews and Essays*, 301). Willard put this view into print in 1861, quoting in her own defense some praise of her theory from a physician who wrote that members of the profession "whom science has only *perfumed*, are the most apt 'to look down with proud disdain' on any discovery originating 'with individuals not indoctrinated.' They do not make the proper distinction between selfish quacks who seek publicity" and "those 'who, prompted by some mysterious power,' come forward against their interest, and at the risk of their reputation" (*Theory*, 19).

In a move that defied all criteria of Baconian theory building, Willard even claimed divine inspiration. In *Respiration* she exults:

> Was there in the whole wide world another person beside myself,
> who would have taken such a living corpse, dragged it out of doors,
> and set it upright, on feet which could not feel, with the expectation
> that it might breathe out death—breathe in life—and be restored? I
> alone had that faith. Faith in truth leads to wisdom in conduct;
> whereas, faith in falsehood leads to folly. The result of my conduct
> showed, that my faith was a faith in TRUTH. (57)

She was still using the tactic in 1861: Her theory, "while it indicates the wisdom of the Almighty in the formation of the animal frame, it shows itself to be His true interpreter" (*Theory*, 12). In publicizing her name along with her theory—she dubbed it the "Willardan" theory—Willard showed her thirst for the imagined personal glory accruing to scientific discovery, the glory of being recognized as a great intellect.[8]

*F*rom the time her discovery of a comet became public knowledge until her death, Maria Mitchell was known as the one "real" woman scientist in the United States.[9] In a number of short essays written for the general public over the years, she spoke authoritatively about the practices and institutions through which science is produced. This makes her work quite different from other writing in this era by women interested in science. She defines science as a set of procedures rather than a set of outcomes; she sees science as group activity rather than lonely exploration. Original discoveries in science remain the finest expressions of human genius, but to her, these are not prerequisite for calling oneself a scientist. She writes: "It is the highest joy of the true scientist that he can reap no lasting harvest—that whatever he may bring into the storehouse today will be surpassed by the gleaners tomorrow—he studies Nature because he loves her and rejoices to 'look through Nature up to Nature's God'" (cited in Wright, *Sweeper,* 168). The bow to Natural Theology is conventional; less so are the metaphors of science as a cumulative storehouse and scientists as gleaners.

Even as she outlined this view of science as group activity, Mitchell recognized that women—her own apparent exception to the rule notwithstanding—had no access to the group. The scientific culture she was explaining and celebrating was profoundly masculinist. In the 1840s a network of influential scientists, men who humorously styled themselves the "Lazzaroni," began working deliberately to redefine science in the United States in a way that would increase its prestige.[10] Among other endeavors, they altered the image of scientist from whimsical gentleman amateur to well-networked, certified professional. The gender of this figure, however, remained male, even as the figure of the amateur was discredited in part by feminizing it. (As I have observed in chapter 5, this feminization and democratization of the amateur became an opportunity for genteel women.) Alexander Dallas Bache, Mitchell's chief sponsor, thought that "science was by definition an activity that only men seriously would pursue" (Slotten, 183 n. 12).

Yet Mitchell herself understood the transformation of science from aristocratic individual endeavor to meritocratic group activity as an opportunity for women and science alike. Even before Mitchell became a teacher of women, her popular writings figured science as the ongoing cumulative work of multitudes, a view strikingly opposed to the image of the scientist as solitary hero, especially as an isolate bucking the establishment. The collaborative image, which comported with the Baconian ethos of atheoretical fact-gathering, corresponded to the actualities of the surveys through which most new science was being conducted in the United States before the Civil War. It also opened a space for women that the heroic image denied them.

Ordinary people on Nantucket Island in Mitchell's youth were well versed in the interrelated subjects of mathematics, navigation, and astronomy. New England's was a numerate as well as literate population.[11] For the many whose livelihoods depended directly or indirectly on merchant shipping, astronomy was a vocational subject, figuring less as occasion for abstract theology than as essential tool. It was taught mainly to help people determine "longitude and latitude, time and tide" (Bruce, 348). As a tool, astronomy might seem paradigmatically male—it did so to Sarah Hale, who, we might remember, complained in an "Editor's Table" column in the *Lady's Book* for April 1870 about Vassar's preference for male astronomy over female chemistry. Astronomy is "no doubt an interesting science and of essential use in navigation. But unless the fair students all intend to follow the sea, it really seems that the relative position of the two sciences in the course should be reversed" (80:348).[12] Still, not only did some Nantucket women go to sea with their captain or mate spouses, many more had reason to follow their families' time and tide–determined fortunes. Maria Mitchell studied mathematics and astronomy in school as a matter of course. She taught them when she set up, briefly, as a teacher herself.

Reliable astronomical observations could not be made by solo investigators, because if they were to be precise, the observer could not leave the telescope to check the clock or record an observation. This called for an assistant. Caroline Herschel's memoir—compiled and published in 1876 after her death—compellingly describes rooftop vigils on freezing nights (she wore several pairs of stockings for warmth), punctuated by running downstairs, stopwatch in hand, to record and compute her brother's sightings in a lighted room, and then racing back up for the next observation (224). (It also describes the process of tempering the lens for the famous forty-foot telescope with cow dung.) Although the memoir had not appeared when Sarah Hale published *Woman's Record*, her entry on Caroline Herschel shows that Caroline's exertions were common knowledge and that the physical demands of doing astronomy were well understood: Hale uses the word *arduous* twice and comments on the rigors of work that must be conducted "till daybreak, without regard to season, and indeed chiefly in the winter" (354).

Working alongside her father, Maria Mitchell might well have remained one of the hundreds of "lost" women who provided physical and intellectual help to men across all the sciences—whose presence, had they been recognized, might have allowed for a very different conception of what doing science involves from the image of the solitary genius-hero. But when the two Mitchells became part of Alexander Dallas Bache's huge network for the U.S. Coast Survey, and Maria discovered a comet on her own, she remained anonymous no longer. Bache, who became director of the survey in 1843, made it the best financed, most ambitious, and best publicized of all the many scientific undertakings of the era. Hundreds of investigators "engaged in simultaneous surveys along the Atlantic, Gulf, and Pacific coasts, developed the use of telegraphy to determine longitudes, carried on astronomical research, including study of solar eclipses, observed the Gulf Stream, made tidal observations, researched life at the bottom of the ocean, and carried on researches in the Office of Weights and Measures" (Miller, Voss, and Hussey, 15).

Bache, who was well networked with European as well as U.S. scientists, eagerly promoted the survey's work to the greatest possible number of people. He and others in his group pressed Mitchell's claim to have discovered the comet. In 1831 the king of Denmark had instituted a system of medals recognizing the discoverers of comets, with a definite protocol for establishing priority. The system bolstered the ideal of individual achievement; by definition, almost, the competition increased competition among would-be "discoverers." When Mitchell failed to report her discovery on time to George Airy (the British astronomer designated to receive the information), "a full statement of the circumstances of the discovery having been made to the King of Denmark, his majesty ordered a reference of the case to Professor Schumacher, who reported in favor of granting the medal to Miss Mitchell" (Loomis, 152). It was not Mitchell who made this "full statement," but a group of the scientists who knew her—and knew her father.

Mitchell's supporters worked less for her than for national science. The very year she won the medal, Elias Loomis gave her a whole (although very short) chapter in *The Recent Progress of Astronomy; Especially in the United States.* In the preface to his 1856 revision of the book, Loomis expressed the hope that "the future progress of astronomy is to be no less brilliant than the past; and that henceforth America may be even more distinguished for her contributions to science, than for her progress in material power and wealth" (iv). Throughout, Loomis pointed out how much more good work like Mitchell's would be accomplished if governments and schools built bigger and better observatories; that is, he made her exemplary rather than unique.

Mitchell's earliest publication for a general audience, "The United States Coast Survey" in the January 1852 *Christian Examiner*, publicizes the work of the survey with an emphasis on its collaborative nature. The essay contains no mathematics but defines the survey's science in mathematical and technological terms, describing the measurements required and the techniques deployed by the survey—a collective noun through which she unifies the work of thousands of people. The scientists are mere ciphers in an activity dominated by technology—from "the observer at the zenith telescope" who "adjusts his instruments in altitude, sees that the clamp in azimuth is properly placed, and waits for the notice of the time from his assistant, who sits at the chronometer," to those in the "office at Washington" who collate observations and "check the work of the field," to those who do the "drawing, engraving, electrotyping, publishing, printing, and instrument-making" (92, 95).

As she puts it, the survey—"a plan of operations far-reaching as the country, a series of investigations almost as extensive as the field of science itself" (77)—aims to translate the illegible national topography into a set of accurate, usable measurements that will forward the productive exploitation of national resources. These measurements require a huge accumulation of discrete observations and calculations, each dependent on instrumentation and vulnerable to numerous sources of error. In fact Mitchell makes the correction of error her essay's motif, describing human and instrumental unreliability at length. "A small error in a base of five or six miles in length, on which is raised a superstructure of triangles whose sides sometimes extend to sixty, seventy, and even a hundred miles, becomes very considerable in the course of calculation" (79); "the observations are so much affected by meteorological phenomena, that they must be made at different times of day, and extend through several days" (82); "no instrument is so perfect as to require no variety of position to balance its errors; the atmosphere of no region is so steady as to be unvarying in its influence, and the observer himself differs at different times in his reading of the same angle" (83); "the connection between eye and ear is not nice; the ear is supposed to be a far from delicately discerning organ; the judgment of fractions of a second involves error, and the fingers require considerable time to make their record" (87); "when clouds are every moment threatening, as in our variable climate, when a long interval may occur, as in prime-vertical observations, between the east and west transit, the observer is almost sure to be affected by his trembling anxiety" (90). Mitchell works here to demystify heroic science but to remystify science as self-discipline in the service of a common cause.

She never suggests in this essay that the professional model suits women better than the genius model. Not until after the war did she begin to elaborate the gender implications of her position. Yet her lifelong views of gender and genius appear in the second essay she wrote before the war, a piece about Mary Somerville published in the May 1860 *Atlantic Monthly*. In discussing the iconic Somerville, Mitchell makes the relation of women to the higher reaches of science—that is, mathematized science—central. She defines three levels of mathematical aptitude: the ability to understand most mathematical works (easy); the ability to understand the most profound of them (requiring "a high order of intellect"); and, finally, the "far-reaching" ability to understand principles of mathematics in sufficient depth to create a theorem ("Mary Somerville," 568).

This last equals great science. Granting that Somerville had impressive mathematical abilities—the most impressive of any woman of the age and perhaps of all time (at this point the only other possible candidate, Caroline Herschel, is dismissed as "the patient, helping sister of a truly great man," [568])—Mitchell still designates Somerville a second-rank intellect. Somerville understood Laplace (a first-order intellect) well enough to translate and annotate his work in a way that made it "comparatively easy to understand" (570); but she was no Laplace. Her *Connexion of the Physical Sciences* and her *Physical Geography* were "vast collections of fact," showing "an amount and authority of learning to be compared only to that of Humboldt" (570)—but she lacked Humboldt's synthesizing creativity. In short, Somerville—the highest historical expression to date of female scientific genius—turns out to be a high-level scientific publicizer, an affiliate after all.

Mitchell's position at Vassar College was only the second science chair in a U.S. college to be occupied by a woman.[13] Prestigious as this appointment might seem, teaching was not Mitchell's career of choice. She referred bluntly to the disjunction between the requirements of good research and good teaching. If the scientist "pursues his science in all his intervals from his classwork, his classes suffer, on account of his engrossments; if he devotes himself to his students, science suffers" (Mitchell, cited in Kendall, 223). The question of science careers for women accordingly took on a personal urgency that, together with her strong commitment to intellectual discipline and the instruction that might encourage it, led her to offer a kind of preprofessional training in all her classes. For nine years, from December 1872 until January 1881, Mitchell contributed a column of her students' astronomical observations to the *Scientific American* almost every month. Designed for "everyday readers," it was called "Astronomical Notes" and described the position and activity of easily observable planets and their satellites, sunspots, meteor showers, comets, and other timely celestial events. Each column began by reminding readers of the author's indebtedness to students "for the items of meteorological and astronomical observations, and for some of the computations" (see, e.g., the December 7, 1872, issue, page 356). Mitchell's aims were to emphasize the women's capabilities for useful astronomical work along with its collaborative nature.

Even as she increasingly accepted the need to be more public about her own views, she hesitated to endorse popularization as a way to disseminate scientific information. She told students in 1866 that the phrase "popular science" had in it "a touch of absurdity. That which is popular is not scientific" because "the laws which govern the motions of the sun, the earth, planets, and other bodies in the universe cannot be understood and demonstrated without a solid basis of mathematical learning" (Mitchell, cited in Kendall, 185). She told them again in 1874 that "the reader of popular scientific books is very likely to think that he understands the science itself, when he merely understands what some writer says about science" (Mitchell, cited in Kendall, 221).

In a review of the popularization *Other Worlds than Ours,* she offers the "grave objection" to all popular science books that they give the reader "no conception of the difficulties of the subject. Mr. Proctor says, 'If Mercury had a satellite, we could tell her weight at once.' That is, after years of observing with the utmost care, and after wearisome and laborious calculations." She suggests that "observatories well endowed, and well furnished with observers, would do much better scientific work than the many ill-supported ones which are springing up all over the land" ("Other Worlds than Ours," 472).[14]

But, as a founding member and president of the Association for the Advancement of Women—chair of its science committee and collector of statistics on the participation of women in science around the country—Mitchell took a somewhat different approach, downplaying the difficulty of science to feature its accessibility to the mass of ordinary women, providing they were well trained. Her brief introduction to the translation of the French popular book *The Wonders of the Moon* proposes that the book's appropriate readers are "those whose occupations do not afford them time for study, or who, from defects in their early training, believe themselves incapable of mathematics. From the first page to the last there is not a problem; not a triangle is drawn" (iii). At first it seems that the best to be hoped for from such a book is that "the narrow boundaries of ordinary daily life may be extended" (iii); "the mission of the popular scientific works is mostly that of suggestion" (iv). Yet, and especially in the case of "young women," there is the possibility after all of an awakening to science intense enough to produce a professional commitment:

> Scattered all over our country are thousands of young girls, leading aimless lives, to whom science might open new worlds. They have the very requisites necessary for observations of phenomena; in general their perceptive faculties have been cultivated beyond all others; they have been trained in minute details and in routine work. They could gather in valuable facts which might lead to new views of nature and new interpretations of its lessons. They could scarcely be observers of phenomena, without taking the next step, and becoming seekers after law. (iv–v)

Mitchell identifies ordinary attributes as those which science needs: a good eye for detail and a high tolerance for fixed routine. She also links the possession of these attributes to women through their training in specifically female tasks: sewing, embroidery.

She is on record as hoping to emancipate women from stitchery: "It seems to me that the needle is the chain of woman, and has fettered her more than the laws of the country. Once emancipate her from the 'stitch, stitch, stitch,' . . . she would have time for studies which would engross as the needle never can" (Mitchell, cited in Kendall, 25–26).

But she celebrates the qualities developed by needlework when she appropriates them for the telescope:

> The perceptive faculties of women being more acute than those of men, she would perceive the size, form and color of an object more readily and would catch an impression more quickly. The fine needle work and the embroidery teach them to measure small spaces. The

same delicacy of eye and touch is needed to bisect the image of a
star by a spider's web, as to piece delicate muslin with a fine needle.
The small fingers too come into play with a better adaptation to delicate micrometer screws. A girl's power of steady endurance of mo-
notonous routine is great. (cited in Wright, *Sweeper,* 139–140)

She proposed in an 1876 talk, "The Need for Women in Science," that
working as science popularizers (which after all was what science teachers
did, even at the college level) might be the best women could realistically
aim for at the moment. If they became scientifically competent enough to
lecture in schools and in public, to write for periodicals, to translate, their
work might make it easier for future women to become professional scientists as a matter of course. For this to happen, she concedes fatalistically, requires the "slow change of the ages; the conversion of public sentiment" and
"a struggle to which hardly anyone is equal"; even then, women may turn
out to lack scientific aptitude. Ultimately, "until able women have given their
lives to investigation, it is idle to discuss their capacity for original work"
(cited in Wright, *Sweeper,* 203–204).

In 1869 Mitchell took a group of students to Burlington, Iowa, to record
a solar eclipse. She wrote about the expedition in "The Total Eclipse of 1869"
for *Hours at Home*, concealing the gender of her students until the final sentence, where it transforms the essay into a celebration of women's capacity
for doing science. The essay repeats points made in her essay on the Coast
Survey: error ("The data may be wrong"); instrumentation ("Our instruments
consisted of an equatorially mounted telescope of four inches aperture, by
Doland; a small one of two and a half inches, by the same maker; and a very
perfect little instrument of three inches, by Alvan Clark"); and collaboration
("We paired off two and two at the telescopes, one to watch the phenomenon
through the glass, the other to count time and to make notes") (558).

Especially interested in the opportunity to view the corona, Mitchell
will of course describe what was seen, but she will simultaneously point out
that seeing is an imperfect business. The need to look through colored glass
distorts every observation: "Beside the different perception of the eye, in its
normal state, the retina cannot instantly lose the effect of the colored glass. I
had just left an orange glass, and was quite insensible to that color; while
one of our party who had been using a green glass declares [sic] the protu-
berances to be orange-red" (559). At the finale, overexcited people in other
parties neglect their scientific tasks to look around during the vital instants
of total darkness. But, says Mitchell, "my assistants, a party of young stu-

dents, would not have turned from the narrow line of observation assigned to them if the earth had quaked beneath them." They knew their duty and did it; might this be, she asks rhetorically, "because they were *women*?" (560).

Mitchell's last published essay appeared in the *Century* magazine for October 1889, four months after her death. It is a reminiscence of the three Herschels, assessing Caroline's life and contributions to science as a way of understanding the interaction of gifted scientific women with social possibilities and constraints. In Caroline's memoir, now published, one might read her strenuously self-abasing analysis of her capacities, which the memoir's editor (Mrs. John Herschel) features as praiseworthy: "I am nothing, I have done nothing; all I am, all I know, I owe to my brother. I am only the tool which he shaped to his use—a well-trained puppy-dog would have done as much" (ix).

In light of Caroline's self-abnegation, Mitchell reads her not as she had earlier—as a woman with no strong talents—but as one whose innate scientific talent was strangled by time and place. "It seems probable that her gifts were as fully bestowed as those of her brother," but "she was left uneducated and undeveloped." When "she kept the records, so systematically and so scientifically that after nearly one hundred years they are still valuable, every line that she wrote was an argument for the higher education of women" ("Reminiscences," 908). But Mitchell does not put all blame on the culture; although Caroline's opportunities were constricted by poor education, she should have done more with her talents:

> The woman who has peculiar gifts has a definite line marked out for her, and the call from God to do his work in the field of scientific investigation may be as imperative as that which calls the missionary into the moral field, or the mother into the family: as missionary, or as scientist, as sister, or as mother, no woman has the right to lose her individuality. . . . If what Caroline Herschel did is a lesson and a stimulus to all women, what she did not do is a warning. Has any being a right not to be? When Caroline Herschel so devoted herself to her brother that on his death her own self died, and her life became comparatively useless, she did, all unconsciously, a wrong, and she made the great mistake of her life. (908)

In words almost identical to those she had used in "The Need for Women in Science," Mitchell concludes: "To discuss the question whether women have the capacity for original investigation in science is simply idle until equal

opportunity is given them" (908). Mitchell tells women with scientific ambitions that they have a moral duty to pursue their goals and, also, that they
should expect to be defeated. In a roundabout way, Caroline Herschel's becomes a narrative of martyrdom like Willard's. And, insofar as Herschel stands
for all women in science—not least Maria Mitchell, a daughter-assistant to
an amateur astronomer—this is Mitchell's narrative also.

CHAPTER 8

Emily Dickinson and Scientific Skepticism

Emily Dickinson's unwillingness to publish sets her apart—as she meant it to—from the crowd of nineteenth-century women who claimed the print domain for themselves and other women. Nevertheless, the rich scientific texture of her poetry invites scrutiny in a study like this. At the least, her scientific facility testifies to the ubiquitous presence of scientific information in the general culture.[1] At most, she deploys her scientific lexicon to draw strikingly different conclusions about science and religion from those prevailing in this same culture.

Without exception, those who affiliated with the sciences insisted that to know science was to know God's benevolence and wisdom, and, implicitly, to know that he existed. Every sign of adaptability or functionality in the creation, according to the tenets of Natural Theology, demonstrated the fact of an intelligent creator. Women who campaigned for science seldom made theology the centerpiece of their efforts—they were not theologians—but they always praised the sciences as aids to rational piety.

Dickinson, however, used any and all of the sciences to argue that knowledge of God's existence and attributes was exactly what science could not provide, and what moreover it never claimed to provide. From her perspective, those who used science to prove religious truths were naive, self-deceived, or downright hypocritical. Foremost among those to misuse science like this were the intellectual leaders of her own native Amherst.[2] Dickinson turned science against its Amherst advocates, making it a powerful weapon in her lifelong private battle against Amherst complacency and conformity.

The science in her poetry is extensive. I count more than 270 poems containing scientific language; this is about 15 percent of the total.[3] A sampling of terms purloined from scientific discourses includes: *amplitude, axiom, axis, concave, condense, corrode, entomology, equilibrium, experiment, hypothesis, ignition, momentum, ornithology, parallax, perihelion, perpendiculars, phosphor, prism, pyrite, species, terrestrial, valves, and velocity.*

From botany, along with vernacular terms like *blossom, bud, pod, bulb, stem, stalk,* and *flower,* she refers to *corolla* (1261, J1241—wherein the "Scientist of Faith" has just begun his research and "The Flora unimpeachable / To Time's Analysis—" resides "Above his Synthesis"), *calyx* (367, J339; 523, J606; 1261, J1241), *stamen* (117, J70), *sepal* (25, J19), and *plant embryo* (1413, J1386; 1507, J1475; 1549, J1524).

In chemistry, at least eleven poems connect atoms to basic chemical or physical laws. The atom, the smallest unit of matter, is impermeable and indestructible; material substances can be almost infinitely compressed, pulverized, or stretched, but the atoms of which they consist do not change (e.g., 581, J376; 423, J410; 653, J515; 516, J600; 279, J664; 1067, J889; 1070, J954; 1168, J1178; 1222, J1191; 1226, J1231). Fire dominates among chemical processes, as in poem 401 (J365) about the soul at white heat. A dozen poems describe ether scientifically. Mechanics provides concepts of velocity and momentum, oil and axle (1016, J983), the technology of rivets and solder, and the understanding underlying the wedges and levers of the "columnar self" (740, J789).

Astronomy contributes the names of a few stars (e.g., Arcturus), constellations (e.g., Orion), and planets (Mercury and Saturn) along with terms like *crescent* (used at least eleven times), *eclipse* (at least nine), *parallax* (once: 1269, J1286), *retrograde* (three times: 1067, J889; 828, J904; 1049, J1089), *perihelion* (once: 1375, J299), and *transit* (twice: 285, J673; 1762, J1744). Dickinson devised metaphors from the facts—available equally from astronomy or geography—that the moon controlled the tides, planets orbited elliptically around the sun, and the earth's revolution created the seasonal phenomena of a year and its rotation the alternation of day and night. She refers often to the telescope and the microscope, the latter especially via many allusions to compound vision.[4]

She refers to electricity some six times. Poem 628 (J440), one of several that equates electricity with the life force, says electricity activates the "curl" of the Clematis. There are also poems 1424 (J1392), 1448 (J1431), 1556 (J1585), 1618 (J1593), and 1631 (J1597), which propose that the heart is motivated by electric impulses. The well-known fact that lightning is electricity turns up in 1263 (J1129). From geology (or perhaps geography) comes the idea of mountains growing, hence having a history (768, J757). Poem 747 (J724) is one of several that identify human death with the concept of species extinction and, accordingly, obliquely deny immortality. Poem 1641 (J1599) refers to igneous and aqueous geological theories in a speculation about how the world might end.

Dickinson uses arithmetic mostly for metaphors of bookkeeping and banking, but she also refers to *ratio* (78, J88; 109, J125; 317, J257), *bisect* (38, J11; 960, J928; 1421, J1411 [where what is bisected is this life from the next, with the result that we can at best "infer" Paradise, never really "know" it]; 1470, J1445; 1772, J1738), and *circumference,* a much-analyzed term used at least seventeen times. From logic, adjunct to geometry, Dickinson draws among other concepts that of *inference,* which shows up in some fourteen poems to signify knowledge that, because it is not empirically demonstrable, is not knowledge (e.g., 1192, J1163). If one grants the premise of the logical argument and reasons correctly from it, then the conclusion is proven—but that does not make it empirically true, for the simple reason that the premise may have been empirically false to begin with.

If every mention of heart, lungs, blood, veins, breath, mind, and brain (not to mention eyes and ears—optical and acoustical information redundantly available from natural philosophy) is ascribed to physiology, then this subject becomes by far Dickinson's most frequently cited science. Physiology was the era's closest approach to biology or life science; its centrality is entirely appropriate in the work of a poet preoccupied with the moment when a living creature becomes a dead one. Ultimately, to Dickinson as to so many in her era and perhaps in ours as well, religion is ultimately about the promise of some kind of afterlife, and the afterlife reduces to the promise of reunion with the beloved dead. If the sciences have nothing to say about the hereafter, they have nothing to say about the only theological question that truly matters.

The vitalist approach that predominated in the nineteenth century, as Ernst Mayr explains, held "that living organisms had properties that could not be found in inert matter and that therefore biological theories and concepts could not be reduced to the laws of physics and chemistry" (2). This is exactly what Dickinson would have learned about life, whether through Calvin Cutter's elementary physiology text in use at Mount Holyoke, or Peter Parley's *Glance at the Physical Sciences* ("the phenomena manifested by all organic bodies are the results of an inherent power, which is generally termed *vital principle*—a power, the essence of which is enveloped in mystery, and upon which science sheds no light" [339]), or Almira Phelps's *Chemistry for*

Beginners (chemists are "ignorant of what constitutes the principle of life in a plant, an insect, or a man" [75]).

Dickinson used this distinction between vital spirit and inert matter just as her scientific textbooks used it—to represent death as a moment when the organic (or organized, in her era's terminology) body becomes inorganic, a species of material whose "laws are only of mechanics, chemistry, and electricity" (Parley, 340). But she used it against the conclusion, drawn from the discipline of Natural Theology, to which these textbooks resorted—that the existence of a vital principle of life guarantees some kind of survival after death.

*I*n making this argument about Dickinson's poetry of science I am contesting the leading critical view, which sees it as evidence of a heroic struggle to reconcile an abiding religious faith with the destabilizing implications of scientific findings.[5] My claim is that because using science as evidence for what science cannot demonstrate is the "Amherst" way, Dickinson turns the claims of "Amherst" theology against those who advance them. Rejecting the Amherst synthesis, widening the abyss between science as knowledge of this world and religion as faith in the next world, she affiliates with science and against religion. "Their Height in Heaven comforts not—" she writes, "Their Glory—naught to me—/ 'Twas best imperfect—as it was—/ I'm finite—I can't see" (725, J696). Approached from this perspective, her scientific poems look less like expressions of religious agony—although they are agonized enough for other reasons—and more like principled attacks on the religious orthodoxy permeating local intellectual life. An inveterate deflator of patriarchal pretensions, Dickinson in her science poetry relentlessly pries apart the synthesis of science and faith to which Amherst College and its satellite institutions—Amherst Academy, Mount Holyoke Female Seminary—were programmatically devoted.

Amherst's dominant intellectual voice was that of the college, a conservative evangelical institution founded in 1821 (among the founders was Dickinson's grandfather) specifically to train young men for Calvinist ministries. Edward Hitchcock (1793–1864), a Silliman-trained polymath, both epitomized and shaped the college's goals. Author of a best-selling geology textbook and other scientific works, director of the geological surveys of both Massachusetts and Vermont, Hitchcock had been raised as a Unitarian but converted as a young man to a zealous Calvinism. He was Amherst College's first professor of chemistry and became its professor of geology and Natural Theology (a conjunction of titles on which he insisted). He also served as college president from 1845 to 1854.[6]

In his invaluable *Reminiscences*, Hitchcock says science entered the Amherst curriculum for two converging reasons. First: the school, founded to "raise up ministers and missionaries," necessarily recruited from "the indigent classes" because "this was the most reliable source of supply" (294). Students from poor backgrounds, unlikely to attain pastorates among the affluent, did not need the cultural capital of belles lettres. The sciences, associated with technology and hands-on work, suited much better. Second: the presumption of early nineteenth-century Natural Theology that nature study led inevitably to nature's God—more, that it led inevitably to a Christian god—was increasingly embattled. In 1851, Hitchcock proclaimed the natural sciences an outpost of "the enemy" who have, "within a few years past, intrenched themselves within the dominions of natural science" so that "there, for a long time to come, must be the tug of the war" (*Religion of Geology*, ix). Because anyone who "studied the sciences only briefly and superficially" was "certain to be worsted in an argument with an accomplished naturalist who is a skeptic" (x), students training as ministers had no choice but to learn science in sufficient depth to defend their theology. Hitchcock never doubted that science, rightly understood, conduced to orthodoxy; he was arguing that right understanding called for substantial immersion in scientific subjects.

A generous, energetic, and committed man, Hitchcock lectured indefatigably over the years: on geology, botany and zoology, chemistry, anatomy and physiology, astronomy, and all divisions of natural philosophy—to Amherst students, Mount Holyoke students, and the general public in Amherst and neighboring towns. He headed the official state geological surveys of Massachusetts and Vermont, and he wrote the reports. As an original researcher he was known for discovering and classifying dinosaur fossil footprints that he unearthed, literally, in the Connecticut Valley. The evidence these footprints provided for the earth's development over time did not unsettle his faith. He held that the great age of the earth was inferable from a right understanding of the language of Genesis. Philology and common sense explicated the six days of creation metaphorically. He reconciled extinct fossil species with Holy Writ by accepting a catastrophist theory of periodic interruptions in earth history; the Bible, for him, spoke only to the last—presumably final—creation, when human beings had been put on earth.

In the introduction to *The Religion of Geology*, Hitchcock explained that understanding the bearings of geology on the Bible required knowledge of geology, zoology, botany, and comparative anatomy; also "sacred hermeneutics, or the principles of interpreting the Scriptures"; and, last, "a clear conception of the principles of natural and revealed religion" (vi–vii). He was saying that while no mere scientist, no matter how learned in his specialty, could authoritatively pronounce on the Bible, neither could a mere theologian, no matter how well-versed in tools of biblical exegesis, refute skeptical scientists without knowing their science. Learned theologians, who have written works with "no accurate knowledge of geology," have "awakened disgust, and even contempt, among scientific men, especially those of sceptical tendencies, who have inferred that a cause which resorts to such defences must be very weak" (vii). On the other hand, "prejudices and disgust equally strong have been produced in the minds of many a man well versed in theology and biblical exegesis by some productions of scientific men upon the religious bearings of geology, because they advanced principles which the merest tyro in divinity would know to be false" (vii–viii).

Hitchcock's energies were crucial in making of Amherst College an institution possessing one of the strongest scientific curricula in the nation. But, as might be supposed, Hitchcock fostered the sciences at Amherst quite specifically to acquaint young ministers "with the grounds on which religion has been attacked, and from which it has also been amply illustrated." Far from imagining the college as a training ground for scientists, he maintained that he would "be content if only instruction enough were given in geology and natural history to qualify the graduates to understand the religious bearings of these sciences" (*Reminiscences*, 114). In Wolff's words, in Amherst's science-heavy curriculum, "all science learning was a form of religious education" (82).

Hitchcock also helped shape the curriculum at the Amherst Academy, where the town's elite youth—including Emily Dickinson from 1840 to 1847—received instruction from recent Amherst graduates.[7] Hitchcock also worked very closely with Mary Lyon, a close friend, whose Mount Holyoke Female Seminary at nearby South Hadley Dickinson attended for ten months after graduating from the academy.

Now insofar as science in all these locations authorized itself through appeals to piety, Dickinson's poetry of science extracted the sciences from the Amherst grip. To do this work was not to question science; it was to contest the Amherst understanding of what science was all about, thus suggesting that Amherst's scientific divines failed to understand religion and science equally, and locating the author firmly in the skeptical camp that Hitchcock had described as the enemy. Whether the ministry was self-deceived or hypocritical, Dickinson finds it at the least to be foundationally obscurantist. And she proposes that the obfuscation is meant to mask a deep anxiety: "Much

Gesture, from the Pulpit—/ Strong Hallelujahs roll—/ Narcotics cannot still the Tooth / That nibbles at the soul" (373; J501).

Behind this rejection of authority stands not only Dickinson's lifelong bias against patriarchal dominance, but also a logical rigor that defines uncertainty as the precondition for faith. This rigor, even though it is "masculine" in character, becomes an anti-patriarchal weapon all the more powerful for being wielded against those who flaunt their logicality as a sign of manly superiority.[8] If faith demands uncertainty, then certainty removes the need for faith. "Too much of Proof affronts Belief" (1240, J1228). Faith is the bridge "To what, could We presume / The Bridge would cease to be / To Our far, vascillating Feet / A first Necessity" (978, J915).

Throughout her many poems deploying scientific metaphors and facts, Dickinson's critique runs in one direction only—from science to religion—because she interprets any divine who relies on science as a man of weak faith. "'Faith' is a fine invention / For Gentlemen who *see*! / But Microscopes are prudent / In an emergency!" (202, J185). Amherst's dependence on science reveals the crisis of orthodoxy that Amherst denied but on which its training was obsessively focused, unmasking its Calvinist version of Natural Theology as a gigantic hoax.

Still, although she wrote many poems in which science demolishes orthodoxy, although almost every poem with scientific references works to this end, Dickinson's scientific affiliations are only provisional and strategic. The sciences in themselves held little interest for her. They are mere tools. As a lyric poet she aimed neither to expound scientific theory nor to teach scientific fact. As a poet who refused to publish, she ignored the campaign to demonstrate the scope of the female intellect; the last thing that occupied her was the work of popularizing. A person who believed that publication was "the Auction / Of the Mind of Man" (788, J709) could hardly be expected to participate in the work of disseminating science to the masses.

*I*n fact, many women in Dickinson's circle affiliated with the sciences in conventional ways. Her mother, as biographers have recently discovered, had attended a school whose ties to Yale University produced a particularly strong science curriculum for its time (Ackmann, 17). Her beloved sister-in-law Susan Gilbert Dickinson taught mathematics before she married, did calculations for intellectual pleasure, played mathematical games with her children, and was overheard as an aged lady (she lived until 1913) querying an Amherst professor about Einsteinian space-time (Bianchi, 145).

Orra White Hitchcock, one-time principal of the girls' department at Amherst Academy, drew the charts for her husband Edward's geology classes and illustrated his textbooks. Edward's *Religion of Geology* is dedicated to her, the "beloved wife" who not only "in a great measure, relieved me of the cares of a numerous family" but also portrayed scientific facts much more vividly with her pencil than he has with his pen.

> It is peculiarly appropriate that your name should be associated with mine in any literary effort where the theme is geology; since your artistic skill has done more than my voice to render that science attractive to the young men whom I have instructed. I love especially to connect your name with an effort to defend and illustrate that religion which I am sure is dearer to you than every thing else. . . . In a world where much is said of female deception and inconstancy, I desire to testify that one man at least has placed implicit confidence in woman, and has not been disappointed. (iii–iv)

Mabel Loomis Todd—known to Dickinson scholars for her long romance with Dickinson's brother Austin and her early editing of Dickinson's poetry—accompanied her astronomer husband on expeditions in the 1890s and wrote astronomy textbooks, including the classroom staple *Total Eclipses of the Sun* (Higgins, 469).

The most important woman proselytizer for the sciences in Dickinson's milieu was Mary Lyon (1797–1849), who established the Mount Holyoke Female Seminary at South Hadley in 1837 and remained its principal until her relatively early death. Lyon, born in poverty, published only for the purpose of raising money for her school, which recruited from the "middling" classes—by which is not meant the genteel bourgeoisie but farmers, artisans, and mechanics. Hitchcock, in his eulogistic memoir of her life, observes that "the wisdom of Providence was manifested, in taking her from the lower ranks of society, and causing all the early part of her life to be spent among those classes upon whom she was to operate, and for whose special benefit she was afterwards to labor. She thus learnt how to sympathize with their principles and feelings, and to meet their idiosyncrasies" (*Power*, 444).

It was perhaps this social background that gave Lyon—according to Hitchcock—a mind "better shaped for giving instruction in science than in literature" (451). Her own inclinations merged with the life prospects of her students to suggest that science should be central in the three-year Mount Holyoke curriculum. Of the seven sciences taken by students who completed the school's three years of study, Lyon's own specialty was chemistry, which she taught to second-year students in a course of nine weeks' duration (Shmurak and Handler, 318).[9]

To learn how to do experiments and teach her students to do them, Lyon boarded for a summer with Amos Eaton, the great champion of scientific education for women in the 1820s, who had trained Almira Phelps and tutored Emma Willard. She lived with the Hitchcocks during the period she was establishing the seminary. Edward helped her prepare her algebra and chemistry lectures; Orra instructed her in scientific drawing (Elizabeth Green, 167). After the school opened, Lyon often accompanied the Hitchcocks and their teams on geological surveys during summer breaks. Hitchcock lectured regularly at Mount Holyoke, bringing his own equipment along for demonstrations. For physiology instruction he donated a costly papier-mâché manikin to the school that could be opened to display the internal organs (Elizabeth Green, 239–240). Mount Holyoke students were invited along on the annual geological outings undertaken by his Amherst class; in a wonderful enactment of gender roles, the women did not climb hills but waited for the men to come back and share the picnic lunch Mount Holyoke had provided.

Dickinson's exact courses of study at both the Amherst Academy and Mount Holyoke are not fully known (Sewell, 349). The academy offered chemistry, natural history, mineralogy, geology, botany, and astronomy, along with mathematics and geography, but her letters mention only botany and geology. Similarly, of Mount Holyoke's seven sciences—excluding algebra and geometry from the count[10]—Dickinson seems to have taken astronomy, physiology, and chemistry. She mentions Silliman's textbook in one letter and writes to her brother Austin (17 February 1848), "Your *welcome* letter found me all engrossed in the history of Sulphuric Acid!!!!!" (*Letters*, 1:62). Ten months would not have allowed for any depth of study in a three-year curriculum.

Regardless of what particular sciences she studied, in the 1840s there was no mistaking either the academy's or the seminary's character as abridged versions of Amherst College. Mount Holyoke in particular meant to train young women, as the college trained young men, to support themselves as teachers and missionary workers. The most widely publicized features of the school during Lyon's tenure were, first, an invasive, consuming interest in the state of student souls with a concomitant instigation of annual religious revivals (Amherst College also initiated annual revivals); second, the requirement that students do all the housekeeping.

The housekeeping provision was both a cost-control measure to make the school affordable to its target population, and a preparation for these women's likely future lives (Hitchcock, *Power*, 189). Predictably, genteel students went elsewhere. Leyda quotes Helen Fiske (later Helen Hunt Jackson, daughter of Deborah and Nathan Fiske, Amherst's professor of Latin, Greek, and moral philosophy) on not attending Mount Holyoke, where she would learn "to make hasty pudding and clean *gridirons*. . . . What sort of a figure do you think I shall cut, washing floors, before breakfast, and cleaning stew pans after dinner?" (1:108).

Thus, while biographers have speculated at length about why Dickinson stayed at Mount Holyoke so briefly, the more puzzling question is why she went there at all. She knew well that in many ways the school was unsuitable for her. In a letter to her friend Abiah Root (6 November 1847) she is delighted and surprised to find "ease & grace a desire to make one another happy" among students from whom she had expected "rough & uncultivated manners" (*Letters*, 1:55). But, that it was her choice to attend is also clear in the correspondence; an earlier letter to Abiah (26 June 1846) says she is "fitting to go to South Hadley" and asks, "are you not astonished to hear such news? You cannot imagine how much I am anticipating in entering there"; "I fear," she continues, "I am anticipating too much, and that some freak of fortune may overturn all my airy schemes for future happiness" (*Letters*, 1:34).

What schemes did she imagine could have been fulfilled by mingling with the rough and uncultivated at Mount Holyoke?[11] Whatever the answer, Dickinson did not stay long. Depressed by bouts of homesickness, out of school for two winter months on account of illness, and unwilling to join the converted during spring revival, she left the seminary at the end of the spring term.[12]

Mary Lyon's health was already failing when Dickinson attended Mount Holyoke; she spoke at assembly but did not teach. Dickinson mentions her moralizing addresses a few times; it is intriguing to think that Lyon's penchant for moralistic scientific analogy might have influenced Dickinson's poetic practice. For example, Lyon applies to human beings the comparative anatomy platitude that a trained anatomist can infer an entire animal from "but one bone or one tooth"; she compares this to leaving the ironing room untidy, which "might be a straw but it showed the way of the wind" (Elizabeth Green, 283). Dickinson's early poem 147 (J100) spins this clichéd single bone away from the ironing room into a characteristic query about future life: As the single bone unfolds the whole perished organism to comparative anatomists, so the "eye prospective" sees rose, lily, and "countless Butterfly" in a winter flower.

In another occasion recorded by Hitchcock, Lyon describes student interactions through chemical analogy: As "some of the rankest poisons were made by the union of the most valuable and inoffensive elements," so "many young ladies, who were harmless oxygen and nitrogen by themselves, if brought together, would make nicotine or strychnine" (*Power*, 374). One might think here of poem 913 (J952) on the dangerous effect of harsh words on a sensitive nature: "Let us depart—with skill—/ Let us discourse—with care—/ Powder exists in Charcoal—/ Before it exists in Fire." Other elliptical formulations—"quartz contentment, like a stone" (372, J341) or "shuts the valves of its attention" (409, J303)—similarly mine the natural sciences for psychological metaphors. Thus a technique long associated with Dickinson's supposed reading of the metaphysical poets may have originated in Mary Lyon's homely scientific discourse.

Over the long run, however, it seems that Dickinson's diverse connections to local women of science did not involve their scientific pursuits. She had little or no intellectual companionship with her mother, whom she disloyally described to Thomas Wentworth Higginson as unlearned and uninterested in ideas.[13] Many of the poems she sent across the hedge to Susan Gilbert Dickinson over the years queried God's goodness, but few are scientific, and no more than a half dozen use the mathematical terms that would have acknowledged her sister-in-law's special interest of study.[14] Epistolary references to the Hitchcocks are about attending social galas at their home; Mary Lyon barely figures in her correspondence. These women were scientific in the mold of Amherst, and Amherst's way of being scientific was not Emily Dickinson's.

*N*atural Theology, as an academic subject, insisted that the presence of function and adaptation in the cosmos implied an unseen but not less real creator, just as a watch implied a watchmaker. It used the gaps in what empirical science could discover to argue not just for religion, but for a specifically Christian Revelation. If the cosmos implied a wise and benevolent creator, then death implied some form of afterlife, because a benevolent God would not have left his creatures—no matter how faulty they were—without consolation. Working from the other side of this divide, however, even devout Baconian scientists recognized that while induction and analogies were useful for generating hypotheses, they proved nothing. Even Hitchcock's *Religion of Geography* conceded this when it explained that the "grand aim" of physical science is "by an induction from facts, to discover the laws by which the material universe is governed. These laws do, indeed, lead the mind almost necessarily to their divine Author. But this is rather the incidental than the direct result of scientific investigations, and belongs rather to natural theology than to natural science" (2–3).

Dickinson simply refused to accept this reasoning. She would not relinquish the expectation—scientific, after all—that hypothesis would be demonstrated or disproved empirically. If no proof was possible—and experimental verification of the afterlife is foundationally impossible ("None see God and live" [1353, J1247]), then the intensity of human longing for another world to correct and complete this one was entirely irrelevant. In fact, if it testified to any kind of God, he might be anything but benevolent. If no empirical evidence could be adduced for or against "immortality," neither did logic make the case indisputably. The project of Natural Theology could be completely derailed by the simple expedient of denying the major premise: God's goodness. These two lines of attack recur throughout the Dickinson corpus, sometimes running parallel, sometimes converging:

> I reason, Earth is short—
> And Anguish—absolute—
> And many hurt,
> But, what of that?
>
> I reason, we could die—
> The best Vitality
> Cannot excel Decay,
> But, what of that?
>
> I reason, that in Heaven—
> Somehow, it will be even—
> Some new Equation, given—
> But what of that? (403, J301)

In poem 259 (J287), the importunities of the bereaved are met with "cool—concernless No." Poem 1668 (J1624) reminds readers that the frost's accidental beheading of a "happy flower" is certified by an "approving God."

The impossibility of determining the existence of an afterlife seems to be the issue in the only poem for which the specific influence of Hitchcock has been theorized.[15] Sewall, whose analysis of poem 1070 (J954)—"The Chemical Conviction"—has been widely accepted, proposes that it takes off from the chapter on spring in Hitchcock's *Religious Lectures on Peculiar Phenomena in the Four Seasons*. There, Hitchcock tries to understand what Saint Paul might have meant when he said human beings were raised after death as "spiritual" bodies.

The conservation of matter—the thesis that no material atom ever disappears—was foundational to modern chemistry, which we recall Dickinson studied, briefly, at Mount Holyoke. It is found in every chemistry text of the time, and in more popular venues as well. Parley's *Glance*, for example, brings it into a discussion of properties of matter: "Although matter, in many instances, seems to disappear, as in the cases of burning and evaporation, yet chemistry distinctly proves that it is incapable of annihilation, and that the original particles, in all cases, still exist" (77). Parley quotes Yale professor Denison Olmsted to the effect that "not a particle of matter is lost; it merely changes its form; nor is there any reason to believe that there is now a particle of matter either more or less than there was at the creation of the world" (78).

But religious skeptics had long pointed out that, if no new atoms had entered the world since creation, every material body was perforce constructed from the detritus of other material bodies. How, then, could all those bodies resurrect themselves on the final day? There were manifestly not enough atoms to go around. It was a common joke question whose body, in the case of a missionary eaten by a cannibal, would rise to the seat of judgment. Although Hitchcock was no biblical literalist, he took the Pauline promise seriously. The idea of insufficient material comported with the idea that the resurrection would not be material; but, still, Paul had said the risen body would be a body. Hitchcock solves the dilemma of the bodiless body by suggesting that, while the "spiritual body" cannot be atomic as human beings understand the concept, it might be that the extremely attenuated substance of ether, although still a form of material, would fit the Pauline promise. There might be an ethereal body as well as an immaterial spirit enclosed within the material shell; this body would rise after death.

Hitchcock presents the idea that by "spiritual" Paul might have meant ethereal as an original speculation. But the triune body—material, ethereal, and immaterial—was a standard tenet of Spiritualist doctrine. That the orthodox Hitchcock was flirting with Spiritualism—which had come into its own as a powerful religious force after the famous "Rochester rappings" of 1848—might be interesting for Hitchcock students (if there are any) or students of midcentury U.S. science. But for Dickinson it is beside the point, because just that hypothesis discarded by Hitchcock—the resurrection of the body in its material atoms—is what poem 1070 is about.[16]

At the same time, the poem's idea that perhaps a single material atom might contain the whole structure of the person—such that the post-mortem dispersal of the physical body's atoms need not preclude bodily resurrection—

also had common currency. I find it, at random, in the popular *Memoirs of the Life of Mrs. Elizabeth Carter* (who was a celebrated eighteenth-century English bluestocking skilled in languages, theology, and science, translator in 1739 of an Italian popularization of Newton's *Optics* "for the ladies"). Carter writes: "The real essence of every individual body may perhaps be comprised in a single particle, of a texture so constituted, as to resist all the waste and impression of time and accidents, and capable of being expanded into all the proportions of an organized form" (2:403–404).

Thus I read poem 1070 as insisting on the material body as a precondition for a happy hereafter. The speaker asks whether, if she will see the "faces of the atoms" in the afterworld—a big if, to be sure—she will also see all the "finished creatures," that is, the beings as she knew them in life (the dead "departed me"), assembled from these atoms. Because "finished" might also refer to the fact that these creatures are dead, the word stands at once for death and life as mysterious opposites, making it impossible to answer the question as posed.[17] The phrase "chemical conviction" attaches the theological concept of saving grace to the scientific realm; but such a conviction allows at best a "fractured" trust in what comes after death.

"Fractured trust"—a phrase adroitly calling on the lexicon of medicine and physiology, reminding one of the "bones" that will rise again—can be read to mean that the chemical conviction heals, sutures, a broken faith; or it can be read contrariwise to mean that the chemical conviction itself does the fracturing, because it cannot explain what the attributes might be of a (perhaps) nonatomic body.

The second stanza, strikingly compressed and equivocating—"The Faces of the Atoms / If I shall see / How more the Finished Creatures / Departed Me!"—can be paraphrased as: "Even if I see the atoms, and maybe I won't, how would that prove that I'll also see the finished creatures—those who have departed—and see them as they were complete and whole when alive?" The only question Dickinson wants answered—will she see her beloved dead again?—is not to be answered by chemistry or any other science. And it certainly is not to be answered by the promises of clergymen.

To interpret poem 1050 as neither affirming nor disputing Hitchcock on the constitution of the spiritual body is not to dispute the place of "Hitchcock" in her thinking, for this poem like others pries apart the fusion of religious hope and scientific certainty for which he stood. Nor does one need to discover, in any case, a particular source for her scientific information, for in all probability it came not from her course work—she started writing poetry seriously a decade after leaving school—nor from scientific lectures, but from eclectic reading in popular sources.

A home like the Dickinsons' would surely have possessed a gazetteer and atlas. Perhaps they owned one of Parley's many geographies, or his *Glance at the Physical Sciences*, which I have been citing as a kind of paradigmatic popular compendium. "On a columnar self" (740, J789) could have drawn on its description (Parley, 86) of the six mechanical powers: lever, wheel and axle, pulley, inclined plane, wedge, and screw. "In Tumult—or Extremity—/ How good the Certainty / That Lever cannot pry—/ and Wedge cannot divide / Conviction—That Granitic Base—/ Though none be on our side."

From time to time Dickinson might well have read—as Rebecca Patterson proposes in a few cases—a popular science article in *Harper's* or the *Atlantic Monthly*, to both of which the Dickinson family subscribed, and responded at once in verse. In the years when she wrote a poem almost every day, most likely something immediate provoked her—something seen, heard, read. It suited her particular persona as an amateur to assemble her scientific archive as a bricolage of contingent and overlapping popular sources that, under the shadow of the more systematic scientism characteristic of "Amherst," would suit her formal as well as substantive purposes. Her makeshift compendium of concepts and terms, all sufficiently in the public domain to be easily recognized by whoever might read her manuscripts, was her weapon against the Goliath of entrenched and systematized orthodoxy.

If, then (as Patterson maintains), the science in her work represents an "untrained" intellect, one may interpret "untrained" as Dickinson's elected stance. Lack of training is fundamental to her persona and the poetical work she does, whose object is not to flaunt expertise but destroy pretensions. For this attack, Dickinson's attitude that even a child can see what's wrong with this argument almost demands that her sciences be represented as serendipitously at hand rather than the outcome of an academic education or programmatic study.

To repeat: Dickinson's overriding intellectual poetic projects where science is concerned are to query the existence of "heaven"—a territory where life continues after death—and its attributes, and to dismantle the claim that a Divinity who has fashioned a human world (without consulting the humans who inhabit it) so terrible that only "heaven" can, maybe, compensate for it, could possibly be a "good" God. Dickinson's obsessively repeated questions obsessively produce the same answers. Human existence is doubly cruel: Its experienced inadequacies demand a complementary heaven to make life bearable; but there is no proof, no evidence, that any heaven exists, let alone a heaven that conforms to human desire. "He has hid his rare life / From our gross eyes" (365, J338).

Science bolsters her contention that humans have no valid evidence for the existence of such an afterworld as local Amherst religion uses science to argue for. What science says definitively is that knowledge of any other world than ours is beyond its reach, and—insofar as scientific knowledge represents certain knowledge—such knowledge is beyond all human reach. "Medicine Posthumous / Is unavailable" (1260, J1270). One must die for real—not in a "jest" that has "crawled too far"—to know what lies on the other side (365, J338). But one seeks knowledge for the living. The dead, safe in "Alabaster Chambers," are "Untouched" by such questions (124, J216). Among scientifically anti-theological texts making this point are poems 403 (J301), 610 (J354), 623 (J437), 373 (J501), 659 (J539), 725 (J696), 747 (J724), 1070 (J954), 1240 (J1228), 1261 (J1241), and 1776 (J1748), where "The only secret neighbors keep / Is Immortality."

Poem 610 (J354) argues against design as it follows a butterfly emerging from her cocoon (a favorite analogy in Natural Theology) "Without Design—that I could trace / Except to stay abroad / On Miscellaneous Enterprise" through to sundown, when "Afternoon—and Butterfly—/ Extinguished—in the Sea."

Poem 623 (J437) describes prayer as "the little implement" through whose means "Men reach / Where Presence—is denied them," flinging their speech in God's ear; it may or may not work: "If then he hear—/ This sums the Apparatus / Comprised in Prayer."

Poem 659 (J539) says that just as nobody who is not already saved can save another, neither can anybody who has not endured "Dissolution" understand "The Science of the Grave"—which is to say, nobody. Poem 747 (J724) links geology's discovery of extinct species with astronomy's discovery of new stars and comes to an opposite estimate of God's goodness from that of Natural Theology (though not an opposite estimate of divine power): "The Perished Patterns murmur—/ But His Perturbless Plan / Proceed—inserting Here—a Sun—/ There—leaving out a Man." Poem 1776 (J1748) analogizes from the volcano that never tells in advance when it will erupt, to the (unnamed) theologians—babblers—who ought to stand "admonished" by the volcano's "buckled lips."

In "'Faith' is a fine invention" (202, J185) Dickinson characteristically trusts science over doctrine, respecting science for its willingness to define limits and stay within their logic, denigrating "gentlemen" who keep micro-scopes in reserve for emergencies. The shortcomings of analogical reasoning are the specific subject of a poem already cited: "I reason, earth is short" (403, J301). The poem uses the algebraic metaphor of a "new equation" given in an afterlife that makes all come out equal: But, she rhetorically points out by the iterated "but what of that," this reasoning has no necessary relation to the empirical truth of its own conclusions. In short, Dickinson concluded against Hitchcock that responsible science could not be put to the work of defending religion, and that responsible theologians would not draw on it. Her point was never that science was false, but rather—just as so many scientists of the day were saying—that its investigation of secondary causes authorized no conclusions about primary causes and opened no doors to the attributes of a world elsewhere. Consistently and ruthlessly, she dismantled the treasured Amherst synthesis of religion and science to unsettle religion, not science.

Approached through her use of science in this way, Dickinson emerges as a profound skeptic whose language unmasks the logical contradictions of orthodoxy. Silently, she played the role of Hitchcock's, or Amherst's, adversary. Her chief understanding of human life was that it terminated; afterward, whatever happened, one was no longer human. And her poetry cares far less about the frightful certainty of her own mortality than the frightful need to continue living in a world marked by the deaths of those one has loved. Interrogating and rejecting her culture's pietistic consolations, her poetry of mourning refuses to be comforted. For her purposes science, rather than pushing the boundaries of the unknown, only makes these boundaries more intensely visible: All we know is the "uncertain certainty" (1421, J1411).

Dickinson's mode of affiliating with scientist and scientism has little in common, clearly, with those of the women, from Phelps to Agassiz to Mitchell, who entered the print arena on behalf of science. Her affiliation with science also assumes none of their responsibility to society. Not having entered public life on science's behalf, she has no need to parade her credentials. Even Susan Cooper, whose class-based representation of amateurism might seem at first glance—at least structurally—to be something like Dickinson's in its denial of expertise, publicized her interests in science as a form of doing good and assured readers that she had striven for accuracy. Cooper's insistence that she was merely a learner may look superficially like Dickinson's professions of childish ignorance, but it ultimately contrasts with Dickinson's as the good apprentice contrasts to the bad. By demonstrating a keener logic, a quicker apprehension of the bearing of facts on the issues they are supposed to address than those who instruct her, Dickinson outsmarts her teachers. But when she attacks this male orthodoxy, she does not define herself as specifically feminine against a masculine norm. To the contrary, she distinguishes herself from fellow scholars who parrot rather than question received wisdom.

In affiliating with the sciences, finally, Dickinson shows no interest in promulgating scientific ideas. She accepts no obligation to learn science. She accepts scientific ideas but assumes that scientists did not need her help to make their case.

The question properly arises in this discussion whether, anywhere in the corpus, she disaffiliates from science. Certainly she adapts scientific language from time to time to nonscientific purposes. Circumference and ratio equal knowledge and justice, the wheeling cycles are eons of time, the "Pleiad" (the supposed lost star in Taurus) means vanished friends, the axle of a turning wheel is the stable center of a personality. Allusions to a soul at white heat or a columnar self are not scientific in the sense of alluding either to material heat or to concrete columns. Through these metaphors an insubstantial mental reality acquires weight and presence.

But using science in this way neither affirms nor denies science as a source of reliable knowledge. A small number of poems do seem, at first, to offer a critique of science; but ultimately they do not deliver on the threat. They all involve questions of scientific terms rather than of scientific fact or law, and they connect to Dickinson's insistence that many experiences cannot be expressed in language. The earliest poem of this type, poem 117 (J70), is a humorous complaint from an old-fashioned girl who is being educated into up-to-date scientific terminology—being tutored to say "Arcturus" instead of "star," "resurgan" or "centipede" instead of "worm," "zenith" instead of "Heaven." The poem prefers the attractive vernacular to tongue-twisting taxonomy. A few other poems ask more directly whether scientific language can represent reality by creating within the receiver an accurate simulacrum of the stimulus. The double-pronged answer is that if reality is subjective and experiential, then scientific language, which is designed to generalize, cannot convey it; and if reality consists of the vital principle, then of course science cannot represent it either, because science itself tells us it cannot represent this principle. As poem 798 (J811) says, humans have to "conjugate" nature's skill while nature itself "creates and federates / Without a syllable." This is not to attack science but simply to separate the representational work of science from the creative work of nature.

Where felt experience is concerned, poem 429 (J420) proposes that "by intuition, Mightiest Things / Assert themselves—and not by terms—/ 'I'm Midnight'—need the Midnight say—/ 'I'm Sunrise'—Need the Majesty?" Poem 721 (J668) says that "nature" is what we see, hear, and know, but "have no Art to say / So impotent our Wisdom is / To Her Sincerity." In 962 (J812), "a Color stands abroad / On Solitary Fields / That Science cannot overtake / But Human Nature feels." But here, more than scientific language is going by the board. In poem 429, after all, midnight and sunrise are deemed incommensurate with the reality—but these are not scientific words. All nouns are ultimately inadequate.

Yet, as one sees in several poems I have talked about, analogies based on science often express something that is otherwise beyond words. As long as analogy stopped short of claiming that it was the real thing—so long as it accepted the status of analogy—it could not only be admitted into discourse, it could work to the poet's advantage. Occupying a middle ground between inexpressible subjective particularity and inexpressible mysterious vitality, the sciences define a place for Dickinson's particular kind of poetic work. Because—given the facts that the culture had already ceded the work of expressing personal experience and subjective apprehension to poetry; given that the experiences of struggling with and for faith are nothing if not felt—the poet can do theological work that scientists never pretend to do, and theologians only pretend to do. She can express religious longings and denials in the mode of felt life. Thus, with the help of science, she begins to relocate the arena of faith from theology to psychology. She can write, with excruciating exactness, of how it feels to live in a world where the answers to the most important questions are by their nature unknowable.

I have written throughout this chapter in terms of Dickinson's poetic work, her project, her initiatives, in a mode that unavoidably suggests a public intention. If it were meant to be public, her affiliation with science against theology would become by far the most radical move of any woman I have looked at in this study. But one is returned here to the poet's aversion to publicity with which I began this chapter—her refusal to enter the public arena in which the demonstration of scientific affiliation by women was meant to make a cultural difference. Dickinson carries her persona as scientific amateur to the ultimate degree, refusing to perform on a public stage for public consumption. From this exigent framework, of course, Dickinson's work is also the ultimate expression of an amateur poet.

CHAPTER 9

The Sciences in Women's Novels

*U*nlike Emily Dickinson, most American women poets avoided scientific topics and scientific metaphors. Occasional examples of science-centered poems by women did appear in outlets like the *Lady's Book* (see chapter 2), but I find no U.S. parallel to the English writer Charlotte Smith's long poem of 1807, *Beachy Head,* which is full of geological terms and facts. Lydia Sigourney's forty-line "The Coral Insect"—the only poem I have found in her three-hundred-page collection of 1847 that alludes to scientific fact—makes a good contrast to Smith. The poem is quoted in full in Parley's *Glance at the Physical Sciences* (278–279). Says Parley: "The wonderful labors of the zoophites have been commemorated in the following lines by Mrs. Sigourney." The opening lines—"Toil on! toil on! ye ephemeral train, / Who build in the tossing and treacherous main"—lead at once to a meditation on mortality. Sailors are drowned by crashing into a submerged reef composed of the bodies of dead coral insects—"the thronging dead." This geological or zoological fact helps Sigourney portray the globe as a pile of intermingled insect and human bones.

There is little science in the vast quantity of floral verse written by women throughout the century, which in fact openly allied itself with a specifically female emotive register, in part precisely by rejecting the scientific, factual approach. The many schoolgirl floras appearing in the first half of the nineteenth century "feminized" botanical material through poetic citation. In Louisa May Alcott's 1873 *Work,* one of the heroine's jobs is assistant to a florist; she arranges bouquets to convey messages through the folk language of posies. She "heroically" labors to learn the taxa (290) but dislikes "dry botanical names and facts" and favors knowledge of "all the delicate traits, curious habits, and poetical romances of the sweet things" (236). Sweet things gets it exactly right; through women's sympathetic identification with flowers, they defined themselves also as sweet things. Serving as an alternative to the everyday, flower poetry exalted women's sensibilities above the drudgeries to which ordinary life had condemned them. The settler woman, Caroline Kirkland wrote in *A New Home—Who'll Follow?*, is "the first to attempt the refining process": she makes "small additions to the more delicate or showy part of the household gear" in an effort "to throw over the real homeliness of her lot something of the magic of [the] Ideal" (147).

Fiction by women, as well as women's poetry, tended to an esthetic approach to female subjectivity. Even in the antebellum decades, when didactic novels about exemplary young women dominated the marketplace, science did not find a home in fiction. To be sure, a web of allusions—to planetary rotation, the age of the earth, the size of the galaxy, the composition of rocks, the life cycle of plants, and other scientific fundamentals of the age—spins through these novels. But it is rare to find a protagonist, even a bookish one, whose great intellectual passion is science. Novels in which the sciences as subjects get much space are rarer still.

This dearth has a generic explanation: Even now, the plot-driven form of the novel coexists uneasily with any substantial amount of sheer facticity. Encyclopedic American novels—whether by Herman Melville, or Thomas Pynchon, or Richard Powers—have always had a cult, not a general, following. But genre merges with gender here. It is not an accident that novels of this type have all been written, and mostly been appreciated, by men. The scarcity of science in women's belletristic writing is most directly accounted for, I think, by the fact that the feminization of belles lettres came about in historical conjunction with ideas of women as more intuitive, emotional, and imaginative than men. In my study of historical novels by U.S. women, I found that the special attribute women brought to nation building was their refinement (*American Women Writers*, 155–156). Throughout the nineteenth century, polite letters increasingly became the preserve of the emotive as opposed to the referential—a situation that I. A. Richards was belatedly to codify for criticism in *The Meaning of Meaning* (1923); simultaneously, polite letters were increasingly appropriated by and reserved for women. In the 1830s, Sarah Hale had bemoaned the "almost exclusive attention of women in her mental pursuits to subjects of taste, sentiment, and devotion" ("Science and Sentiment," 273; see chapter 3). To urge science on women had been from the first an effort to resist this gendered division between fact and fancy. In women's poetry and fiction, fancy counterattacked.

After the Civil War art and science increasingly went separate ways and women increasingly became the chief patrons, if not producers, of high cultural artifacts. (C. P. Snow was roundly scoffed at in the 1950s for his theory of two intellectual academic cultures, but as any employee in a research university knows, he was entirely right.) When, in addition—and by no means coincidentally—the art novel began to supplant the conduct novel as the favorite form used by serious woman writers, the rational heroine of antebellum fiction became an endangered species. Women authors of art fiction were more than ready to exploit, or reanimate, the traditional gender stereotypes that Enlightenment-inspired women had worked to overcome. Art writers proposed that because women were essentially unqualified for abstract reasoning and laborious fact gathering—because, that is, women were essentially unscientific—they were therefore especially suited for the superior realm of the esthetic.

Many male writers, anxious to maintain the fine arts as a preserve for their own sex, countered that women were suited for producing neither art nor science. The struggles of men to reclaim literature for masculinity (and the counter-offensive by women to keep it for themselves) are, in some general ways, the stories of literary realism and literary modernism. But these intraliterary conflicts had little effect on the larger culture, which continued to become ever more scientific and ever more ideologically masculinist. The idea of art as feminine—or, worse still in a homophobic age, effeminate—became standard in the waning years of the nineteenth century.

More and more, women's novels mobilized the rhetoric of an exaggerated estheticism to signify the feminine nature. In the 1860s and after, a prevalent women's writing style, described by Alfred Bendixon in the case of Harriet Prescott Spofford as constituted by "a love of poetic language, of richly sensuous description, of striking phrases and extravagant images" (xi), came to the fore. Of course women could have written less mannered prose; and they did—but they did so less and less in fiction. The baroque rhetoric of women's fiction and poetry enunciated a specifically female perception of imaginative reality, whose imaginary opposite was utilitarian, earth-bound science.

Certainly, the sciences themselves played no small part in such discursive differentiations. High Victorian (or, in the United States, antebellum) science had shared, in Gillian Beer's words, a "common language" with "other educated readers and writers of their time"—a language that was literary, nonmathematical, and "readily available to readers without a scientific training" (6). But the late-nineteenth-century sciences—increasingly specialized, increasingly mathematical, increasingly dependent on sophisticated instrumentation—were speaking in tongues well beyond the interpretive abilities of ordinary people of both sexes. Lexical difficulty was of course the necessary result of the kind of work the sciences were now doing. But scientific argot also worked to install the gate-keeping and credentialing devices that made science the exclusive possession of practicing scientists.

At the same time, the expansion of the sciences throughout U.S. economic and educational life called for many more scientific workers than had been needed earlier in the century. Women began at last to make up a measurable (although still very small) part of this new labor pool. This is why all historians of women scientists in the United States begin their accounts around 1870, when higher education provided training for women who wanted to enter the scientific professions.[1]

We have already seen that women who had gone to school learned some basic science; inevitably, scientific allusions appeared now and then in their fiction and poetry. It seems less important, however, to list such allusions than to focus on the occasional significant foray into scientific subject matter, or the occasional protagonist for whom science is importantly formative. It also seems worthwhile to contemplate novels where the conflict between art and science gets gendered expression. In what follows—postponing discussion of women in medicine for chapter 10—I survey some of the more important of these novelistic moments, concentrating on texts that were best-sellers or were produced by women of influence.

*T*he first (and to some extent, the only) attempt to bring science and fiction together is Almira Phelps's 1833 *Caroline Westerley; or, The Young Traveler from Ohio*. This is a juvenile fiction; it was reissued by Harper's in 1844 as part of a "Boy's and Girl's Library." By 1833 Phelps's botany text was a big success; she was planning to write other scientific textbooks; she was publishing the lectures comprising her *Fireside Friend, or Female Student* (see chapter 2). The *Fireside Friend* attacked novels for creating "a distaste, almost amounting to disgust, for the homely beings" and "every day scenes of life" with which a young girl was typically surrounded. Reading a novel demanded of the young women "a strong and painful effort to regain that mental equilibrium so necessary for prudent conduct and amiable deportment" (9). Yet there was no gainsaying the attraction of stories; *Caroline Westerley* is thus a novel that is not a novel, depicting prudent conduct and amiable deportment in connection with a love of science that amounts to a love of fact over fiction.

The novel consists of journal letters written by Caroline to her younger sister Louisa back home in Ohio, as she travels with her father along the Erie Canal en route to a New England boarding school. The preface tells readers that Caroline's example in "describing the events of her journey, and the various objects which she saw, is a very good one, and may induce some other young persons to set about acquiring the same habit." To write as well as Caroline requires practice in composition, as well as knowledge of "history, geography, and the natural history of the various objects which the earth exhibits—minerals, plants, and animals"; also chemistry, natural philosophy, and the "philosophy of the human mind" (3–4).

The scientific materials in Caroline's letters coexist with materials about history, political science, esthetics, and other intellectual realms that, taken together, transform what might be a boring trip into a constantly interesting event while they turn meaningless terrain into a densely informational text. The letters define the intellectual capacities of a model protagonist; and—in a swerve from the strictly educational into the realm of manners—they show the superiority of educated over idle, fashionable people.

The journey calls on every branch of science: natural philosophy for the steam engine powering the boat across Lake Erie that takes them to the canal, botany for the wildflowers that grow along the canal banks, geology for the rocks through which the canal has been cut, chemistry for table salt and natural gas. "Eaton calls the formation which prevails at the village of Black Rock *cornitiferous lime rock*. This belongs to the *secondary formation*" (78); "sitting down upon a sofa, and emptying in my lap the contents of my basket, I took up a bunch of harebells (*campanula rotondifolia*), and explained to my attentive auditors the meaning of the botanical name" (104). History, systematic esthetics, and Natural Theology also contribute to Caroline's apprehension of her surroundings—no response is unmediated by the discipline of an established factual discourse.

Caroline thinks of her letters as practice for a literary career, an ambition allowing Phelps to make three arguments for female scientific training: self-cultivation; the contributions a cultivated woman may make to family and social circle; and preparation for a useful, respected vocation. Caroline tells her sister: "The talents that God has given us should be improved; and a conscientious desire to do this will stimulate us to exertion; this is very different from the feverish ambition which desires distinction merely as such" (71–72). Caroline's ambitions, which run like her author's toward the work of popularizing science, have been fostered by a mother who believes—also like Phelps—that "while men of strong minds were toiling to dig at the *roots* of science and letters, many women of talents were successfully employed in collecting the *blossoms* and *fruit*, and presenting these to the young in a manner to please their imaginations and invite their taste" (202).

Two modest plot lines advance the narrative. In one, Caroline's letters, read aloud at home, persuade a young tutor—who had doubted female mental capacities—that women are intellectual beings after all. In the second, Caroline and her father triumph socially over a family of empty-headed fashionables. As these people become aware of the Westerleys' social preeminence (conveniently for the plot, Caroline's father is a congressman), the very aspects of Caroline's character that had excited their ridicule—piety, bookishness, and scientific curiosity—produce admiration and a desire to imitate. Phelps's inclusion and foregrounding of science in this repertory exhibit ways in which the sciences ought to function in forming an admirable female character.

Although *Caroline Westerley* apparently had little circulation, its program strikingly foreshadows the work of several of the era's great best-sellers, including the books that set the agenda of what I have called woman's fiction, *The Wide, Wide World* (1850) by Susan Warner (1818–1885) and *The Lamplighter* (1854) by Maria Susanna Cummins (1827–1866). Both novels feature the same intellectually hungry protagonist who persuades skeptics of the quality of the female intellect, and whose intellectual and moral worth— merit, in a word—are shown to be superior to money and fashion not only through the narrator's rhetoric but also through plots that make her victorious in every competition with well-dressed but fatuous competitors, whether the prize is social approbation or the most eligible bachelor.

The Wide, Wide World is richer in curricular specifics, and more pedagogically explanatory, than any other book of this sort. The special aptitudes of the protagonist, Ellen Montgomery, her innate superiority, her fitness to be a heroine, are indicated early on by her iterated demand, "I want to know why." The motif of a commendable curiosity that is specifically scientific is introduced early, when Ellen is aboard a ship taking her away from her beloved mother in New York City toward her life in upstate New York on Aunt Fortune's farm. Miserable at the separation from her mother, and mistreated by those who had agreed to shepherd her on the voyage (she is laughed at for her unfashionable bonnet and lack of gloves), she is befriended by a gentleman who offers evangelical consolation and a guided tour of the boat.

"The going over the boat held them a long time, for Ellen's new friend took kind pains to explain to her wherever he thought he could make interesting; he was amused to find how far she pushed her inquiries into the how and why of things" (76). Warner, like Phelps, builds pedagogically from curiosity—innate in girls as well as boys—about the how and why of the material, nontextual world around her. Like Phelps, Warner is almost programmatically attentive to the full range of current sciences.

When Ellen asks Van Brunt, manager of her aunt's farm, why "the sun shines first upon the top of the mountain, and then comes so slowly down the side," he can only answer that he supposes it always did so. Yes, "but that's the very thing,—I want to know the reason why" (131–132). Van Brunt's stolid, rural fatalism contrasts with Ellen's agile, urban inquisitiveness; the episode opposes a prescientific mentality to the scientific worldview—exemplified in a girl child. Ellen and her eventual mentors, the Humphreyses, are intensely pious, but they firmly expect natural phenomena to be explained by secondary causes. I want, Ellen says, to learn "French, and Italian, and Latin, and music, and arithmetic, and chemistry, and all about animals and plants and insects" (140); thus the sciences are worked into a program for full mental development.

In hours filched from Fortune's demands, Ellen works on "sums and verbs and maps and pages of history" using the battered schoolbooks she has brought from the city (144). Alice Humphreys's shelf of "precious books" is her "greatest treasure" (194), but her cabinet of natural history is a close second. "There I keep my dried flowers, my minerals, and a very odd collection of curious things of all sorts that I am constantly picking up," she remarks, and then asks Ellen: "Are you a lover of dead moths, and empty beetle-skins, and butterflies' wings, and dry tufts of moss, and curious stones, and pieces of ribbon-grass, and strange bird's [*sic*] nests?" (163). The book, with a benevolent and pious young woman serving as the child's informal teacher, models a pedagogical ideal of intergenerational relations between women. The intimacy between Alice and Ellen begins when Alice, having promised to answer Ellen's questions, keeps the promise by explaining—to Ellen and to readers—why, in fact, the sun shines first on the top of the mountain and then comes so slowly down the side.

The novel reports more than Ellen's questions; it dramatizes them like a Marcet textbook. What is this "curious brown stuff" that grows "all over the rock," Ellen asks, "like shriveled and dried-up leaves? Isn't it curious? part of it stands out like a leaf, and part of it sticks fast" (120). The book also reports the answers, sometimes at length, thereby modestly introducing readers to physics, astronomy, plant physiology, botany, chemistry, and geography, as well as history. To Ellen's query, "What makes the leaves fall when the cold weather comes?" for example, Alice first responds that the answer can't be provided "in a breath"; but when Ellen counters that Aunt Fortune had answered this same query by telling her to "hush up and not be a fool," Alice launches into a compensatory minilecture on vegetable physiology:

> The tree could not live without leaves. In the spring the thin sap which the roots suck up from the ground is drawn into the leaves; there by the help of the sun and air it is thickened and prepared . . . and goes back to supply the wood with the various matters necessary for its growth and hardness. After this has gone on some time the little vessels of the leaves become clogged. . . . The hot sun dries them up more and more, and by the time the frost comes they are as good as dead. (186)

Approached this way—through what might be called an urban middle-class rather than rustic proletarian worldview—the country is translated from a venue of cheerless toil and ignorance into a spectacular textbook of natural science. What's the purpose of pouring water on the grindstone? Why salt the pork? Why does the moon look larger when it rises than it does later on? (136, 233, 409). Intellectual boundaries expand: How delightful it is to travel with Alice "in thought, to the south of France, and learn how the peasants manage their vines and make the wine from them; or run over the Rock of Gibraltar with the monkeys; or . . . sail round the world with Captain Cook" (336). Van Brunt is pressed into service for his knowledge of botany.

> Their talk often ran upon trees, among which Mr. Van Brunt was at home. . . . He tried to teach her how to know each separate kind by the bark and leaf and manner of growth. The pine and hemlock and fir were easily learnt; the white birch too; beyond those at first she was perpetually confounding one with another. Mr. Van Brunt had to go over and over his instructions; never weary, always vastly amused. (337–338)

Only think, she says to him later in the novel, "of my not having been to look for flowers before this spring," as the two collect anemones, liverwort, yellow bells (the name "uvularias" is provided parenthetically by the narrator), Solomon's seal, cowslips, wild columbine, and corydalis (420–421). An unpromising adult has been conscripted for the child's didactic needs. After Ellen finishes studying ancient history via Rollin's famous text, she progresses to physics (via Marcet's *Conversations on Natural Philosophy*): "I have done with Rollin now," says Ellen, "I am ready for the moon" (410).

The "curious brown stuff" introduces notions of plant classifications (120); pouring water on the grindstone involves mechanics and hydraulics (136); salting the pork speaks to chemistry (233); the changing size of the moon invokes optics (409)—it is not enlarged, it is only magnified by the atmosphere, which reaches only about forty miles up between us and the moon. Sailing around the world with Captain Cook invokes physical geography—that is, the nonrandom dispersal of natural objects around the globe as outcomes of landforms and climate, as these were presented in popular accounts of scientific travel and exploration (272, 302, 304).

That few novels after *The Wide, Wide World* were as detailed in their curricular dispensations suggests that writers hesitated to follow Warner's example to the letter. Yet the novel's huge circulation suggests that her approach was acceptable, even efficacious. There is comparatively little scientific information in *The Lamplighter* (1854); yet much is conveyed about the child protagonist when Cummins says she is attracted to "comparatively solid" reading and is especially fond of a little book about astronomy (70–71).

Approaching this allusive code from the opposite direction, Elizabeth Stoddard's mordant attack on New England in *The Morgesons* (1862) makes science education one of its many targets. The first-person narrator reminisces:

> Miss Black called me in to her desk. "I think," she said, "you had better study Geology. It is important, for it will lead your mind up from nature to nature's God." . . . It was the first time that I had heard of Geology. The compendium she gave me must have been dull and dry. I could not get its lessons perfectly. It never inspired me with any interest for land or sea. I could not associate any of its terms, or descriptions, with the great rock under grand'ther's house. It was not for Miss Black to open the nodules of my understanding with her hammer of instruction. She proposed Botany also. The young ladies made botanical excursions to the fields and woods outside Barmouth; I might as well join the class at once. It was now in the family of the Legumes. I accompanied the class on one excursion. . . . I declined going again. . . . I made no more advance in the humble walks of learning than in those adorned by the dissection of flowers, the disruption of rocks, or the graces of composition. (37–38)

The geological metaphor of nodule and hammer reveals a narrator who has learned more from science than she admits; but the book is nevertheless resolute in its representation of a gendered literary and esthetic sensibility profoundly resistant to systematic learning. Yet this sensibility is only ambiguously celebrated; the author shows it up as dreamy, escapist, narrow, lethargic, provincial, and, ultimately, profoundly passive. In resisting New England ideologies and exposing New England hypocrisies, this rebellious sensibility also condemns itself—as the plot goes on to show—to a life of passive misery.

No popular woman novelist in the nineteenth century made greater claims for female intellect than the southerner Augusta Evans (1835–1909).[2] Her novels' recondite allusions were much satirized (and end-of-century reissues often deleted the more arcane of them). Evans, however, responded by making each successive novel even more encyclopedic, and each successive protagonist even more intellectually ambitious and more justified in her intellectual self-esteem. The motif of intellectual ambition is situated within plots of conflict between the protagonist's allotted social functions and her God-instilled ambition to achieve great things. The whole is packaged in a highly wrought style loaded with erudite allusions. "I suppose it did me good," one reader of her 1869 novel *Vashti* recorded, "for it kept me running to the dictionary or to an encyclopedia" (Susan Harris, "Responding," 267).

Evans's intellectual protagonists are more interested in theology than in science; but they believe that the sciences, rightly understood, support Christian orthodoxy. The eponymous protagonist of *Beulah* (1859), for example, says: "I believe . . . the day is already dawning, when scientific data will not only cease to be antagonistic to scriptural accounts, but will deepen the impress of Divinity; . . . I honor the tireless laborers who toil in laboratories; who sweep midnight skies, in search of new worlds; who upheave primal rocks, hunting for footsteps of Deity; and I believe that every scientific fact will ultimately prove but another ramp, planted along the path which leads to a knowledge of Jehovah!" (419). As she works to demonstrate how science and religion converge, the character accepts a womanly obligation to piety; but her ambition takes her well beyond the safe haven of doctrinal acquiescence. She also develops a career as professional popularizer, using belles lettres against the tenor of the times to circulate the knowledge she herself has attained.

But in aspiring to serious popularizing, she finds herself in a battle with received practices. For example, Edna Earl, the main character in her blockbuster *St. Elmo* (1867), must battle stereotypes to publish a novel summarizing her philological research on ancient religions. One skeptical editor warns her that "people read novels merely to be amused, not educated; and they will not tolerate technicalities and abstract speculation in lieu of exciting plots and melodramatic *dénouements*" (237). He continues: "Persons who desire to learn something of astronomy, geology, chemistry, philology, etc., never think of finding what they require in the pages of a novel, but apply at once to the text-books of the respective sciences" (237).

Edna counters that for "habitual novel-readers" who will not read text-books, it is the novel or nothing. Popular novelists demean themselves and their audience writing about such trivialities as whether the heroine "wore blue or pink tarlatan to her first ball" (237); Edna holds that women have a "right to erudition," that "in the nineteenth century, it was a woman's privilege to be as learned as Cuvier, or Sir William Hamilton, or Humboldt, provided the learning was accurate" (151). Edna wants indeed to do more than popularize a scholarly subject; she wants to elevate the novel, the prototypical woman's genre, so that it and the reading of it become serious intellectual work. Edna's novel's great success proves the rightness of her plan.

But the great success of *St. Elmo* itself proves no such thing, because it is a conflict-filled and highly romantic fiction with a Byronic hero, as much as it is a disquisition on Edna's own favorite topics. The many bookish protagonists in antebellum best-sellers show that readers generally liked the idea of a learned heroine; it does not mean they wanted to sit in the library with her.[3] Evans's straw-man editor, although bested in her fiction, may have been right in fact. The fact that two of Edna's allusions are to scientists (Humboldt and Cuvier) and that three of the editor's are to sciences (chemistry, geology, astronomy) suggests obliquely that science and scientists were especially what readers did not expect to find in fiction.

Edna has a great success, which proves the editor wrong. But her success falls far short of her innermost ambitions. In *St. Elmo*, as in many of her novels, the Evans heroine retreats from the public sphere into marriage. I have argued elsewhere that Edna's withdrawal capitulates to sexual desire from a perspective in which the demands of body and brain are incompatible ("Women's Novels"). One can also interpret it as capitulation to the class expectations of her more conservative southern culture. And one can interpret it as withdrawal from a cultural scene in which the best possible for women is not enough, is pathetically limited in comparison to their ambitions.

In 1864, Evans published *Macaria; or, The Altars of Sacrifice*, the novel containing the strongest representations of science and a scientific woman in her corpus and, arguably, in any woman's novel of the century. *Macaria* is also a passionately pro-South book about the Civil War. Dedicated to the Confederate army, supposedly composed on scraps of paper as the author sat at the bedsides of wounded soldiers (Fidler, 95), selling over 20,000 copies in the South before war's end (Faust, xvii)—*Macaria* has been understandably analyzed much more for the relation of white women southerners to politics than for its science. But Drew Faust (xxiii) and Suzy Holstein (123) both note in passing that two sacrifices are demanded of the protagonist, Irene, the daughter of a fabulously wealthy southern planter: She loses the man she loves, who is killed in battle (she had little chance of marrying him, however, since her father had opposed the match); and she abandons her astronomical studies in favor of charitable activities categorized by the author under the rubric "Womanly Usefulness" (380). Even though—as Faust also points out—astronomy teaches Irene the lesson of "religious submission" (xxiii) and thereby prepares her for what she must eventually do, the fact that she gives up astronomy might seem to suggest that doing it is in itself neither useful nor womanly. But it also suggests, contrariwise, that—because the only meaningful sacrifices are those that go to the quick—astronomy is an externalization of Irene's truest self.

This truest self may, however, be devotional, not scientific; for, although from childhood Irene loved to study the celestial and terrestrial globes along with "the index of the thermometer, and barometer" (38), her earliest interests had been theological. This focus makes clear that she is not scientific because she is a skeptic, but just the reverse, because she is innately pious. This puts her firmly within the feminine camp, an important authorial strategy, because her love of science itself is seen as a womanly anomaly. One of her early tutors had fused religion with science by counseling her to study the natural sciences for religious purposes:

> As these furnish data for almost all branches of investigation now-a-day (there being a growing tendency to argue from the analogy of physics) you can not too thoroughly acquaint yourself with all that appertains to the subject. The writings of Humboldt, Hugh Miller, Cuvier, and Agassiz constitute a thesaurus of scientific information essential to a correct appreciation of the questions now agitating the thinking world; and as you proceed, you will find the wonderful harmony of creation unfolding itself, proclaiming, in unmistakable accents, that the works of God "are good." As time rolls on, the great truth looms up colossal, "Science and Christianity are hand-maids, not antagonists." (109–110)[4]

Thereafter, her path is set: she will study science as a way to worship God and defend his ways. Because "from her earliest recollection, and especially from the hour of entering school, astronomy and mathematics had exerted an over-mastering influence upon Irene's mind," astronomy becomes her chosen science. With the help of her teacher in New York she "possessed herself of all the most eminent works bearing upon the subject, sending across the Atlantic for tables and selenographic charts" and books "not to be procured in America" (176). But over the long run, and long before she gives it up entirely, her scientific practice has subsided into a form of solitary worship; defending God's ways to others disappears as a motive.

Irene's scientific intellect is denoted masculine by Evans even as it is sited within an extraordinarily beautiful female body. She is doubled by a foil, Electra, who, as an artist, is more conventionally feminine. Differentiating the scientific and the artistic as analytic and intuitive, respectively, Evans in the earlier parts of *Macaria* discusses difference among women and asks what a scientifically inclined woman might do with her talents. She offers a taxonomic analogy: While all human beings must develop according to scientifically certain laws, these laws are far from being known. In the present state of uncertainty, it is impossible to decree that all women are or ought to be identical, especially when so much evidence goes the other way. They may constitute a species, but every species is characterized by variation: "Linnaeus and Jussien [*sic*], with microscopic aid, have classified and christened; but now and then new varieties startle modern *savans*, and so likewise new types stalk among men and women, whose elements will neither be lopped off nor elongated to meet the established measure" (125).

Making Irene the protagonist, Evans implies that the scientific mind is a higher type than the artistic—or, at least, a more interesting type. Yet, Irene is no genius, not even brilliant. "Her intellect was of the masculine order, acute and logical, rather deficient in the imaginative faculties, but keenly analytical"; she is "a patient rather than brilliant thinker, and with singular perseverance searched every nook and cranny, and sifted every phase of the subject presented for investigation. Her conclusions were never hasty, and consequently rarely unsound" (38). One might infer from this description that Evans denies scientific genius to Irene to make clear that scientific competence in a woman is useless. Electra is no genius either, but there is something she can do with her talent in the world. A poor girl who needs to make a living, she goes to New York City to study art because there exists such a thing as the professional woman artist. After she leaves school Irene can do no more than pursue her observations in solitude; there is no profession for women scientists.

The description of Irene doing astronomy, which occupies the whole of chapter 17—and is unique in women's fiction—deviates markedly from the picture of laborious astronomy as Maria Mitchell conveyed it. Here it is a form of private worship, a playing at research, not the real thing. Irene owns a "fine telescope" and, weather permitting, "never failed to make her nightly visit to the observatory" in which she has installed it (176). In her observatory, while waiting for the appearance of "a small star," Irene consults her sidereal clock, readies her blank book for noting the observation, and begins to calculate. When the star is due to arrive, she sights it through her telescope, notes the exact moment and position in her register, and then continues her calculation, which she must repeat three times before it comes out right "according fully with the tables of Leverrier by which she was computing" (175). Of course this whole scene is a fantasy; but intentionally or not, the scene Evans describes is profoundly amateurish. When an uncle asks Irene what object she can possibly have in view carrying out "all this laborious investigation" with no outcome, her response barely conceals its own contradictions:

> Are you sceptical of the possibility of a devotion to science merely for science-sake? Do my womanly garments shut me out of the Holy of Holies? . . . You men doubt women's credentials for work like mine; but the intellectual bigotry and monopoly already trembles before the weight of stern and positive results which women lay before you—data for your speculation—alms for your calculation. In glorious attestation of the truth of female capacity to grapple with some of the most recondite problems stand the names of Caroline Herschel, Mary Somerville, Maria Mitchell, Emma Willard, Mrs. Phelps, and . . . Madame Lepaute. (174)

To be devoted to science merely for science's sake cedes the profession to men, because it acknowledges that her work has no practical use. She has indeed published an article—on Leverrier—in an astronomy journal. He is her hero for having propounded the theory of the universe revolving around a central star.

> Night after night she gazed upon the pleiades, singling out Alcyone, the brilliant central sun of the mighty astral system, whose light met her eager eyes after the long travel of five hundred and thirty-seven years; and, following in the footsteps of the great speculator, she tried to grasp the result, that the period of one revolution of our sun and

system around the glittering centre was eighteen millions two hundred thousand years. (177)

At her best Irene is only a fanciful follower in the footsteps of great astronomers, not a contributor to astronomy's work. It does not distort the novel's tendency to say that *Macaria*'s story is not about a woman who either becomes, or sacrifices her desire to become, a scientist. Notwithstanding Irene's list of women astronomers, who seem to offer a precedent for female professionalism, it is the story of a woman who cannot become a scientist because no such possibility exists for a woman in her culture.

By the novel's end, Irene has found useful work in a traditional path for wealthy women: charitable giving. This socially responsible activity is quite unlike her solitary scientific studies. And this, after all, may be Evans's real point about science as a female pursuit. Irene's favorite charitable project is to fund a women's school of design directed by Electra. In light of her devotion to science, one is justified in wondering, Why not an academy to train science teachers for women's schools, or a technical school to train women as chemists, or a woman's medical college with professorships for women in anatomy, physiology, and *materia medica*? The point seems to be that Evans cannot imagine science for women in any terms other than a private pursuit, hence an indulgence, a luxury.

Elizabeth Stuart Phelps (1844–1911) is best known today for her *Story of Avis* (1877). A novel about a gifted woman painter whose talent is destroyed by marriage and motherhood, it is perhaps the best of the postbellum U.S. *Bildungsromane* (or rather, failed *Bildungsromane*) with which authors tried to deal with the new reality of career paths for women.[5] Set in the New England college town of Harmouth, the novel features Avis Dobell, who has developed her extraordinary talent with four years of demanding study in Europe. The leading man, Philip Ostrander, is a handsome, clever scientific polymath who turns out to be an emotional weakling. The conflict of masculine science versus feminine art is complicated by his dilettantism, which loses him the job of geology professor at Harmouth and transforms Avis into a surrogate mother rather than a wife. The female-male binary is thus replaced by a mother-child one; or, perhaps, Phelps insinuates that true women are essentially maternal (rather than sexual) beings, which makes Avis's conflict internal as well as between her and Philip.

One generation up from Avis and Philip, her father, Hegel, and her aunt Chloe—who moved in to raise the eight-year-old Avis and run the household when Avis's mother died—repeat the gender difference in interesting ways. The aptly named Hegel is Harmouth's professor of philosophy and Natural Theology; Chloe is a talented housekeeper whose secret ambition had been to become a botanist. The kindly Hegel exemplifies an abstract if benevolent male reason, along with unselfconscious assumption of male privilege; Chloe represents old-style New England female domestic faculty and principled self-sacrifice. If Philip and Avis stand for science and art, Hegel and Chloe stand for abstract logic and empirical practice. Chloe is to Avis as the ordinary to the talented woman—yet Chloe is not a cipher. And her story is oddly repeated with variations in the life of the niece who seems so unlike her.

Chloe abandoned her dream when she married; Avis imagines she will not need to abandon hers, but she is wrong. She is undone by household cares, child rearing, and the burdens of living with a professionally incompetent and personally selfish man. But Avis is also clearly complicit in the events that demolish her ambitions. Chief among her shortcomings is a dreamy idealism, which manifests itself not only in the obvious overvaluing of Philip typical of romantic love, but also in a curious undervaluing of Chloe. Avis resolutely disregards real-world practicalities; Philip's theoretical science is a closed book to her, and Chloe's practice of domestic science strikes her as a joke. The inspiration for her greatest painting comes through a drug-induced vision.

By the end of the novel, with Philip and her first-born child, a boy, both dead, Avis finds herself without talent and drive. She elects to become an art teacher, leaving to the next generation the task of becoming a real woman—which, we finally learn, she never was. Unlike Evans's Irene, a woman for whom the time has no place, Avis is too much a woman of her age. The narrator speculates, in great physiological detail, on what is needed to create the woman Avis ought to have been, the woman who does not yet exist:

> We have been told that it takes three generations to make a gentleman; we may believe that it will take as much, or more, to make A WOMAN. A being of radiant physique; the heiress of ancestral health on the maternal side; a creature forever more of nerve than of muscle, and therefore trained to the energy of the muscle and the repose of the nerve. . . . Such a woman alone is fitted to acquire the drilled brain, the calmed imagination, and sustained aim, which constitute intellectual command . . . in whom emotion intensifies reflection, and passion strengthens purpose, and self-poise is substituted for self-extravagance. (246)

Accepting the essential physiologic difference of women from men as a matter of finer nerve versus firmer muscle, Phelps imagines a physical specimen of womanhood that is not at all like Avis. Rather, Avis's nervous susceptibility is the exact source of her talent, which means that the art she is capable of may well be at best something minor.

Even the narrator herself, whose master discourse encircles the other characters—who is better versed in domestic economy and horticulture than Chloe, in philosophy and Natural Theology than Hegel, in esthetics and artistic matters than Avis, in the sciences than Philip—may be far from that ideal. Still, the narrator's facility with scientific materials is central to her self-presentation. She is comfortable writing such lines as: "A harmonious home, like a star in its orbit, should move of itself. The service of such a home should be a kind of blind intelligence, like a natural law, set in motion, to be sure, by a designer, but competent to its own final cause" (140). She voices Hegel's complaints about Philip:

> He bends himself to too many things. Now it is electricity; now it is magnetism; then it is a process for utilizing coal-gas. Just now it is a new method for blowing up caterpillars—blowing up fiddlesticks! Every fossil ought to be a poem to him. He shouldn't be able to say *Old Red Sandstone without a thrill!* . . . There is a soul in science: he should have handled her body reverently for her soul's sake. He should have overwhelmed that class with his inspirations, as the deluges have overmastered the mountains. When every man in it worth educating could get an enthusiasm out of a chip of granite . . . then he might have taken to his magazine-writing, and his what-not, and the more welcome. (173)

My count of scientific references identifies at least seventy of them, displaying knowledge of astronomy, geology, metallurgy, chemistry, natural history, botany, horticulture, physics, optics, mathematics, logic, physiology, and anatomy. Avis's best friend says, offhandedly, "I should as soon look for a Belvedere in the third tertiary strata" as expect to find a handsome man on a college faculty (60). The narrator describes Avis as "ready to be fed with any full, rich nutriment which seemed to promise fibrine to a growing soul" (31); she calls Philip's a "refractive," not an "absorbing" nature (90); she characterizes the phrase "saving souls" as "well-rasped, not to say worn, but indestructible as an atom, and poetic as a fossil" (122).

Unbleached cotton, to Avis, "like x in the algebra, represented an unknown quantity of oppressive but extremely distant facts" (123). Avis's baby seems at first "a mere little ganglion of quivering nerves" (150); the combination of baby and nurse is a "fair equation" from which, presumably, it "was not too much to expect a clear solution" (151). After three years, Avis's marriage is like sulfur that, "past the point of fusion, at a higher degree of temperature, consolidates again" (179); the strong wife (which Avis finally becomes by sacrificing her talented individuality) is "a rock in the topography of a man's life," a "corner-stone of granite in a human home" (214).

But this allusive language is finally esthetic in its impact—that is, science is incorporated into poetry, the male materials subjected to female rhetoric. The narrator brings the sciences into her own repertory as a lower form of discourse than the artistic, thereby defining herself as the artist that Avis was not able to be. The movement among and between metaphors and different discursive registers can sometimes be quite striking: "The gorge was a vein of deep purple lava, which to Ostrander's educated eye told the story of a terrible organic divorce" (42); its two sides "are thrust apart by flood or fire. They were originally of one flesh. It was a perfect primeval marriage" (46).

Hegel insists that there is a soul in science, but to this narrator science is no more vital than the earth itself, when the earth has not been transformed through poetic vision. Philip is followed at Harmouth by one Professor Brown, "the man who had recently detected the precise difference between the frontal sinuses in the white and grisly bears. A brilliant career was predicted for him" (198). So, while the narrator gives the reader plenty of science, she gives the reader much more esthetics, transmitted through the rococo language by which that approach announces itself. Esthetic discourse permeates virtually every page of the novel, enclosing its geology, its astronomy, and its chemistry within its own superior forms of representation:

> Through the opaque air he could see rudely defined, like the values
> of a vast, unfinished sketch, the waves leap and slip and fall upon
> the glazed cliffs, and across the narrow reef from which the light-
> house shot sheer against the sky. . . . The well-defined metallic tints
> common to the New-England coast—the greens and reds and um-
> bers, the colors of rust, of bronze, of ruins—covered the reef. (42)

In short, *The Story of Avis* is a conflicted antiscience salvo launched from a position in which the feminine merges with the esthetic under the romantic sign of the highly excited imagination. This position assumes that women will not be suited for science, and that science will not appeal to them. It proposes that esthetics is superior to science, so that women are superior to men. Yet, it also intimates that at some future time, when women's brains are drilled, imaginations calmed, aims sustained, emotions intensified but clarified by reflection—when, in short, they are no longer the feverish creatures they are today—then esthetics may disappear. The very excesses of the narrator's rhetoric in *Avis* might be interpreted to testify to an ideal of the calm, rational female—the scientific female, after all.

In a sense, therefore, *The Story of Avis* is an art novel that undercuts itself, in which an esthetic style is doubled by the plot of a failed woman esthete. Science, although satirized in the novel, works indirectly to suggest an alternative. Few novels by women are as ambiguous as *Avis* in their approach to the esthetic perspective; but always, I think, women's work in various forms of "art" literature cannot be separated from the rapid extension of scientific values into every corner of U.S. life. This is true even if science plays no overt role in any given work. More and more, women and men are characterized as emotional versus rational. Among pertinent novels from the later nineteenth century, one thinks almost automatically of Kate Chopin's *The Awakening* (1899), where Edna's artistic talent (not to mention that of the pianist Mlle. Reisz) is contrasted to her best friend Adele's domestic practicality, where the whole novel is enclosed within a rhetoric of strongly gendered avant-garde estheticism, and where Edna's husband, Leonce, is a kind of paradigm of masculine instrumental rationality.

I have already referred to Elizabeth Stoddard's *The Morgesons*, an early art fiction indicting didactic narratives as hypocritical and useless, even as it indicts romances as dangerously false to life. Harriet Beecher Stowe, in *The Minister's Wooing* (1859), contrasted female estheticism, in the form of a kind of intuitive rapport with the natural world, with male logic, according to the heart-and-head polarity that inevitably mapped directly onto art and science (Susan Harris, "Female Imaginary"). Even as Louisa May Alcott's *Work* advocated female discipline and usefulness, it wrote about flowers in a sensuously esthetic fashion:

> A group of slender, oriental trees whispered in the breath of wind that blew in from an open sash. Strange vines and flowers hung overhead; banks of azaleas, ruddy, white, and purple, bloomed in one place; roses of every hue turned their lovely faces to the sun; ranks of delicate ferns, and heaths with their waxen bells, were close by; glowing geraniums and stately lilies side by side; savage-looking scarlet flowers with purple hearts, or orange spikes rising from leaves mottled with strange colors; dusty passion-flowers, and gay nasturtiums climbing to the roof. (229)

The highly estheticized writings of Harriet Prescott Spofford (1835–1921) from the 1860s register technical information about light, jewels, flowers, and so forth, while burying this information in esthetic language. Her 1864 novel, *Azarian*, has an artist protagonist whose flower paintings offer a female way to "do" botany that is unfettered by Alcott's sense of propriety:

> The likeness of a bunch of gentians just plucked from the swampy mould, blue as heaven, their vapory tissue—as if a breath dissolved it—so tenderly curled and fringed like some radiate cloud, fragile, fresh, a creation of the earth's fairest finest effluence, dreams of innocence and morning still half veiled in their ineffable azure. The other, only a single piece of the wandering dog-tooth, with its sudden flamy blossom starting up from the languid stem like a serpent's head, full of fanged expression, and with its mottled leaf, so dewy, so dark, so cool, that it seemed to hold in itself the reflection of green-gloomed transparent streams running over pebbly bottoms. (8)

Juxtaposing this prose to Phelps's *Caroline Westerley*—"Sitting down upon a sofa, and emptying in my lap the contents of my basket, I took up a bunch of harebells (*campanula rotondifolia*), and explained to my attentive auditors the meaning of the botanical name" (104)—one recognizes a wholly different rhetorical world. By century's end, many women novelists and poets had developed a conscious feminine esthetic as a gendered alternative to masculine science. Estheticism extended to areas where it might not seem obviously appropriate, for example, to regional writing, a genre long associated with New England women writers (see Donovan). The tendency of women regionalists to estheticize the rustic objects of their regard has recently been recognized and attributed to an unreflective urban cultural imperialism, an expression of the touristic imagination (Brodhead). In part, however, it may have involved a narrative idealization of backwater lifeways precisely because they were prescientific. Late-century poetry and fiction by women argued for the superiority of an otherworldly feminine estheticism over masculine science. That this happened just when women began to pursue scientific interests directly means that women of letters and women of science were now journeying on diverging paths.

In women's writing, esthetic superiority merged with a sense of spiritual superiority; to produce esthetic objects and represent themselves as lovers of beauty rather than utility was to demonstrate for women an otherworldliness that connected fairly obviously to ideas of the occult and the supernatural. This late-century turn to estheticism by women has a history internal to the development of female literary professionalism—women writers who presented themselves as artists were rejecting the antebellum image of women writers as schoolteachers. Esthetic women were adults speaking to adults, while didactic women were adults speaking to children. To the women involved, the rise of female estheticism signaled women's literary coming of age.

But among other things, the schoolteacher had been a science teacher. The trope of the esthetic female thus also made a statement about the fit between women and science. In major ways, the strategies of estheticism confirmed cultural stereotypes of the feminine no less than did the strategies of schoolteacherly didacticism. Throughout the century, if not right up to our own moment, the moral mother and the decorative object divided the province of womanhood between them. Female estheticism was far less transgressive than it claimed to be.

Not only did being esthetic prove more culturally acceptable for women than being scientific; the implicit femininity of estheticism made it much more culturally congenial for women performers than for men. "Literature, and poetry especially, has, since the time of the Romantics, been in a state of conflict around imputations that there is something intrinsically feminine in its constitution. Very many poets and novelists have been women, despite the attempts of academic English to write them out of the story, and a hint of effeminacy lurks around many male writers" (Sinfield, 85). "The language of expertise and scientific method" contrasts "to that of amateur appreciation (associated with feminine—or effeminate—producers and consumers" (Hughes, 48).

The different connotations of the terms *feminine* and *effeminate* make clear that to identify the esthetic with the feminine worked against men and worked for women. And—to close the circle here—it worked for women in part because the women esthete ceded the more culturally prestigious domain of science to men. Estheticism pointed indirectly to its nonscientific character through flamboyantly nonscientific language and an impressionistically subjective approach to representing reality. From the point of view of women of letters who advocated science for women, the colonization of literature by female esthetes was at best irrelevant and at worst a sign of female willingness to occupy abandoned terrain. Having dramatized both their lack of interest in, and lack of fitness for, science, women esthetes apparently left science to the men and the schoolmarms.

It would be men's work to insist that to do literature and literary study were just as manly as doing science. The efforts of male realists in the late nineteenth century, and male modernists in the twentieth, to displace women in the house of literature are well known. As for literary criticism, Elizabeth Renker has shown in her work on U.S. literature studies at Johns Hopkins that the "rhetorical and institutional masculinity of science exerted pressure on 'fields' of knowledge to 'defeminize' themselves in order to be adequate to the university culture's demands" (347).

CHAPTER 10

Women of Letters
and Medical Science

$\mathcal{B}$efore the middle of the nineteenth century, medical practice in the United States was entirely unregulated. The earliest academic scientists were almost all doctors who taught anatomy, physiology, and *materia medica* to a small cohort of medical students; few medical practitioners went to college.[1] Moreover, medical *science* as we understand the concept developed only in the late 1860s on the heels of work by Louis Pasteur and Robert Koch.[2] Despite the shakiness of their claim, however, doctors of all stripes called themselves "men of science." And because the number of professional scientists was so small, most ordinary people's encounters with doctors would likely constitute all they knew firsthand about self-styled scientific men.

Most doctors employed "regular" or "allopathic" or "heroic" therapies—bleeding, blistering, and purging—designed on Galenic principles to restore the balance of body fluids. Because these therapies had observably poor cure rates and were painfully invasive, regular physicians in fact often simply prescribed bed rest, fluids, cold or hot compresses, and perhaps a placebo, helping self-limiting illnesses run their course. But the specter of heroic medicine produced a host of "alternative" or "irregular" or "sectarian" theories, including Thomsonianism (herbs—especially hot peppers—and sweat baths), hydropathy (saturating the body inside and outside in cold water), and homeopathy (miniscule doses of the substance thought to have caused the disease).[3]

Allopaths defended themselves by forming protective gatekeeping associations like the American Medical Association (founded in 1847) and installing increasingly rigorous scientific schooling as prerequisite for the newly necessary medical license. Irregulars responded by establishing their own schools and licensing systems. It took a long time for the process to sort itself out (perhaps it has still to do so); but the prestige of science weighed heavily in favor of professionalization—the professionalizations of science and of medicine were parallel, interconnected cultural developments.

Whatever the role of the doctor, it was women, and mothers in particular, who tended the sick. Female kin and neighborhood women relieved each other by swapping sickbed chores.[4] Colonial women had also been midwives, diagnosticians, and respected herbalists; but nineteenth-century medicine appropriated these activities for male professionals. Domestic advice manuals attempted to imbue women's household chores with scientific dignity (see chapter 4); but advice books also cautioned mothers to consult doctors in serious cases. Catharine Beecher, even as she defined women's domestic work as a form of applied science and centered on family health, distinguished crucially between mothers and physicians. The mother's work was to prevent illness by constructing the home as a healthy physical container for the bodies it housed; when illness struck, she was to follow the doctor's orders. Feminist historians who describe scientific medicine as a deliberate attempt by upstart male professionals to wrest power from traditional women healers may exaggerate (e.g., Ehrenreich and English, 11; Lerner, 19); but it does seem clear that medical science, like professional science more generally, tried to define women as consumers rather than as producers of expertise.

This is the turbulent context in which the movement for trained women doctors arose (see chapter 3). Inevitably, advocates for women physicians demanded scientific training for women identical to that of men. (This means that, for at least some scientifically minded women, studying medicine was a sure way to learn and do science.) Reformers agitated for the formation of women's medical schools. But, at the beginning, there were of course no such schools, and no regular college or university admitted women.

Sectarian schools, by contrast, "often welcomed women students"; therefore many in the first generation of women doctors graduated from such institutions (Morantz-Sanchez, 31). It is not so much that nurturing women were more attracted to noninvasive antiheroic therapies, as some believe. Comparing the obstetrical procedures of nineteenth-century men and women doctors in Boston, for example, Morantz-Sanchez found "only minor variations" in their use of heroic approaches (215). Moreover, by 1870 heroic medicine was in decline everywhere. Quite simply, women who wanted medical licenses attended schools that admitted them. This association between women and alternative medicine allowed allopathic male doctors to accuse women of inadequate preparation, if not of outright charlatanism.

There may well have been proportionately as many women charlatans as men in medical practice. The physician Marie Zakrzweska recalled her problems finding office space in New York City; people assumed that a female physician would be "a spiritual medium, clairvoyant, hydropathist" (152–153). The supposed passivity and intuitive plasticity of a woman's nature gave women special status in mesmerism. Having been mesmerized (or having mesmerized themselves), clairvoyants looked through the patient's flesh to perceive diseases of bone and inner organs.

To make matters worse, the phrase "woman physician" in the antebellum era was code for abortionist, and even before abortion was criminalized throughout the United States around 1870, abortionists operated covertly. Among motives for becoming a doctor, Elizabeth Blackwell cites a passionate wish to retrieve women's medicine from abortionists: "That the honourable term 'female physician' should be exclusively applied to those women who carried on this shocking trade seemed to me a horror. It was an utter degradation of what might and should become a noble position for women" (*Pioneer*, 30). The most notorious of these abortionists, who called herself Madame Restell, practiced in New York City, where her name appeared regularly on the police blotters.[5]

By the end of the nineteenth century, even as medicine became ever more scientific and standardized, there were more and more women doctors. Some two hundred of them were practicing around 1860, twenty-four hundred around 1880, and more than seven thousand at the turn of the century, with the high point coming around 1894 (Walsh, 186).[6] This burst of professionalism might have produced writings by and about women doctors that celebrated women's breakthrough into scientific professionalism. But new gender-specific professions had arisen that gave women an alternative to the M.D. These, including visiting nurse, social worker, hygienist, kindergarten teacher, nutritionist, and the like, arose quite specifically as female nonscientific alternatives to medical study. And, typical texts by and about women doctors represent them as nurses and teachers who happen to have medical degrees. These doctors may know some science, but except for setting an occasional broken bone, they are shown only counseling, soothing, instructing.

These idealizations constitute strongly conservative statements not only against the professionalism and scientism of modernity, but also against the scientific woman herself. With one exception, no woman glorifies the woman doctor for her scientific acumen or endorses a woman's right to pursue a profession just like a man, for a man's supposed reasons. Women doctors in women's texts about medicine are motivated by a love for suffering humankind (especially womankind) that is both Christlike and maternal, not by interest in chemistry or anatomy or physiology, or the challenges of diagnosis, or the possibility of contributing new knowledge to the understanding of disease.[7]

Only Dr. Mary Putnam Jacobi—the era's best-known woman physician—insists that women should go into medicine for the science of it and that without science a doctor is worthless. As a teacher of women medical students, Jacobi is especially sensitive to the appeal of a sentimentalized ideology of the woman doctor. For example, in an 1882 essay, "Shall Women Practice Medicine?" she writes: "It is impossible to be a physician on the basis of personal sympathies alone. If the interest in the disease be not habitually greater than the interest in the patient, the patient will not profit, but suffer. He may gain a nurse, but he loses a physician" (*Pathfinder*, 373).

*T*he memoirs of three important antebellum women doctors—Harriot Keziah Hunt (1805–1875), Elizabeth Blackwell (1821–1910), and Marie Zakrzweska (1829–1902)—recount great struggles to acquire necessary scientific training. They also frame these struggles by an ideal of women's medical practice as a way for women to serve other women. The stories are redundantly gendered; from the inception of medical ambition to the achievement of medical practice and beyond, the fact of being a woman is all-determining. At once defiant and acquiescent, the accounts imply a felt need to justify the professional choice in gender-specific terms. Gender is both motive and impediment.[8]

The unlicensed, self-trained Hunt was the most successful woman doctor in Boston before 1850. Her 1856 *Glances and Glimpses* explains that she thought of becoming a doctor in reaction against the heroic therapies to which her younger sister was subjected over a forty-one-week period when doctors made 106 professional calls, administering blisters, mercurials, and leeches (83), failing utterly to cure the unknown disease.[9] This awful process led her to fantasize a kind of doctoring that would keep people from becoming ill. "Setting aside medication, we endeavored to trace diseases to violated laws, and learn the science of prevention. That word—preventive—seemed a great word to me; curative, was small beside it" (122).

This kind of approach had already been enunciated, for example, by the Scottish phrenologist George Combe (142), whose *Constitution of Man, Considered in Relation to External Objects,* had been published in Boston in the 1830s and who lectured there in that decade. (*The Constitution of Man,* later reprinted by the New York City firm of Fowler and Wells—the major publishing house for alternative health materials—was in its twentieth edition by 1850.) Combe described three levels of universal law: physical, organic, and moral. Using gravitation as his example, he explained that a wholly *physical* object, like a wooden plank, cannot help but fall. Animals, who are both physical and organic, instinctively avoid falling. The human, alone in the world possessing a moral as well as a physical and organic nature, learns to avoid falling by observing the painful consequences of a fall. Unlike planks and dogs, humans may disobey the law. But law is never abrogated; disobedience exacts punishment. Because punishment is not an unpredictable, unmediated act of an angry God, however, but the outcome of knowable causes, the moral law is a pedagogical device installed by a benevolent God to help humankind improve itself.[10] Every sickness points to the broken law that caused it and indirectly teaches people how they can avoid it.

Combe's lectures gave Hunt the foundation for a highly successful practice; but nevertheless she longed for a scientific education. She and her sister, who worked with her for several years, read medical textbooks; but book study did not strike her as adequate preparation. She petitioned Harvard twice to attend anatomy lectures, assuring the medical faculty that "it is mind that will enter the lecture room, it is intelligence that will ask for food; *sex* will never be felt where science leads, for the atmosphere of thought will be around every lecture" (266). On the first attempt, the faculty rejected her. The second time they admitted her but withdrew permission when students rebelled against a woman's presence in the classroom. She would have to pursue her way in "a new, true, elevating path for woman" (267) on her own.

Hunt's desire to learn medical science points to her discomfort with her anomalous situation, her recognition that without scientific expertise she was rightly consigned to a lower rung on the professional ladder, and, perhaps, her real interest in the human organism as a subject for scientific investigation. At once defensive and aggressive, she veers within paragraphs, even within sentences, from praise to censure of the scientific medicine she cannot practice:

> Medical science, full of necessary details, lacked, to my mind, soul;
> it was a huge, unwieldy body—distorted, deformed, inconsistent, and
> complicated. Pathology, so seldom taking into consideration idiosyn-

crasies, temperamental conditions, age, or the state of the spiritual
body, would have disheartened me, had I not early perceived that the
judgment—the genius—of each physician must decide his diagnosis. Therapeutics—think of the many hundred volumes on that subject, which it would blind the eye and confuse the brain of any student
to wade through!

General and special anatomy,—shall I ever forgive the Harvard
Medical College for depriving me of a thorough knowledge of that
science, a knowledge only to be gained by witnessing dissections in
connection with close study and able lectures? Physiology, with all
its thousand ramifications, had a fascination for me beyond all other
branches—use, abuse—cause, effect—beginning, and end—all were
significant in the light of a science undarkened by technicalities,
doubtful assumptions, tedious dissertations, controversies, and contradictions. My mind was greedy of knowledge. (121–122)

Hunt's description of her practice suggests that she was mostly a purveyor of commonsense health rules, offering strictures about cleanliness, diet,
exercise, counseling women on child rearing, and deploying a range of
noninvasive therapies. She prescribed medications (whose components she
did not reveal) more because she recognized that patients needed the reas-
surance of a prescription than because she believed in the efficacy of any
particular concoction. "I am the disciple of no medical sect," she proclaimed;
"I am not the proselyte of any special school. It would hardly be an exaggeration to say that in my practice I have availed myself of all" (171). She
splits herself into the professional practitioner whose decisions are beyond
the grasp of the lay public, and the popularizer whose mission requires the
belief that education will make people healthier.

Hunt specialized in women's diseases not only because this was the only
route for women to follow, and "not only because they were beyond the reach
of mere medication, and had no nomenclature in the list of maladies, but because the male practitioner could not have drawn their diagnosis, without that
confession from the patient which could not be given in most cases with delicacy except to a woman" (155). She augmented her practice by delivering
public lectures to women on anatomy and physiology; and, over time, she
began to believe—perhaps thereby contradicting her laws-of-life approach—
that the ignorance and neglect she hoped to overcome by instruction were as
much a product of sociosexual asymmetries as they were women's own fault.
The culture's insistence on female "purity" was self-defeating. More and more,

Hunt writes, "was the conclusion forced upon me, that the false position of our sex had much to do with their diseases" (159).

Following this line of reasoning, Hunt became an advocate of women's rights. In fact, many nineteenth-century women's rights activists came to feminism through a concern for women's health. Mary Gove Nichols (1810–1884) and Paulina Wright Davis (1813–1876) are two of the better-known such women. Nichols became a hydropathic therapist around 1832 and edited the *Water Cure Journal*; she also seems to have been the first woman in the nation who lectured publicly on anatomy, physiology, and hygiene (Blake, 627). Davis, an organizer of the first National Woman's Rights Convention in 1850, delivered popular lectures on physiology and anatomy to women, using a scandalous female manikin imported from Paris (Tyler, 445). As a doctor, however, Hunt also pushed women's claim to enter the medical profession on behalf of other women, taking the exclusion of women from medical science as itself a leading indication precisely of the "false position" of women in society.

Elizabeth Blackwell dedicated her tellingly titled *Laws of Life* (1852) to American women as "the first fruits of my medical studies" and offered to them "as an earnest of future work." As a doctor, she promises that she "would gladly render aid, and give the right hand of fellowship" to any woman wishing to become a doctor (64), but she cautions that "studies in relation to the body, necessary to the medical student, and to the woman who would intelligently perform the noble duties of a mother and a rational member of society, are widely different, and it is productive of much mischief to mingle the former with the latter" (64–65). Her medical credentials authorize her to circulate nonmedical information; she draws a boundary, like Hunt, between the professional and the popularizer while invoking her professional standing to vindicate her popular work.

Blackwell had emigrated with her family in childhood from England. When she graduated in January 1849 from the eclectic Geneva Medical College after a fourteen-month course of study, she became the first licensed woman physician in the United States. Dissatisfied with her training at Geneva, she broke more ground by studying in the clinics of London and Paris. Despite these attainments, she had no professional success until the lectures published as *The Laws of Life* attracted attention and garnered support from public-minded women who would normally distrust the claims of a female physician. A reassuringly conservative book, *The Laws of Life* made it clear that Blackwell was no medical charlatan.

Thanks to this support, and along with her younger sister Emily who received a medical degree from Western Reserve in 1854, Elizabeth Blackwell was able to found a dispensary for women in New York City in 1853, the New York Infirmary for Women and Children in 1857, and—capstone of her U.S. career—a Woman's Medical College in 1868. Because the college used the infirmary for clinical practice, this was one of the women's schools that most closely resembled a regular men's medical college at the time.

In 1869 Blackwell returned permanently to England, where she moved decisively from clinical medicine to public health. She said that Florence Nightingale, her close friend, awakened her belatedly "to the fact that sanitation is the supreme goal of medicine, its foundation and its crown" (*Pioneer*, 176). Unlike Nightingale, however, she never accepted the germ theory of disease. In her 1895 memoir, *Pioneer Work in Opening the Medical Profession to Women*, she gave three reasons for her early medical ambitions. First, although she was always in love (with men), "whenever I became sufficiently intimate with any individual to be able to realise what a life association might mean, I shrank from the prospect, disappointed or repelled." Second, she was "rather encouraged than otherwise" when cautioned that becoming a doctor was impossible for a woman; "the idea of winning a doctor's degree gradually assumed the aspect of a great moral struggle, and the moral fight possessed immense attraction for me" (28). Third, she wanted to rescue the women's medical profession from its association with abortionists. Madame Restell, she recalled, was "known as a 'female physician,' a term exclusively applied at that time to those women who carried on her vile occupation. Now, I had always felt a great reverence for maternity—the mighty creative power which more than any other human faculty seemed to bring womanhood nearer the Divine" (30).

The Laws of Life may also incorporate this anti-abortion perspective, for Blackwell attributes her motive for giving these lectures to a reverence for motherhood. She assumes that her auditors are all mothers; her aim is to show them "how to make the human race stronger and more beautiful. I must therefore digest for you the endless multiplicity of medical facts, and present you the result thus obtained. I must give you knowledge which you can use, and teach you how to use it" (65).

Supposing that the essence of organic life is its power of self-originating motion, and that the muscles and nerves are motion's instruments, Blackwell decrees exercise the organism's basic need and opposes every aspect of modern U.S. child rearing, from the laziness of pregnant women to the horrors of schooling—a sort of enforced immobilization, whose practices are "diametrically opposed to the true principles of growth" (122). Her

lectures contain an all-out attack on Enlightenment-inspired female education, with its stress on book learning and its division of mind from body. She
counsels that between the ages of seven and sixteen children should have no
formal schooling at all, because these years are meant by nature for physical
rather than mental growth (123). Blackwell attacks each and every specific
subject to which a girl is exposed "during these long years of school, at such
a sacrifice of physical strength":

> The logic has not taught her to reason well on any subject—the men-
> tal and moral philosophy will furnish her no guide to goodness or
> happiness—the chemistry will never aid *her* in the preparation of
> wholesome food, or taking stains out of her furniture—the botany
> will not render more interesting the country rambles that she does
> not care to take. She will never use her natural philosophy to make
> the fire burn, or ventilate her house. . . . Little *real knowledge* is
> gained, but an evil habit of mind has been acquired; a habit of care-
> less, superficial thought, an inability to apply the mind closely to
> any subject—and *this habit* unfortunately cannot be dropped with
> the superficial acquirements which produced it. (136–137)

Blackwell tests every subject by its suitability for traditional female
domesticity. This intense social conservatism, equating female destiny with
motherhood, coexists with Blackwell's own radical desire to be a doctor; or,
perhaps, it justifies the radicalism. The woman doctor escapes motherhood
in one sense while she embraces it in another, helping others fulfill their
maternal function. In her memoir Blackwell argues that the movement for
women doctors

> was only a revival of work in which women had always been
> engaged . . . in an advanced form, suited to the age and to the en-
> larging capabilities of women.
>   The clear perception of the providential call to women to take their
> full share in human progress has always led us to insist upon a full
> and identical medical education for our students. From the begin-
> ning in America, and later on in England, we have always refused to
> be tempted by the specious offers urged upon us to be satisfied with
> partial or specialised instruction. (199)

Blackwell insisted that future women doctors would preserve and even en-
hance the inherent differences between the two sexes:

Our medical profession has not yet fully realised the special and weighty responsibility which rests upon it to watch over the cradle of the race; to see that human beings are well born, well nourished, and well educated. The onward impulse to this great work would seem to be especially incumbent upon women physicians, who for the first time are beginning to realise the all-important character of parentage in its influence upon the adult as well as on the child— i.e. on the race. . . . We may look forward with hope to the future influence of Christian women physicians, when with sympathy and reverence guiding intellectual activity they learn to apply the vital principles of their Great Master to every method and practice of the healing art. (*Pioneer*, 252–253)

Marie Zakrzweska's 1859 *A Practical Illustration of Woman's Right to Labor: A Letter from Marie E. Zakrzweska, M.D.* is a third important memoir by a woman physician. Zakrzweska (1829–1902), an immigrant from Berlin, had been clinically trained and licensed there as a midwife. In New York City she had to take a variety of unskilled jobs. Discovered by the Blackwell sisters, who paid for her English lessons and helped her get a medical degree, she spent two years working in their infirmary before moving to Boston. At first she taught obstetrics and the diseases of women and children at the New England Female Medical College, but, discovering that this school had a bad reputation, she resigned in 1862, being unwilling to "grant women medical diplomas simply because they were women" (Morantz-Sanchez, 83, 84). Later she founded the New England Hospital for Women and Children.

Zakrzweska's memoir appeared in Boston just before she moved there. Edited by the women's rights activist Caroline Healey Dall, its narrative of immigrant life in New York City addresses Dall's own interests in social purity and rehabilitating fallen women. Almost alone among antebellum women, Zakrzweska attributed prostitution to systemic causes:

One can live in this way for a little while, until health fails, or the merchant says that the work has come to an end. You will think this terrible again. Oh, no! this is not terrible. The good men provide in another way. They tell every woman of a prepossessing appearance, that it is wrong in her to work so hard; that many a man would be glad to care for her; and that many women live quite comfortably with the help of a *friend*. (133–134)

This unusually blunt text clarifies Hunt's allusions to the origins of women's diseases in the social structure. But, whereas Hunt had pointed to sexual ignorance and, perhaps, covert indiscretions among middle-class women, Zakrzweska writes about working-class women who are being culti-vated for the business of sex. Her work as a physician justifies this analysis because she encounters the results of prostitution in the illness of women who both are and are not sex workers.

The leitmotif of Zakrzweska's autobiography is her intense compassion for stigmatized women, whose condition is to be improved, first, by the in-terventions of women doctors trained as men are, and, second, by social changes whose shape she can scarcely begin to imagine. Women doctors will meliorate the condition of their suffering sisters until society develops a more just perception of what is actually meant by "women's right to labor." These women doctors need men's training to do their women's work.

*W*omen doctors' self-image as science students only as a preparation for service is repeated in late-nineteenth-century novelistic treatments of women physicians, the two best-known of which are Elizabeth Stuart Phelps's *Dr. Zay* (1882) and Sarah Orne Jewett's *A Country Doctor* (1884). Both novels analyze the medical profession in relation to women's conventional lives and duties. They are typically studied as variants of the marriage-versus-career novel (see, e.g., Fulton, Masteller). As marriage-and-career stories, both novels feature a love plot, although in *A Country Doctor* this part of the story is perfunctory. *Dr. Zay* ends with marriage in prospect. *A Country Doctor* as-serts that no woman who wants to be a doctor can marry:

> While a man's life is strengthened by his domestic happiness, a woman's must either surrender itself wholly, or relinquish entirely the claims of such duties, if she would achieve distinction or satis-faction elsewhere. The two cannot be taken together in a woman's life as in a man's. One must be made of lesser consequence. (360)

Unquestionably, the marriage-versus-career motif is central to these novels. But, from the perspective of this study, it is important to note that the choice of career is not arbitrary. Both novels contribute to debates about how and why women might become doctors, the specific ways in which women ought to practice medicine, and the extent to which an interest in science ought to propel them. Both concede that women can and must learn the necessary sci-ence and attain the expected legitimating credentials. They insist however that the profession, as it is shaping up, is overly focused on impersonal scientific expertise, so that the compassionate practice of the woman physician represents a higher form of medicine.

Phelps's and Jewett's women doctors cure their profession as much as they cure their patients. *Dr. Zay* makes a point of how much scientific training its eponymous heroine[11] has received but shows how fully she has transcended it; through its heroine, Nan Prince, and her male mentor, Dr. Leslie, *A Country Doctor* frankly attacks the scientific trend in modern medicine. *Dr. Zay* imagines a spiritualized, deeply compassionate, feminized medical practice that women doctors are just beginning to create; *A Country Doctor* imagines that such a practice once existed but is now giving way to impersonal professionalism. In this context, Dr. Zay is a member of the advance guard, while Nan Prince is dedicated to preserving the old ways.[12] No matter, however, whether the best doctoring is still to come or lies in the past—women doctors bring much-needed sensibilities to the profession, which are womanly precisely to the extent that they are nonscientific.

Dr. Zay is focalized through Waldo Yorke, a young man who becomes Dr. Zay's reluctant patient when he has a serious carriage accident in the remote country town where the doctor is working. He gets a quick education in gender fluidity as he learns to appreciate the elegant, well-dressed—she usually wears a black dress of "almost extravagantly fine cashmere," with "a carmine ribbon around her high, close collar of immaculate linen" (73)—utterly feminine-appearing "woman of science," who is cast as estheticism's other. "'You speak in figures,' said the woman of science, curtly. 'I am a person of facts. I fail to follow you'" (131).

As some critics have noted (Kelly, 76–78; Kessler, 67–69), the esthete Yorke, who is beautiful himself, and also highly appreciative of beauty, is no stereotyped example of masculinity; in many ways, he turns out to be a less traditional example of his gender than the scientific Dr. Zay is of hers. The likelihood that this romance will succeed requires a shuffling of the stereotyped deck; opposites continue to attract, but gender attributes have, at least to some degree, been reversed: "In the subdued light of the sick-room all the values of his face were deepened; he looked whiter for its setting of black hair, and his eyes were darker for the pallor through which they burned. But the doctor was not an artist. She observed, and said to herself, 'That is a *cinchona* look'" (61).[13] "She came out presently, with that cool, scientific eye which stimulated more than it defied him" (133). The "woman of science" is like a woman of business: "She took his wrist in a business-like way" (51). "She had the decisive step which only women of business acquire to whom each moment represents dollars, responsibilities, or projects" (97). "It was impossible to draw her within telescopic sweep of a personality" (118). "The young man experienced a certain embarrassment. The physician gave evidence of none" (51).

Dr. Zay's power "of absorption in the immediate task" is called "far more masculine than feminine" (133). She treats Yorke impersonally and authoritatively; according to the narrator, when she tells him he has suffered "a nervous strain," she uses a phrase that "stands with a few others (notably among them 'the tissues,' 'the mucous membrane,' and 'debility') that science keeps on hand as a drop-curtain between herself and a confiding if expectant laity" (69). Yorke stands for readers of both genders who must come to terms with professional, scientific medicine, and who must also adjust to this instance of scientific professionalization in a woman who is so unlike the standard idea of "doctresses," who are "a species of higher nurse,—poor women, who wore unbecoming clothes, took the horse-cars, and probably dropped their 'g's" (63).

This description, reeking of class bias, shows ultimately how far Dr. Zay goes beyond science in her commitments to women in the crude rural population she has chosen to serve. Despite all the rhetoric of cool masculine scientism, at the core Dr. Zay is burningly feminine in her desire to sacrifice herself for others, and in particular for other women. The science is exposed as only the means to the far more important end of reclaiming fallen womanhood.[14] "Why did you select this wilderness to bury yourself in?" Yorke asks (74). She answers:

> "I had learned how terrible is the need of a woman by women, in country towns. One does not forget such things, who ever understands them. There is refinement and suffering and waste of delicate life enough in these desolate places to fill a circle in the Inferno. You do not know!" she said, with rare impetuousness. "No one knows, Mr. Yorke, but the woman healer." (75)

In her final illness Dr. Zay's own mother had been helped by women doctors; "I said, When she is gone, I will do as much for some one else's mother" (77). The book is defining medicine as a timely way for women to give themselves to service to other women, to mothers above all. If "woman physician" was code for the abortion provider, *Dr. Zay* refutes this image in a key medical sequence wherein the doctor "heals" by brokering a marriage between a pregnant, seduced woman and her seducer (Morris, 142–143).

The holy nature of this commitment to life, in contrast to the implied work of the abortionist, is made clear in the rhetoric through which Yorke imagines the scene. Emerging from the house where this "poor girl" lives, Dr. Zay says: "She has just told me who it is that is to blame!"

> Nothing of the sort had occurred to him, when she spoke about her "poor girl." Nothing could have revealed to him, as did this little shock, the gravity and sacredness of her work. Alas! What could have so betrayed to him the gulf between her dedicated life and his own.
>
> "Excuse me, Mr. Yorke . . . I was overborne by the poor thing's trouble. . . . And the women all depend on me so; they think there is nothing beyond my power. Why, she clings to me as if she thought I could undo it all—could make her what she used to be again!" (138)

Indeed, Dr. Zay almost achieves that feat by persuading, in fact virtually coercing, the guilty man—whom she has rescued from a mill accident—into marrying his victim. A loving god to fallen women, Dr. Zay unites the divine with the womanly in her own person, becoming much more than a mere "woman of science" and, by that token, becoming more woman than scientist. The landlady, a useful narrator's tool, assures Yorke and us that "there's more *woman* to our doctor than to the rest of us, just as there's more brains" (86); "there's *woman clear through that girl's brains*" (101). The importance of Dr. Zay as a doctor is that she is one of those women who "love *women,* Mr. Yorke, care for 'em, grieve over 'em, worry about 'em, feel a fellow feeling and a kind of duty to 'em, and never forget they're one of 'em, misery and all . . . and they lift up their strong arms far above our heads, sir, like statues I've read of that lift up temples, and carry our burdens for love of us, God bless 'em!" (88–89).

Dr. Zay redeems more than particular other women; she redeems the entire sex by transcending their womanly weaknesses. And, if she is stereotypically feminine in her self-abnegating ideal of service (toward the end of the book she contracts diphtheria while she attends to a village epidemic), she is also so in her profound piety, as she herself makes clear, telling Yorke that "a woman usually—naturally perhaps—is the guide in matters of belief. Spiritual superiority belongs to her historically, and prophetically too," such that part of her mission is "to heighten or deepen" a man's ideal of the feminine (170–171).

In the novel's world, however, Dr. Zay is the only example of this supposedly "natural" woman, a point that identifies her with the progressive development of womanhood toward its ultimate historical expression. It is clear here that Dr. Zay's exceptional spirituality, far more than a "taste for science" (84), has drawn her to this "ummatched" profession:

Even the clergy have a poor one beside us. We stand at an eternal confessional, in which the chance of moral escape or evasion is reduced to a minimum. It is holding human hearts to count their beats. When you add the control of life and death, you have a position unique in human relations. When I began, it seemed to me like God's. (161)

*F*or Sarah Orne Jewett in *A Country Doctor*, medicine is also a divine calling. In one of many mini-sermons larded through the book, the author-narrator says:

Nobody sees people as they are and finds the chance to help poor humanity as a doctor does. The decorations and deceptions of character must fall away before the great realities of pain and death. The secrets of many hearts and homes must be told to this confessor, and sadder ailments than the text-books name are brought to be healed by the beloved physicians. Teachers of truth and givers of the laws of life, priests and ministers,—all these professions are joined in one with the gift of healing, and are each part of the charge that a good doctor holds in his keeping. (364–365)

The novel's heroine, Nan Prince, orphaned in childhood, finds her life's work in doctoring. The book presents doctoring as a profession suited to a type of woman who is now appearing in large numbers, as the century wanes and "civilization" (Jewett's iterated word) advances beyond the need to dedicate all women exclusively to procreative purposes. Contesting stereotypes about womanhood, Jewett shows that this new type, although essentially unsuited for marriage and motherhood, is also an evolutionary advance. Dr. Leslie, Nan's guardian and the novel's idealized spokesman, recognizes early on that Nan is unlikely to marry. He describes her, in social-Darwinian terms, as a "typical and evident" example of a new species variety (360).

At first he suggests that this new type is neither better nor worse, but only different, from the more common species of womanhood. She represents "the class of women who are a result of natural progression and variation, not for better work, but for different work, and who are designed for certain public and social duties," a class "that must inevitably increase with the higher developments of civilization" (360). In all centers of civilization, "the majority are women"; evidently, therefore, some women must be "set apart by nature for other uses and conditions than marriage" (361).

But he goes on to say that the number of single women is bound to grow because woman are only now ready "to use the best resources of their natures, having been later developed, and in many countries but recently freed from restraining and hindering influences" (361). Nan, to Leslie, will grow up to be

> one of the earlier proofs and examples of a certain noble advance
> and new vantage-ground of civilization. This has been anticipated
> through all ages by the women who, sometimes honored and some-
> times persecuted, have been drawn away from home life by a devo-
> tion to public and social usefulness. It must be recognized that certain
> qualities are required for married, and even domestic life, which all
> women do not possess; but instead of attributing this to the disinte-
> gration of society, it must be acknowledged to belong to its progress.
> (358)[15]

Leslie and Jewett argue that the single woman is superior to the married woman because her womanly sentiments are not focused on her own offspring exclusively, and because she is liberated from domestic drudgery. At the very moment that civilization is producing more such women—women for whom the profession of physician is an obvious calling—the medical profession is declining into a site of scientific careerism. Through Dr. Leslie's views of medicine, which Nan adopts, *A Country Doctor* attacks modern medicine as a materialist, competitive, faddish, theory-driven, status-hungry departure from the pastoral ideal of the doctor as counselor, confessor, and spiritual healer.

Dr. Leslie, his friend Dr. Ferris, and the narrator join in a chorus of complaints over a profession that thinks operations are brilliant despite their damaging results, that favors useless theories over a patient's health, that applauds the young scholar-author of a "puzzlingly technical paper" and neglects the old practitioner who conquers a malignant disorder single-handed (266). Dr. Ferris gripes about today's "army of doctors" who can only "find out what is the matter with their patients after all sorts of experiment and painstaking analysis, and comparing the results of their thermometers and microscopes with scientific books of reference" in contrast to Leslie's "true gift for doctoring" wherein "whatever comes to you in the way of instruction simply ministers to your intuition" (216).

More than good medical intuition is involved in Leslie's practice; he has a wholly different view from the new professionals of what it means to medicate. *A Country Doctor* is laced with laws-of-life rhetoric; Leslie keeps Nan out of school according to the very regimen advised by Elizabeth

Blackwell, allowing her to develop physically before she begins to study. He tells Ferris: "A man has no right to be a doctor if he doesn't simply make everything bend to his work of getting sick people well, and of trying to remedy the failures of strength that come from misuse or inheritance or ignorance" (216); the true doctor "tries to keep human beings from the failures that come from neglect and ignorance. . . . While half-alive people think it no wrong to bring into the world human beings with even less vitality than themselves, and take no pains to keep the simplest laws of health, or to teach their children to do so, just so long there will be plenty of sorrow of an avoidable kind, and thousands of shipwrecked, and failing, and inadequate, and useless lives in the fullest sense of the word" (265).

Leslie is much more than a teacher; he is, as Nan will become, a veritable Christ, and in this he looks back to a golden age of doctoring rather than to a professionalized future. He inspires Nan to do more than provide "medicines and bandages and lessons in general hygiene for the physical ailments of her patients" and offer "a tonic to the mind and soul"; to "go about doing good in Christ's name to the halt and maimed and blind in spiritual things" (364). "When we let ourselves forget to educate our faith and our spiritual intellects, and lose sight of our relation and dependence upon the highest informing strength, we are trying to move our machinery by some inferior motive power" (218); and, anyway, "it is our souls that make our bodies worth anything" (218–219).

From the standpoint of an intuitive doctoring that means to cure souls rather than bodies, or that values bodies only as the soul's housing, scientific medical education is mainly a waste of time. Leslie and Nan agree on her need for a medical degree, but they regret the need. "Almost without any discussion it was decided that she must enter the medical school to go through with its course of instruction formally, and receive its authority to practice her profession. They both felt that this held a great many unpleasantnesses among its store of benefits" (269). Nan resents having to pass many weeks "listening to inferior instruction before gaining a diploma, which was only a formal seal of disapproval in most persons' eyes" (270). At the novel's end— despite many offers of residencies in modern scientific hospitals (Jewett has her cake and eats it too)—Nan returns to work and study with Leslie, "for she knew better than ever before that she could find no wiser teacher" (364).

But if medical school does nothing for Nan beyond bringing her professional certification, she does something for the school and the profession. Leslie sees that students at this women's college are, happily, not "such doctors as several of whom he reminded himself, who were disgracing their sex" (i.e., abortionists), but they strike him as women "whose lives were ruled by a pettiness of details, a lack of power, and an absence of high aim." He consoles himself that, "like all new growths," the college "was feeble yet, and needed girls like his Nan, with high moral purpose and excellent capacity, who would make the college strong and to be respected" (270). She will strengthen the college and the profession by her high moral purpose, thus restoring values that scientific medicine is abandoning. Jewett opens a medical profession to a woman whom she has defined in deliberately archaic terms. Although she is an advanced variety of the species woman, Nan turns the clock back on scientific medicine.

$\mathcal{M}$ary Putnam Jacobi (1842–1906), the daughter of publisher George Putnam, was the most accomplished and famous U.S. woman physician of her day. Although she never became the chemical researcher she had originally wanted to be, she used her clinical practice as the basis for many scientific articles on diagnostics and therapeutics. After getting a medical degree in New York City, she went to Paris, where she was admitted to the clinics of several hospitals, as well as to Paris's School of Medicine. Indeed she was the first woman admitted to that school, the second to get a diploma there.

After her return in 1871, she began a long association with the New York Infirmary for Women and Children, holding the position of professor of *materia medica* and therapeutics there between 1873 and 1889.[16] She organized the Association for the Advancement of the Medical Education of Women in 1872; one might say that the main theme of her public life was to advance an ideal of a women's medical education as equally scientific in every respect to that of men. In 1873 she married Dr. Abraham Jacobi, one of the nation's leading pediatricians. The couple had three children, but only one survived to adulthood. They worked together on issues of public health and gave the lie in their own lives to the platitude that a woman had to choose between marriage and career.

Jacobi used her popular writings and public addresses (many of which were published) to emphasize women's need to accept professional standards. This, for her, meant they had to relinquish all self-serving and evasive sentimentalizations of womanhood by which they avoided scientific discipline. In an odd way, although the reform of womanhood was not her intent, she harkens back to Almira Phelps's early-century program to produce better women by making them more scientific. Morantz-Sanchez says Jacobi believed in science "with an earnestness that was almost extreme" and viewed scientific research unambiguously, "as an absolute good because it added to the fund of human knowledge" (192). Jacobi was troubled by the conventional feminine "stress on the primacy of the maternal qualities of sympathy and instinct"; she objected to "female-centered, moralistic, and separatist standards for women" (197).

In attacking what might now be called "difference" theories of women, Jacobi did not so much deny difference as denigrate it; this "almost extreme" position may be explained in large part by the ways in which, in her view, women were making excuses for their unwillingness to work hard by invoking their emotional, intuitive, spiritual superiority. Whether emotionality and intuition were superior to science and reason was, however, not the question for her. The question was whether emotional, intuitive women could be good doctors; and her answer was resoundingly negative.

While living in Paris, Jacobi dispatched monthly medical letters to the New York *Medical Record* (inverting the initials of her name—Mary Corinna Putnam—she signed them P.C.M.), establishing herself as the first U.S. woman medical journalist. She summarizes publications, lectures, therapeutic debates, and her own clinical experiences. The letters aim to encompass the entire disease inventory, both to master taxonomy and to distinguish one disease from another according to fine variations of symptoms, so as to dictate appropriate therapy. An incomplete list of her topics includes: albuminuria, anesthetics, aphasia, cholera, coxalgia, difficult births, dyspepsia, empymema, gonorrhea, jaw fractures, kidney cancer, lithotomy, liver abscess, metrorrhagia, muscular atrophy, naso-pharyngeal polyps, osteomalacia, ovariotomy, psoas-iliac abscess, rheumatism, skin diseases, spinal curvature, syphilis, tracheotomy, tuberculosis, uterine retroversion, vaginal cysts, and wound suture (Jacobi, *Pathfinder*, 1–170 passim).

Nothing could be further from medical intuition and pastoral idealism than the care with which she recounts the different appearances of a variety of kidneys in a series of letters on Bright's disease.

> The pathognomonce appearance of the amyloid kidney is only observed after the addition of iodine and sulphuric acid. A drop of solution of the iodated iodide of potassium, added carefully to the slice under the microscope, colors the malpighian corpuscles a transparent carmine by transmitted light, orange by reflected. . . . The same reagent colors orange red the black opaque deposit that surrounds and invades the convoluted and straight tubes. On the addition of a drop of sulphuric acid, the color changes to dark purple, blue, and finally, after a quarter of an hour, deep red, brown, and black. (156)

The core of her public writing and lecturing is the insistence, already clear in these letters, that good medicine means science, science, more science. Her inaugural address at the opening of the Women's Medical College of the New York Infirmary (October 1, 1880), declares it impossible as yet to say whether women are capable of medicine, because "the preparation afforded to the mass of women students is still inferior to that which is attainable . . . by men" (350).

And as I have suggested, she holds women accountable at least in part for the poor quality of their schooling. During the thirty years that women have been studying medicine in the United States, she says,

> there have always come forward a much larger number to claim the right to practice than to crave the privilege of being thoroughly well educated. This unfortunate majority has been the cause of immense injustice to the higher toned minority, because they have constantly tended to drag the conditions of medical education down to the level of their capacity, or intention to fulfill them. (355)

Even serious (high-toned?) women are held back by their social conservatism, which makes them "hesitating, undecided, timid," and works circularly "to justify the social prejudice" against women doctors (351). Women as a class "are never habituated to test their work, and have an almost irresistible tendency to appeal to some personal influence to avert the consequences of its failure"; they are "not trained to achieve anything" and are easily "flattered into a very dangerous over-estimate of their own powers" (352).

Jacobi can be even harsher than this. In "Shall Women Practice Medicine?" from which I quoted earlier in this chapter, she wrote that

> The obloquy heaped upon women students of medicine has been so great that many women of refinement have been repelled from a pursuit to which their natural taste inclined them. Conversely, many women have entered upon it without taste or understanding, but merely attracted by the flavor of notoriety and the enjoyment of something slightly turbulent and very eccentric. . . . The refusal to admit to a disciplined education and to submit to suitable tests the women who were really fitted for both, have merely resulted in the rather extensive education of the unfit. (*Pathfinder*, 374)

Jacobi and Jewett converge here in their attack on women's medical education; but the solutions to the dilemma they jointly expose could not be more different. Jacobi suggests that women seeking to avoid the disciplinary severities of medical study, as well as those discouraged by "social obloquy," are apt to excuse themselves by antiscience arguments. Her inventory of character traits needed by the successful physician is conventionally masculine in its emphasis on rational control and emotional distance; it casts the doctor as a disciplining (male?) parent and the patient as an ignorant, recalcitrant (female?) child:

> The capacity to examine minutely, yet generalize comprehensively; to take large views, yet not overlook the smallest details; to be quick to notice, yet slow to speak; to reason cautiously, yet decide promptly; to be at once very cool and very warm; to be tenacious of one's reputation, yet indifferent to careless opinions; to be sensitive, yet not touchy; to be patient in temper, yet capable of wrath; to be absolutely honest, yet successfully prudent; to be unworldly, yet capable of managing the forces of the world—all these mental and moral capacities are necessary to enable a physician to study practical medicine, to practice medicine, and to build up a practice out of services rendered to a crowd of sufferers, at once helpless, ignorant, exacting, and capricious. (*Pathfinder*, 348)

Yet Jewett too would agree that patients are "half alive," lacking in vitality, ignorant, shipwrecked, failing, inadequate, and badly in need of a paternal counselor. But she would never identify this counselor with science. Jacobi begins her address by establishing the scientific basis of medicine through a hypothetical case—a skull fracture—and discussing what it takes to diagnose it. Without anatomy, "the first science on which medicine reposes," a doctor would not even know there was a brain inside the skull. Without the science of physiology, the physician could not understand why a blow on the head produced loss of consciousness. To understand "the radiation of the fracture, the effect of the rebound of the head from the pavement, and of the brain within the skull . . . a third science must be invoked—that of physics." To analyze the clear fluid running from the ear demands the science of chemistry. "Here, then, are four separate sciences, with entirely distinct methods"; and after all these, "the physician is still at the outset"; knowledge from a fifth and a sixth science—pathology and histology—must also be consulted. The doctor, she says, "must know how to enforce his directions, in spite of the reluctance, or indifference, or carelessness, or stupidity, or forgetfulness of his patients," which requires a fine, "not blubbering," sympathy (*Pathfinder*, 336–338, 347).

Jacobi used her private and clinical practices as materials for articles on diseases of the female reproductive system and of childhood, as well as for papers titled "Anomalous Malformation of the Heart," "Intestinal Obstruction," "Scarlatinous Nephritis," "Fatty Degeneration of the Liver," "Aphasia," "Generalized Tuberculosis," "Embolic Pneumonia," and others. And although social convention confined her to a practice among women and children, she strongly opposed the trend to specialization, especially for women doctors. In an 1882 editorial in the *Archives of Medicine* she argued that while medical researchers necessarily had to specialize because of "the advance of science and of scientific method" (*Pathfinder*, 366), medical practitioners must remain generalists. Women students especially ought never to restrict themselves to an exclusively female practice:

> If women will use this specialty, now often thrust upon them, as a stepping-stone to general medicine; if they will look upon it as the small end of a wedge, and persist in driving it forward to a larger end; then they may assure their position, and that of their successors, by means of this temporary opportunity. But if they do not obtain a foothold on the broad, intellectual basis of general medicine; if they content themselves with claiming this little corner, they will never really gain a high place there. (354–355)

Ultimately, and despite the severity of her critique, Jacobi blames women far less than she blames the culture for the popular ideology of female scientific incapacity. How much "real genius for medical science may develop among women remains to be seen. The conditions for such development do not yet exist" (380). Her words here, resembling Maria Mitchell's, are perhaps tinged with the same kind of fatalistic melancholy. They envisage a long interim during which women's best intellectual endeavors cannot hope to match men's best. And this is not because women are intellectually inferior, but because at every moment, and despite everything she does to counteract this reality, the woman scientist struggles against social prejudice and limited opportunity.

CHAPTER 11

Spiritual Science

*L*ike almost everybody else in their culture, the influential nineteenth-century women of letters working to affiliate women with science thought that science expressed human ability at the highest level. They believed that scientific technologies were literally transporting humankind from the dark ages, through modernity, toward a perfect future. They insisted that progress needed women who were scientifically literate; only such women could develop their own intellects to the highest degree and become equal partners with men in forwarding the course of history. Because scientific power—mental force—was destined ultimately to triumph fully over material power, and because women were so clearly disadvantaged in a world ruled by physical might, these women also saw science as an ally in their struggle for respect and recognition.

This approach of course foreclosed any questioning of the universal benefits or the universal validity of science. There is no sign that these women perceived science as in any way socially constructed. Certainly they saw scientific discovery as a product of their own cherished Protestant-Enlightenment heritage; that fact however was testimony to the superiority of that heritage over other worldviews. The technological results of scientific knowledge, visible everywhere in the nineteenth-century United States, proved redundantly to these people that science was absolutely true. Nor did the kind of feminist attack on science characteristic, for example, of the 1980s and early 1990s have any place in their thinking. That science was a masculine violation and savaging of nature's female body, a Western colonization of non-Western peoples and spaces, or a misogynist dismissal of women—these ideas were beyond conceiving within their world frame. On the contrary, the tendency of science to overcome the advantages accruing from physical strength seemed to them to make it an ally, not an exploiter, of the weak. The ecofeminist view that women are more closely tied to the earth, are more embodied than men (or, more precisely, are more aware of their embodiment than men), runs in the opposite direction from the nineteenth-century idea that women's inferior physical strength compared to men evidenced their relative disembodiment.[1]

We might recall here Harriot Hunt's paean to contemporary science quoted in chapter 1: scientific advance promises "the complete triumph of mind over matter, and the obliteration of that strongest of all distinctions which characterize the sexes, making it possible for woman to *share* in the duties and responsibilities, honors and profits of every employment and office" (244). As machinery increasingly does the "heavy work of the world," men as well as women "will rule by intellectual, and *moral*, and religious power, not by physical strength and material force" (244–245).

More problematically, however—because it was so obvious that brute force retained considerable historical efficacy—these women of letters also believed that a carefully crafted ideology of female exceptionalism had some uses. They were not prepared to sacrifice the privileges their status as women might confer. The core of an ideology of female exceptionalism involved attributing greater spirituality to women than to men. From the perspective of a greater spirituality, it was possible to be critical of scientists for their supposed tendency to opine on matters beyond their ken—specifically, on matters beyond the borders of the material world.

But where exactly were the borders of the material world located? The transformations wrought by applied science in the first half of the century tested the empirical understanding of facticity. Standard criteria for observability no longer seemed to apply in an era of technologies like the telegraph and photography, where one could observe results but not their causes. (Actually, the question of facticity had been raised much earlier by gravity, a force everywhere evident but nowhere visible.) If gravity and electricity and other "imponderables" were scientific facts, then even scientists could not say with any certainty where the material world ended and the immaterial, spiritual world began.

In some very crucial cases, women attempted to merge the assumption of female spirituality with the language of science, thereby crossing the boundaries in a way that made science spiritual, or made the spiritual scientific. They strove to revalue a series of discredited links between women and the occult, women and the spiritual, women and the immaterial, by insisting that modern science had objectively proven the existence of invisible—

spiritual—forces. Because these undertakings took the form of rogue religions, they belong as much to the history of women's breakaway religions, which I am not writing, as they do to this study of women's writings about science.

The three most powerful female-dominated movements of this sort were Christian Science, Seventh-Day Adventism, and Spiritualism. All three relied for authority on a combination of scientific terminology and the claim that because women were more intuitive and spiritual than men, they were better physiologically suited to register vibrations from the beyond.

Mary Baker Eddy's Christian Science attacked the scientific claims of contemporary medical practice, including claims made by alternative therapists, by pointing out that all these claims accepted the real existence of matter. Ellen G. White, the visionary prophet of the Adventists, formulated an anti-evolutionary—hence anti-geology, anti–life science—view that continues to exert cultural influence today in the movement known as "Creation Science." Spiritualist mediums, many of them women, rejected the basic theoretical requirement of the scientific disciplines of the century—that causal explanations must not invoke the supernatural.

But Spiritualists also insisted that there was nothing at all supernatural about the spirit world, that it conformed completely to natural law. In fact, all three initiatives insisted on their scientific validity and credentials. Variously disputing the scientists' own definition of the supernatural (as well as the scientists' prior right to decree what was and what was not supernatural), they insisted that their own work was in complete accord with a right understanding of natural law. That is, they affiliated with the sciences in the very teeth of their own resistance to the particulars of the scientists' worldview, striving to detach the term *science* from standard meanings and secure its prestige for themselves. This strategy signifies the felt need of these groups—these women, who differed among themselves as well as with the "male" establishment—to claim for themselves the authority of science, to affiliate with science after all.[2]

*M*ary Baker Eddy (1821–1910) openly named her religion a science, deploying the term not in its long-obsolete sense of general knowledge, but quite specifically in its nineteenth-century sense: as a method for interpreting and controlling the natural world through knowledge of predictable recurrences designated as scientific laws. She described her religion as the latest, final, fully scientific stage in the same progressive history narrated by other Protestants, a history cherished by scientists themselves—the history of mind's ever-expanding dominion over matter.

"Science is the watchword of our day. Note its advances!" Eddy announced in the 1889 edition of *Science and Health, with Key to the Scriptures*.[3] She named the telegraph, steam travel, photography, penny postage, ocean cable, telephone, and electric street lighting as examples of the scientific progress by which humankind was overcoming the resistance of matter by applying knowledge of the laws that matter obeyed. Christian Science, rightly understood, was merely the capstone of this progress (231), because it simply took the argument to what Eddy saw as its logical outcome. If, everywhere, matter could be subdued by mind, it followed to her that only mind had a "real" existence.

Christian Science, Eddy maintained, was identical to natural science in envisioning science as the progressive victory of mind over matter via its insistence "that law is everywhere, and that there can be no exception to it," and as correlatively denying the status of "miracle" to any event, "if by a miracle is meant any variation from the regular order of divine cause and effect." For "Christian Science devoutly believes the wonderful works performed by Jesus, but affirms that his so-called miracles were in accord with the highest law. . . . All men and women, in proportion as they are true disciples of the Truth, can heal and be healed, even according to the Master's word" (232).

But Christian Science was also not identical to natural science—because it pushed further. To Eddy, every technological development exhibited matter's ontological unreality. To anyone who grasped the real, inner meaning of scientific progress, matter could have no real, inner existence. While Mrs. Eddy rejected any approach that conceived of matter as an existent in its own right, she did grant—as is well known—vast power to the human belief in matter's reality. In fact, the power of false belief was exactly the focus of her religion; but so, for that matter, was every proscience narrative in which science won out over superstition.

Much is made in Eddy biographies of her relationship to the mental healer Phineas Parkhurst Quimby; in this particular matter, however, she is equally a disciple of Ralph Waldo Emerson, who famously advised readers in the conclusion to *Nature* to conform their lives to the mind's "pure idea" and promised that when they did so, "all disagreeable appearances, swine, spiders, snakes, pests, mad-houses, prisons, enemies" would "vanish." To Eddy, as apparently to Emerson, belief in the reality of matter was mere residual superstition, something the sciences themselves were profoundly dedicated to eradicating.[4]

Mary Baker Eddy put aside the obvious victory of mind over matter exhibited in nineteenth-century material technologies to concentrate on what she saw as the work of science in this final stage of human development: achieving the victory of mind over its belief in matter. From her vantage point, earlier scientific work that had divided the world into real matter and real mental force was destined for philosophical obsolescence, regardless of the value of its material accomplishments. Science to this point in history, she said over and over, merely pointed toward the revelation of a truly Christian science.

The practical innovation for which Christian Science has been so roundly condemned was its bypassing, indeed its proscribing, of all material interventions on the grounds that they granted existential status to matter. (Another apparent innovation was to center the idea of "science" more or less exclusively on health; but the stress on cures had been a focus of religious practice for centuries, and the identity of science with improved health and longevity is still, or again, the norm.)[5]

Mary Baker Eddy's distinction between real matter and real belief in matter made her work anathema to established scientists of her day. For them, if matter was unreal, the triumph of mind over matter would be either meaningless or magical. More urgently, perhaps, Christian Science instructed believers to ignore any demonstrable benefits of medical intervention in favor of the ministry of prayer.[6] The antimaterialist essence of Eddy's medical doctrine was that a felt disease expressed a belief in disease rather than a true somatic illness, which by definition could not exist. A failed cure meant, not that the basis of her science was wrong, but that prayer had not been offered with sufficient mental force to overcome false belief.

"To govern the body scientifically," she wrote, "it must be reached through Mind" (19); "mind's control over the body must supercede the so-called laws of matter" (21). "Disease should not appear real to the physician, since it is demonstrable in Science that to make disease unreal to his patient is to cure him. To do this the physician must understand the scientific unreality of disease" (296). Eddy did not argue that drugs never cured; she did argue, however, that "when the sick recover by the use of drugs, it is the law of a general belief, culminating in individual faith, that heals, and according to this faith will the effect be" (94).

Mary Baker Eddy did not base her medicinal arguments on scientific evidence; but in fact her constant use of the term "demonstration" suggested—as Gottschalk points out—a protocol of evidence and proof. And she pointed to successful cures as evidence of the validity of her principles. She could not escape the age's demand for empirical testimony. That she yoked the term *science* to the term *Christian* in naming her religion indicates a powerfully felt need to secure scientific status for her own viewpoint. In basic ways the nomenclature affirmed the significance and authority of science in quite a conventional, mainstream sense.

From a mainstream perspective, equally important as Eddy's disbelief in the reality of matter is the fact that while the mainstream claimed authority for a scientific assertion on the basis of experimental evidence and observation of facts, Mary Baker Eddy derived hers from what she loosely dubbed inspiration. No doubt many scientists arrived at their grasp of scientific law through the exercise of an instructed intuition, but intuition itself never compelled assent. But to Eddy, and despite her use of the terminology of demonstration, material facts could provide no authoritative testimony, because materiality was an illusion. Unlike Ellen G. White and the mediums I consider later, however, Eddy never claimed direct inspiration from any specified or identified supernatural force. Any such force—even a personified Jehovah—smacked too much of, exactly, personification, and therefore of the material. What Eddy claimed to have experienced was more an absorption into the currents of an Emersonian universal mind than a communication from the beyond.

From this vantage point, she attacked the establishment not for being overly scientific, but for being insufficiently so. "The Science of Soul is no more supernatural than the science of numbers; but departing from the realm of the physical, as it must, some may deny it the name of Science" (13). Christian Science, she asserts, "eschews what is termed Natural Science, erected on the unnatural hypothesis that matter is its own law-giver, that law is governed by material conditions, and that these are final, overruling the might of Mind. Not less, but more, do these rejections prove Christian Science to rightly bear this name" (154).

As Stephen Gottschalk, the most useful expounder of Christian Scientist views to non-Scientists, explains: "For Mrs. Eddy, Christian Science had a truly scientific character"; her use of the term "is clearly congruent with its general use in late nineteenth-century thought, in which science was a prestige-laden word connoting the idea of authorities, universality, and infallibility" (26). After her death, he points out, Christian Scientists often claimed in lectures and articles that "the changed concept of matter in the physical sciences from an objective substance to a structure of energies confirmed Mrs. Eddy's discovery" (26-27). If true science was about law, if the universe was truly lawful, if apprehension of the law was an activity of mind, then—obviously, to her—the expansion of the kingdom of mind was identical to the expansion of the scientific.

*E*llen G. White (1827–1914) is less well known today than Mary Baker Eddy, but she may well turn out to have been even more influential. Starting from an entirely different vantage point and working toward completely different ends from Eddy, White also affiliated with the sciences, both by insisting that her literal biblical fundamentalism was a form of science, and by pronouncing on the truth or falsity of scientific assertions. A posthumous selection and compilation from her voluminous works is appropriately called *Principles of True Science*.

The Seventh-Day Adventists, whose visionary prophet she was, had emerged from the Millerite remnants after the "great disappointment" of 1844, when the millennium they anticipated failed to arrive. As millennialists, the Adventists based their theology on belief in a specific, biblically foretold Second Coming. Ellen White backed up her readings of the Bible with the unfalsifiable evidence of her private visions.[7] Through these it was shown to her that accepting the Saturday Sabbath was the final step by which the faithful could separate from the unsaved whose derelictions had prevented the prophesied advent.

From this sabbatarian foundation it followed that there must have been, literally, six days of creation. Not for her the anxious evasions of Natural Theologians or scientist believers who interpreted the six days as six days widely spaced over many eons, or as metaphors for great stretches of continuous time. "Each of these periods Inspiration declares to have been a day consisting of evening and morning, like every other day since that time" (*Education*, 129). Indeed, in one vision she actually saw God creating the world in six days. In those six days, of course, all the extant species were created as they are found, along with some now extinct that are preserved in the fossil record. She responded to complaints that her cosmogony lacked scientific authority by pointing to the instability of scientific authority itself. "When consideration is given," she wrote, to

> how often the supposed deductions of science are revised or cast
> aside; with what readiness the assumed period of the earth's devel-
> opment is from time to time increased or diminished by millions of
> years; and how the theories advanced by different scientists conflict
> with one another,—considering all this, shall we, for the privilege
> of tracing our descent from germs and mollusks and apes, consent
> to cast away that statement of Holy Writ, so grand in its simplicity,
> "God created man in His own image"? (130)

Darwin eventually became the epitome of everything wrong with natural science; but White was anti-developmental from the start. (Her earliest vision occurred about two months after the "disappointment" of October 22, 1844 [Nichol, 30].) She argued that the fossil record demonstrated the destruction of some species by the Noachian flood; that, in other words, rather than testifying to evolution, it testified to the truth of biblical writ:

> Moses wrote under the guidance of the Spirit of God; and a correct theory of geology will never claim discoveries that can not be reconciled with his statements. . . . In the days of Noah, men, animals, and trees, many times larger than now exist, were buried, and thus preserved as an evidence to later generations that the antediluvians perished by a flood. God designed that the discovery of these things should establish faith in inspired history; but men, with their vain reasoning, fall into the same error as did the people before the flood—the things which God gave them as a benefit, they turn into a curse. (*Principles*, 227–228)

In *Darwinism Comes to America*, Ronald Numbers argues that the origins of today's influential Creation Science lie not in any early objections of theologically orthodox scientists to Darwin's ideas. Except for the signal instance of Louis Agassiz, he says, American scientists were generally receptive to Darwin. The origins of Creation Science are found in White's Adventist writings. Francis Nichol, her leading twentieth-century apologist, agrees, differentiating White's anti-Darwinism from that of all the other fundamentalist sects, which, he explains, were too quick to accept the idea of "gradual world reform" implicit in Darwinism, and thus to adopt a "secular conception of world betterment" instead of the vision of a cleansing apocalypse to which White and the Adventists cleaved (302).

In another development, Ellen G. White experienced many visions about hygiene and health. White's health advice, far less radical than Mary Baker Eddy's, was entirely compatible with recommendations of the "laws-of-life" health reformers, whom she claimed however not to have read. Her strictures encompassed a diet rich in grains, fruits, and vegetables; daily bathing; rejection of stimulants like coffee, tea, and of course alcohol; regular exercise; and comfortable dress, especially for women. In Battle Creek, Michigan, where they settled in 1855, the Adventists established a health sanitarium whose first and second directors—John Harvey Kellogg and Charles William Post—made consumer history with prepared breakfast cereals. And until the 1960s, when the Aquarians' interest in so-called natural foods eclipsed the Adventists', Adventists were the chief proponents and merchandisers of organic foods.[8] In this case, White advanced the compatibility of her health visions with scientific findings as evidence of their truths; where geology and zoology were concerned, she denied the truths of scientific findings. In short, she used science in whatever way suited her agenda. What she did not, or could not, do was omit science from the picture.

Neither Mary Baker Eddy nor Ellen G. White claimed that their inspirations had been mediated or conveyed by a particular supernatural presence. This was precisely the heart of the Spiritualist claim.[9] Unlike Christian Science and Adventism, Spiritualism had no women theorists; but it had a huge although indeterminable number of women practitioners and believers. Its most prominent early historian was Emma Hardinge (1823–1899), a poor girl from England eking out a career on the U.S. stage as an actress and singer, who reinvented herself as a successful lyceum speaker with no expertise beyond what she claimed was direct instruction by the spirits. She delivered a series of lectures narrating the scientific history of the world from geological prehistory to the eventual perfection of the race in a spiritual afterlife. The assertion that she had never read a science book in her life was key here; like other "trance lecturers," she emphasized her disadvantages because they testified to the spirit source of her knowledge.

Hardinge is described by the historian of spiritualism E. J. Dingwall as "the most talented and successful propagandist for Spiritualism the movement had ever known" ("Introduction," xvii). Her 1870 *Modern American Spiritualism* was "the most detailed account of the birth, development, and progress of Spiritualism in America ever to appear up to the date of its publication" (xiv). Because Spiritualism lacked formal ecclesiastical structure and creed and had no organized rituals or designated places of worship, the question whether Spiritualism should "count" as a religion is much debated among historians of U.S. religion. But its very informality, to many, is what makes it a particularly "American" kind of religion. Hardinge attributed its origins and success in the United States precisely to a national character impatient with established authority. In no small measure, that character was also practical and scientific—and not least because science also preferred empirical evidence to scholastic authority. In Hardinge's words: "Spiritualism, with a large majority of its American adherents, *is a religion*, separate in all respects from any existing sect, because it bases its affirmations purely upon the demonstrations of fact, science, and natural law, and admits of no creed or denominational boundary" (11).

Modern Spiritualism originated in February 1848, when, a few months after the Fox family had moved into an old house in Hydesville, New York (a hamlet just north of Newark, New York, and only a few miles from the old Erie Canal), mysterious rappings began to disturb them. The rappings, which sounded only when the two young Fox daughters—Margaret and Kate—were present, were ascribed to spirits (by curious visitors rather than by the sisters themselves).[10] Thanks in large part to press coverage—including enthusiastic publicity in Horace Greeley's *New York Tribune*—Spiritualism spread to involve perhaps millions of Americans.[11]

The movement struck many thinkers across the intellectual spectrum as a reversion to pre-Enlightenment credulity. The striking visibility of women in the movement seemed to justify the worst that could be said about the superstitious female mind and its penchant for magical thinking. Yet, historians have discovered that Spiritualists came chiefly from the progressive, utopian churches: Quakers and Universalists above all were drawn to Spiritualism, along with Unitarians. Anne Braude and others have pointed out that Spiritualists were associated with the most progressive reform movements of their time: women's rights, abolition, and utopian socialism. Hardinge claimed that "the great majority of the believers, save and except the residents of the Gulf States, were more or less in favor of anti-slavery" and "only a scattered few attached themselves to the pro-slavery party" (406–407). She observed also that

> Indian spirits play a prominent and most noble part in the Spiritualism of America. Nearly every medium is attended by one of these beneficent beings, guiding, counselling, protecting them, and using their peculiar knowledge of herbs, plants, and earthly productions, to suggest rare and invaluable medicaments for the cure of disease. What a comment on the principles and practices of Christianity does this phase of Spiritualism present! Helpless ignorant beings, nay, whole tribes, that have been despoiled and cheated by Christian cupidity, out of land, home, and life itself, now seem to be the most prominent of all the returning spirits, in practically illustrating the lesson which the Christians so glibly teach and so wantonly falsify by their deeds, namely, to "overcome evil with good," and forgive those who know not what they do. (481)[12]

Spiritualism, thus, was more progressive and more optimistic in its view of world history, as well as curiously more democratic, than any other religion or belief of its day. And, of course, it offered opportunities to women available in no other religion. Although they probably did not form a majority among mediums until the end of the nineteenth century, women comprised as much as 50 percent of the guild almost from the start. Nor were they by any means the passive victims of male mesmerizers represented, for example, in Nathaniel Hawthorne's *Blithedale Romance*. Those who succeeded were often astute businesswomen who booked appearances, collected money, and put themselves into trance states (or did whatever else was needed to impress their clients) through their own efforts rather than depending on a male entrancer.

The remarkable advent of spirit communication was itself taken to be evidence of universal progress. The spirits' accounts of their post-mortem opportunities for further self-improvement opened the blissful prospect of eternal life directed toward attaining individual perfection. One lived, as oneself, as long as it took to become perfect—and then one lived on as a perfect being. Better still, after death one encountered and recognized those who had gone on ahead. The consolatory power of this vision, perhaps even more to those who had lost loved ones than to those who feared death, is inestimable. Its congruence with a belief in divine benevolence—for what good God would terminate his creatures' efforts to become better?—is also symptomatic of an intense will to believe in a historical moment when a vengeful God seemed less and less the right national deity for a democratic people.

Perhaps the loss of loved ones told especially heavily on women. Perhaps, too, the prospect of making good money doing interesting work was irresistible for many women who lived boring, constrained lives. But for this study, the most important aspects of Spiritualism were its insistence that its worldview was entirely scientific, and the alacrity with which women in spiritualism adopted this argument. Mediums and publicists alike insisted that Spiritualism was the only religion to offer scientific proof of the existence of an afterlife and of the persistence of personal identity after death. Spiritualism made unnecessary any division according to which religion was only about faith, science about facts. Ahlstrom says that in the popularity of Spiritualism "one may observe both the threat of modern science to traditional faith and the appeal to empirical confirmation of cherished hopes" (490). In Hardinge's words: "The whole realm of visionary supernaturalism melts away, then, before the morning sun of that glorious light that science brings" (10):

Chemistry, Physiology, Phrenology, Magnetism, and Clairvoyance
have all been steps leading up through the once-forbidden mysteries
of nature into the realm of imponderable forces, bearing the student
onward to the very gates of the temple of mind, within which are

now heard the low, telegraphic knocks of the spirit, inviting the earnest inquirers to enter, and prophesying the great day of revelation,
when man may ascend, as on a Jacob's ladder, that mighty column
where Physics is the base, Science the shaft, Metaphysics the superstructure, and Spiritualism the coronal glory of the capital, whose
starry crown pierces the overarching firmament of Heaven. (22)

Leah Underhill, the oldest Fox sister and impresario of the younger women's
well-attended public appearances, wrote (or had written for her) in 1885 that
"the use of the manifestations of spiritualism" was that they "*demonstrate*
the reality of the survival of man's spirit, or inner self, after that 'death' which
is by birth into another stage of progressed and progressive life, in unchanged
personality and identity; or, in other words, that immortality of the soul (heretofore a mere dogma of unproved and unprovable 'faith'), which is the foundation corner-stone of all religions and of all Religion" (3).

   According to Hardinge, the spiritual rappings first encountered in
Hydesville were a veritable telegraph system "by which invisible beings were
enabled to spell out consecutive messages"; they were "organized by scientific minds in the spirit spheres. It depended mainly upon the conditions of
human and atmospheric magnetisms, and pointed to the ultimation of a science whereby spirits, operating upon and through matter, could connect in
the most intimate relations the worlds of material and spiritual existence" (29).
The particular scientific mind at the helm in the spirit world was generally
thought to be Benjamin Franklin's. As Underhill put it:

Inasmuch as Electricity and Magnetism seem to play some part in
the machinery of this intercommunication, it is not surprising that
the Spirit on the other side who seems to have been the principal
initiator, not to say the inventor of this new development in the evolution of Humanity, was the great man known to earthly fame as the
father of electrical science, as he was one of the great fathers of
American liberty; he of whom it has been grandly written that he
snatched the lightning from the sky, and the sceptre from the hand
of the tyrant: the immortal BENJAMIN FRANKLIN. (55–56)

   Some of the difficulties pertaining to spirit communication, Hardinge
explains, might be simply resolved if one would put aside any presupposi-
tions about how and what a spirit ought to communicate "and simply acknowledge that which seems patent to the communion, namely, that it depends upon
some electrical properties evolved from the physical organizations of

favorably-endowed individuals" (247). In other parts of her history Hardinge elaborates a scientific explanation for the mechanics of the spiritual communication: spirits "manifest through two primitive elements," first "an electro-magnetic element of which the spiritual body is composed; next, a physical aura, which emanates from the medium, or can be collected from material substances, analogous, it is supposed, to the element of 'vitality.'" From the combination of these two, "a third or composite is formed, which is affected by the atmosphere and human emanations." Her explanation continues:

> From the preponderance of the electro-magnetic or spiritual element, the laws of cohesion and gravitation can be overcome, and through this spirits are enabled to dissolve and recompose substances with great rapidity, heave up and carry material bodies through the air, and cause them to float or sink in proportion to the strength of the battery formed. It is this element which enables some spirits highly charged with it, to come into contact with matter, and thus to use pencils, pens, etc., in writing, drawing, and playing on musical instruments. By aid of the physical or human aura—animal magnetism—they cause concussions, raps, shaking of furniture and heavy ponderable bodies; by this also they produce spirit light, gathering it up so as to form an envelope of matter around their own hands, condense sound so as to be heard singing and speaking, and strike upon the heavier instruments. (312)

The Spiritualist poet and abolitionist activist Lizzie Doten explained in the preface to her 1871 *Poems of Progress* that "no other form of faith ever brought this spiritual world so near, *as to banish its supernatural character, and place it within the province of natural law*" (6). "It has been demonstrated," she continues, that the eye, ear, and nerves are "avenues of sense" that serve "to convey the vibrations of the surrounding 'ether' to the central consciousness, which alone is possessed of the power of perception. Since this is so, who shall dare place a limit to the possibilities of that consciousness, of which so little is definitely known?" (6). The "revelations of the spectroscope, and the investigations of some of the great minds of the present day, have determined the existence of a higher scale of vibrations than those which fall within the ordinary range of human vision. . . . That we should be made sensibly aware of this higher life, under certain legitimate conditions, is perfectly *natural*" (7–8).

The overarching Spiritualist assumption was that a new age in the evolution of humanity had begun. Only now were spirits able to communicate widely; only now were more and more people finding within themselves the ability to receive spirit messages. The basis for this theory of new developments lay both in the incontrovertible fact of scientific advance and the historicity of such scientific discourses as geology and evolutionary natural history.

Hardinge's "imponderables," standard items in every natural philosophy textbook, included magnetism, light, electricity, and any other substance that could not be measured or weighed. To scientists as well as lay people, as Lizzie Doten rightly observed, the entire universe had to be permeated by an ethereal fluid. This imponderable allowed scientists to explain action at a distance (for example, the gravitational effects of the distant sun or moon on the earth) as the transmission of one imponderable through another. That the universe could operate without some substance filling the void is impossible for common sense to imagine. Ether did not leave the scientific lexicon until Einstein's calculations made it superfluous.[13]

Spiritualism argued that the next stage of scientific progress was not to be further conquest of the planetary sphere, but a making visible of the invisible ether and the entities that traversed it. And here, even more than in the field of literary estheticism, was a practice in which cultural stereotypes of women could further their careers. For the greater nervousness of women meant that they were more electric than men, and it was taken as a matter of physiology rather than of poetry that women were more ethereal than men as well. It was in fact the greater percentage of ethereal fluid in their nerves that enabled women to register and transmit electrical impulses. This made the scientific case for women being better suited than men to receive spirit messages.

Like Mary Baker Eddy and Ellen G. White, the women Spiritualists are most powerfully nineteenth century, and most remote from the twenty-first, in their assumption of a hierarchy in which the spiritual realm exists above and outside nature, such that women have better access to that realm than men because they are less rather than more embodied than men. Their relative disembodiment allows them more direct access to the truth that the scientific experimenter can arrive at only by "plod[ding] through a regular sequence of logical arguments" (Hale, *Woman's Record*, xlvi). For all these nineteenth-century women, the triumph of mind over matter was the ultimate goal. This, it must be noted, is precisely the grounds on which twentieth-century antiscience feminism attacked science: for separating mind from body, for subjecting body to the exploitation and domination of mind. Nineteenth-century women who affiliated directly with scientific men believed that science was about the conquest and subduing of nature, insofar as nature was the equivalent of material reality. But the Spiritualist women who disaffiliated from scientific men while affiliating with science took exactly the same position. As physically weak women, they all looked forward to the reign of pure mind.

NOTES

CHAPTER 1 *Print and Women's Scientific Affiliations*

1. Because what we now call physics was called "natural philosophy" until after the Civil War, I use "natural philosophy" to mean physics throughout this study.
2. Historians of science place the first use of the term *science* in William Whewell's 1840 *Philosophy of the Inductive Sciences*.
3. For the partnership of religion and science, see especially Bozeman; Gillispie, *Genesis*; Greene; Hovenkamp; Knight; Stevenson; Struick; Leonard Wilson.
4. Kohlstedt's number is 337 (*Formation*), Daniels's is 269. Data include sources such as membership in the AAAS (Kohlstedt); entries in the *DAB* (Bruce); scientific publication (Beaver).
5. For the Wilkes Expedition, see Viola and Margolis. For the Coast Survey, see Slotten. For western expeditions, see Goetzmann, *Army Exploration* and *Exploration and Empire*. Bruce identifies Alexander Dallas Bache above all (he was superintendent of the Coast Survey after 1843), and especially in his collaboration with Joseph Henry, director of the Smithsonian after 1846, as the forger of the synthesis we know as "big science."
6. This summary of scientific institutional change in nineteenth-century America synthesizes especially Beaver; Bozeman; Bruce; Daniels; Guralnick, *Science*; Howard Miller; Knight; Kohlstedt, *Formation*; Slotten; Louise Stevenson; Struick; and L. Wilson. For the content of nineteenth-century science as Americans would absorb it, I have consulted contemporaneous materials, including such general overviews as: Herschel, *Preliminary Discourse* and *Manual*; Humboldt, *Cosmos*, vols. 1 and 2; Somerville, *Connexion* and *Political Geography*; Whewell, *Philosophy* and *History*; Parley (Goodrich), *Glance*. For technology I have looked at Bigelow, Lardner, Mahan, Edward Youmans; for anatomy and physiology Cutter, Hitchcock and Hitchcock, Beecher (see chapter 4); for astronomy Burritt; Dick; Loomis, *Introduction, Progress*; Olmsted, *Introduction*; for botany Phelps (see chapter 2); Asa Gray, *First Lessons* and *Manual*; Eliza Youmans; for chemistry Alonzo Gray; Liebig; Marcet; Silliman, *First Principles*; for agricultural chemistry Dana, Emerson and Flint; for entomology Thaddeus Harris; for geology Alonzo Gray and C. B. Adams; Hitchcock, *Outline*; for mathematics Davies; for physics (natural philosophy) Loomis, *Elements*; Silliman, *Principles*;

Whewell, *Astronomy and General Physics*. Because I am interested in domains of knowledge defined by experts of the time as "science," I ignore initiatives that, even in their own day, were called "pseudosciences" and said to be expounded by "quacks." The differentiation of quacks and charlatans from real scientists was an ongoing struggle throughout the century and one in which academic scientists were much invested. Because women were thought to be especially vulnerable to pseudoscientific claims, science education was often described as a way to protect them from impostors; but, for the same reason, women were deemed less capable of doing original science themselves.

7. Kasson notes such arguments from technology's boosters as: technology made the nation less economically dependent on the Old World; it made consumer goods so widely accessible that the aristocratic taint of "luxury" connected with consumerism disappeared; it countered territorial expansion through centralized transportation and production (50). For technological nationalism see also Marx. On the rising standard of living epitomized in more goods and services, see Bushman.

8. This point is made especially by Bruce and Howard Miller, who suggests that at least some scientists used nationalistic rhetoric opportunistically to forward more purely scientific aims.

9. Today, when numerous professions—business, law, medicine, and many areas of academia—have opened their doors at least partially to women, the absence of women in the sciences is noticeable. For recent statistics, see Rosser, *Teaching the Majority*, 1–211, and "Applying"; Leggon; Valian. For the dearth of women scientists in the nineteenth century, see Kohlstedt, "Periphery"; Rossiter, *Struggles and Strategies*. Other accounts of women scientists in the West, past and present, are: essays in Abir-Am and Outram, especially Shteir, "Botany"; Rossiter, *Before Affirmative Action*; Shteir, *Cultivating*; Warner, "Science Education" and *Graceanna Lewis*; Wells.

10. Shteir identifies botany as the preeminent science for British women, accepting the general belief among historians of women's science that this was the women's chosen subject because flowers were conventionally associated with the feminine. But this hypothesis does not seem to hold for the United States in the same way that it does in England. For one thing, teachers like Phelps stressed aspects of botany other than floral beauty (see chapter 2); for another, chemistry, not botany, was the nation's most taught science for women.

11. In his biography of Faraday, L. Pearce Williams explains that the crowd of privileged young ladies attending Humphrey Davy's lectures at the Royal Society were drawn there because Davy was "the handsomest man in the history of science"; they were drawn "more by his charm and the vivacity of his person than by any passion for chemistry"; it was "to this audience that Mrs. Marcet addressed her *Conversations*, so that Davy's followers could understand as well as admire him" (19). If one shuffles off the biographer's uninstructed sexism as laughable, one is left with testimony to a substantial female audience for chemistry lectures in England. Lindee's research on American use of Marcet's texts supports Sarah Hale's claim in *Woman's Record* that hers was the basic chemistry text for everybody (732).

12. I define geography as a science not only because the subject introduced students to all the other sciences as well as to scientific thinking, but also because it was the dominant scientific approach in the United States "in the first six or seven decades of the nineteenth century" (Reingold, 60). Geography as configured by Alexander von Humboldt involved so comprehensive a view of the natural world that every science could contribute to it. (For "Humboldtian" science see especially Cannon, Livingstone; for its role in the United States, see Bruce, Slotten.) Geographies typically listed mountains, volcanoes, and rivers; they also defined these landforms and explained their history and their effect on the civilizations they abutted or sustained. Geographies offered repellently chauvinistic surveys of other cultures even while they endorsed a progressive ethos of world trade; but—what matters for my purposes here—they explained the basic principles of astronomy, climate, geology, mineralogy, meteorology, map making, navigation, zoology, and botany. And, since by the 1820s most primary schools were teaching geography, one might hazard that every child who went to school at all in the United States had some exposure to basic science. Goodrich alone published differently sized and priced geographies for all uses, from Parley's primary-school text to an encyclopedic *Universal Geography* running to almost a thousand pages.

13. An illustration in the *Scientific American* for 1852, taken from an English magazine, that represents a demonstration of Foucault's pendulum, shows that half of the first-row audience are women.

14. This motive is not dead. Hawking, for example, says a unified theory would further understanding of "why it is that we and the universe exist," which would be to "know the mind of God" (175). For antiwoman implications of Judeo-Christian science, see Noble.

15. Perhaps women had to get access to professional science before they could begin to theorize an intellectual rejection of it. The idea of male bias in science—as opposed to the obvious fact of male bias against women scientists—had to wait for the feminist approach pioneered by Keller in *Reflections*, which builds from Kuhn's early description of science as socially—more precisely, professionally—constructed knowledge.

    Evelyn Keller's biography of Barbara McClintock, *A Feeling for the Organism*, draws on the controversial but influential "different voice" theory of Carol Gilligan to propose that women did science holistically and cooperatively with the organism, while men did it abstractly and antagonistically, seeking to dominate and dissect the nature they studied. Nineteenth-century U.S. women—at least, white "Anglo" women—were only too happy to have nature dominated and dissected.

    Feminist critiques of the antinaturism of science have often merged with theoretical attacks on empiricism from Science Studies specialists, especially Bruno Latour—in *Laboratory Life* (coauthored with Steve Woolgar), *Science in Action*, and *We Have Never Been Modern*. (See also the essays in Biagioli.) Working from another angle, Pratt in *Imperial Eyes* has identified Western science as "local knowledge" (Latour's term) designed to forward Western imperialism and environmental exploitation on behalf of the wealthier nation-states. Environmental and gender concerns have converged to produce the highly factionalized ecofeminist movement.

Contemporary feminist critiques of science thus range from liberal attempts to overcome or at least minimize the various social asymmetries that obstruct women's pursuit of scientific careers (aiming to produce more women scientists), through notations of masculinist myopia that produce obviously bad empirical science, to radical attacks on science as foundationally antilife, antiearth, antiwomen, antichildren, and anti-indigenes (aiming to abolish or at least discredit science altogether). For examples of these diverse approaches see essays in Bleier, especially Fee; Bordo; Gaard and Murphy; essays in Mary Gergen, especially Hubbard and Kenneth Gergen; Haraway; essays in Rothschild, especially King; Harding, *Science Question* and *Whose Science?*; Evelyn Keller, *Reflections* and "Gender/Science System"; Longino; Mellor; Merchant; Noble; Norwood; Ritvo; Schiebinger, *Mind Has No Sex?* and *Nature's Body*; essays in Tuana; Wertheim. These initiatives seem to have peaked in the mid-1990s.

Chapter 2   *Almira Phelps and the Discipline of Botany*

1. Phelps, a New Englander, taught school until she married Simeon Lincoln in 1817. After his sudden death in 1823 she joined the faculty at her sister Emma Willard's school. She left eight years later to marry John Phelps but returned to teaching in 1838 with her husband's encouragement—he was business manager of Patapsco until his death in 1849. Phelps retired to Baltimore in 1855, after her daughter and close confidante, Jane Porter, was killed in a railway accident. She always remained close to Emma Willard. Her books circulated under several names: Mrs. Lincoln, Mrs. Lincoln Phelps, Mrs. Almira Lincoln Phelps, Mrs. Almira Hart Phelps, Mrs. Phelps. Bolzau's is the only full-scale biography; Scott, Slack, Norwood, and Welch draw heavily on it.

2. Phelps's botany text dominated the market until 1836, when Asa Gray brought out his rival book—written, according to Dupree, specifically to counter Phelps's Linnaean approach (52). Gray's text outsold and outlasted Phelps's, but there was no third major botany text in the market and hers remained very widely used. Besides her other science textbooks, Phelps's published work included two female conduct novels, *Caroline Westerly* and *Ida Norman* (see chapter 8 on *Caroline Westerly*); a best-selling introduction to women's education (sometimes called *Lectures to Young Ladies*, sometimes *The Female Student*, sometimes *The Fireside Friend*, it was adopted by the Massachusetts public school library system the year after its first publication in 1833); a joint translation (with Willard) and annotated edition of Madame Necker de Saussure's treatise on child development; and many occasional essays.

3. For botany in the United States as a kind of master science uniting taxonomy to Baconian methodology, see Daniels, 86.

4. This rationale, stripped of its doctrinaire piety, persisted well after the Civil War. For example, Eliza Youmans's *First Book of Botany*, arguing in 1889 for installing the subject as a fourth requirement in elementary education, praises the subject for its systematicity. She says the deepest defect of current education is "the almost total lack of any systematic cultivation of the observing powers. Although all real knowledge begins in attention to *things*, and consists in the discrimina-

tion and comparison of the likenesses and differences among objects," the educational system makes "no provision for the regular training of the perceptive faculties." We "do little to exercise the mind upon the realities of Nature, or to make it alert, sensitive, and intelligent, in respect of the order of the surrounding world." What is wanted is "that object-studies shall become more close and methodic, and that the observations shall be brought into connected and organized knowledge," aims for which botany is suited "beyond all other studies" (4).

5. For the ethos of "republican womanhood," see Kerber, *Women*.
6. McAllister, Eaton's biographer, quotes extensively from his correspondence. See also Smallwood and Smallwood.
7. On plant taxonomies in contemporary biology see Mayr and Niklas.

CHAPTER 3   *Sarah Hale and the Circulation of Science*

1. The journal is typically referred to in critical discussion as *Godey's*, but in its own day it was known as the *Lady's Book*, and that is what I shall call it here.
2. Sarah Josepha Buell Hale (1788–1879) was tutored in girlhood by her older brother Horatio, a Yale student. She taught school from the age of eighteen until her marriage to David Hale, a lawyer, in 1813. David died suddenly of pneumonia in 1822, just days before the last of their five children was born, and for some years thereafter Sarah labored to support the family through sewing. She began her editorial career at the Boston-based *Ladies' Magazine* in 1828; this magazine was absorbed by Louis Godey into the *Lady's Book* when he attracted Hale as editor in 1837. Although the *Lady's Book* was published in Philadelphia, Hale did not move to that city until the youngest of her three sons graduated from college. She never remarried. Louis Godey handled the business side of the magazine and with some important exceptions—he barred references to the Civil War from the magazine until the conflict was over—he left editorial policy to Hale. Besides her editorial work, she published more than fifty books including novels, collections of her stories, poems, anthologies, a much reissued cookbook, a flora, and other works. The cookbook, as I shall iterate later, constituted a signal effort to make cooking systematic and to base it on scientific understanding of human physiological needs.
3. Some feminist scholars have been offended by the political incorrectness of Hale's opposition to woman suffrage and her support of Liberian colonization rather than abolition. Conrad proposed that Hale (in contrast to Margaret Fuller) achieved her reputation by forwarding a conservative, anti-intellectual ideology. Okker, however, has countered convincingly by documenting Hale's campaigns to make editorship a woman's profession, to publish literary fiction (along with the chief women writers of the day she published Hawthorne, Longfellow, Poe, and other men), and to define an intellectualized and activist "women's sphere."
4. In "From Enlightenment to Victorian" I trace the evolution of Hale's ideologies of womanhood as they mutated from the rational toward the more intuitively spiritual. My "Onward Christian Women" and "Sarah Hale, Political Writer" argue for the priority of historical knowledge in Hale's idea of female education. Hale

urged women to study history for two reasons: so they would understand their obligations as republican citizens and so they would recognize their duties as the world progressed from the reign of brute force toward the dominion of mind and spirit. I integrate the historical with the scientific in Hale's program by saying that to her, right understanding meant that women would seek a modern scientific rather than an obsolete, impractical, and perhaps un-American traditional education.

5. On the market revolution and the emergence of consumer culture well before the 1880s and 1890s—the decades with which it is usually associated—see especially Blumin, Bushman, Pessen, and Sellers. Marx has identified the critical, i.e., the antimodernist, antitechnology, strain in U.S. literature with the canonical antebellum figures. He has correspondingly associated protechnology ideology with the uncritical bourgeois majority, although not with women. But given that bourgeois women are frequently identified with the popular audience, it seems quite appropriate for them to be protechnology.

6. According to the *New York Times*, however (February 2, 1999), "even though it seemed for many years that Einstein had consigned ether to the trash heap of obsolete notions," it is enjoying a new "incarnation" as a "universal web of 'quantum fields'."

7. This observation coincidentally foretells what Caroline Herschel herself said far more abjectly, as her 1876 memoirs reported it: "I am nothing, I have done nothing; all I am, all I know, I owe to my brother. I am only the tool which he shaped to his use—a well-trained puppy-dog would have done as much" (ix).

8. Somerville's modern biographer says it added greatly to Somerville's luster that she was an exemplary wife and mother. "Displaying no tinge of blue, she moved easily and graciously in cultivated society, preserving all the traditional female traits and graces, while adding to them extraordinary mental achievements" (Elizabeth Patterson, xii). In chapter 1 I quote from Somerville's draft manuscript of her autobiography, where she bemoans her lack of scientific genius and attributes the defect to her sex.

Chapter 4   *Catharine Esther Beecher and the Sciences of Home*

1. Beecher was sixteen when her mother died; she took the death very hard and continued to memorialize her mother into old age. She was also emotionally attached to her father, though she struggled against and finally rejected his Calvinism. Her fiancé, Alexander Fisher, youthful professor of natural philosophy and mathematics at Yale, drowned at sea in 1822—a mere four months after their engagement. Thereafter Beecher dedicated herself to a life of active singlehood focused on educational reform. With her sister Mary she established a school in Hartford, Connecticut, in 1823. Moving to Cincinnati with her father and his family in 1831, she founded the Western Female Institute in 1832. After the institute folded in 1837, she embarked on a peripatetic life of public advocacy. Besides arguing that women's education should prepare them for women's tasks, she worked especially to raise endowments for women's teacher-training schools and to find employment for New England women teachers in the West, a region she

had come to view—as did her father and brothers—as vulnerable to a papal take-over. She brokered the assignment of some five hundred New England teachers to western schools (Cross, 123). Full-length interpretive biographies are Harveson and Sklar.

2. Harriet Beecher Stowe is named on the title page as coauthor of *The American Woman's Home* and its textbook redaction, titled simply *Principles of Domestic Science*, which was published in 1870. Stowe's contributions, drawn from a se-ries of her essays published in the *Atlantic Monthly* as "House and Home Pa-pers," comprise only a small portion of the text. They are easily distinguishable from Beecher's work because of their topics—home decoration and beauti-fication—and their elegantly rococo style in contrast to Beecher's utilitarian plainness.

3. Beecher published *Woman Suffrage and Woman's Profession* in 1871. This was an attempt to define the profession of homemaking as a satisfying alternative to female enfranchisement, which she opposed, not because it took women out of the physical home, but because it took their minds away from their home duties.

4. Beecher's target audiences in *Treatise* and *American Woman's Home* (cited here-after as *Home*) are women who may or may not have domestic servants, but who are not servants themselves. Servants, in her view, already had a profession. She wrote one book for this group—*Letters to Persons Who are Engaged in Domes-tic Service*—which appeared in 1842, the year after the *Treatise* was published. The book tried to define interactions between servant and employer in terms of a professional exchange, not as an affective relation. Burstyn was the earliest critic to note Beecher's definition of homemaking as a profession (386). See also Tonkovich, xiii. Rossiter, judging the scientific content in Beecher's books by later professional standards, dismisses it as "primitive" but also recognizes its formative influence (*Struggles and Strategies*, 67). Previous criticism has some-times observed but has not analyzed the extensive science in her writing; nor has the way Beecher welds it to a professional ideal been noted. Harveson fo-cuses on Beecher's attempts to professionalize teacher training, not housework. Sklar is more interested in the psychological tensions between Beecher's domes-tic, religious, and careerist thought than in unpacking the scientific tendencies of her work; she calls the *Treatise* "scientific but personal" (154). Tompkins merely remarks on its "wealth of scientific information" (143).

5. Understandably but regrettably baffled by what look like inconsistencies, and ir-ritated by her insistence that women ought to stay home for the good of the na-tion, some feminist critics have dealt with Beecher through satiric references to her plain appearance, her advocacy of homemaking while she herself never kept a home, or her advice to mothers while she herself was childless. I will not cite examples. Amy Kaplan, surprisingly oblivious to scholarship on the politics of early national and antebellum U.S. domestic writing, is shocked—shocked!—to discover that Beecher was an imperialistic chauvinist. But of course advocates of the Protestant-republican synthesis, who saw the home as the cradle of the nation, also thought the nation was the cradle of the world's millennial future.

6. Unlike mainline women's historians and literary critics, all historians of home economics without exception identify Beecher as the discipline's foremother; for

example, Apple, 79; Bevier, *Home Economics in Education*, 108–109; Biester, 549; Marjorie Brown, 1:185; Budewig, passim; Carver, passim; Craig, 4; Shapiro, 29, 40; Vincenti, 11. Her technophilia is briefly acknowledged in Ellul, 326; Giedion, 514–515; Handlin, 56, 405–406; Hayden, 54–63. Giedion approves of her labor-saving kitchen strategies, but Hayden is the only critic to call her technological approach feminist.

7. Like all physiology texts in this era, Beecher's omits the reproductive system (one had to read the so-called marriage manuals to find this information). This elision, which fostered a huge industry of books about sex, had the oddly useful although probably unintended outcome of focusing physiology on the shared rather than the gendered body. No wandering, hysterical womb explains nervous collapse here, because there is no womb; rather, there is bad ventilation, constricting clothing, inactivity.

8. Sklar, however, finds the keynote of the *Home* to be its greatly increased piety (264) rather than its greatly enhanced and updated science.

9. For Richards, see Douty and Hunt.

10. The prevalence of chemists in the first generation of women academic scientists reminds one that chemistry had been the most taught women's science throughout the nineteenth century.

CHAPTER 5   *Susan Fenimore Cooper and Ladies' Science*

1. *Rural Hours* went through seven editions in five years; it was revised and reissued in 1868, and again in 1887. There is no biography of Susan Cooper; Beard's summary in *NAW* is useful. The Cooper family, including three younger sisters and a brother, was close-knit. Susan and her father, James Fenimore Cooper, were especially close. He accompanied her on the excursions described in *Rural Hours* and helped get the book published. Susan Cooper never married; she continued to live in Cooperstown from the time the family moved there in 1836, when she was twenty-three, until her death in 1894. Following the publication of *Rural Hours* (an earlier novel, *Elinor Wyllys* [1846], had not been successful) she wrote essays, edited an English nature journal in 1853 (John Knapp's *Country Rambles in England*), and compiled and annotated a belletristic anthology, *The Rhyme and Reason of Country Life* (1855). From the late 1850s onward she put most of her literary energies into preserving and enhancing her father's reputation. *Pages and Pictures from the Writings of James Fenimore Cooper* (1861) was a lavishly produced, beautifully illustrated anthology of extracts from Cooper's novels interspersed with her astute biographical and critical commentary. She also wrote the introductions to volumes in the Household Edition of his novels (1876–1884). For analysis of *Elinor Wyllys* see Maddox.

2. Although one might suppose that Cooper published anonymously so as not to presume on her famous father, the dedication—"to the author of 'The Deerslayer' very respectfully, gratefully, and most affectionately"—obviously implied a close kinship between author and dedicatee. All the Cooper acquaintances knew the authorship from the start. James Fenimore Cooper wrote home excitedly from New York soon after publication, "Right and left, I hear of Rural Hours. I am

stopped in the street, a dozen times a day to congratulate me" (quoted in the Johnson-Patterson edition of *Rural Hours,* xiii). Throughout my discussion of Cooper's *Rural Hours,* I cite this edition of the 1850 text.

3. For the gentrification of country life after 1840, see Huth; Marx; Stilgoe, *Borderlands*; Thornton. Among important New York writers publicizing an upscale rural style of life were Nathaniel P. Willis (*Rural Letters,* 1849), J. T. Headley (*The Adirondack, or Life in the Woods,* 1849), and the Hudson River Valley horticulturalist and landscape architect Andrew Jackson Downing. For the class aspirations of the Cooper family—and their interest in the value of real estate—see Taylor.

4. See chapter 2 and Keeney for the vogue of natural history, especially botany, in the United States; for Great Britain, see Allen, Barber.

5. Likely English models for Cooper's work include Leigh Hunt's perambulatory almanac *The Months* (London, 1821); William Howitt's calendrical *Book of the Seasons,* published in London in 1831 and in Philadelphia soon thereafter; Howitt's sociological *Rural Life of England* (London, 1838); John Knapp's *Country Rambles, or Diary of a Naturalist,* published in London in 1829 and edited for Americans in an 1853 edition by Cooper herself, brought out by a publisher in Buffalo; Gilbert White's *Natural History and Antiquities of Selborne,* first published in London in 1789 and many times reprinted; and Mary Russell Mitford's five volumes of popular sketches, *Our Village,* published between 1824 and 1832 in London and New York.

6. Humboldt's history of attitudes toward nature in the first volume of *Cosmos* is heavily mined by Cooper for her introduction to *The Rhyme and Reason of Country Life.* For an excellent popular biography of Humboldt, see Botting. For Humboldt's impact on scientific practice in England and the United States, see Bowen, Bruce, Cannon, Livingstone, Slotten.

7. Of course Thoreau's *Walden* comes to mind here, with its challenging insistence that traveling a great deal in Concord is equivalent to world voyaging and its truculent finale about the superficiality of actual travel as opposed to inward exploration. Thoreau cites Cooper's work in his journals, and many discussions of *Rural Hours* deviate at some point into discussions of Thoreau. Some scholars propose that Thoreau got *Walden's* seasonal form from Cooper. But, if she was his model, she was also his challenge; his masculine farmer's persona neatly counters her genteel femininity as a model of how to live in the country. For a development of this point, see Baym, "English Nature"; for the influence of Humboldt on Thoreau's own scientific writing, see Walls.

8. Neither the original journals nor the book manuscript seem to have survived; using local weather records, Hugh MacDougall has shown that she combined materials from at least 1848 and 1849, and perhaps 1850 as well, incongruously—and perhaps fatally for any project demanding scientific environmental accuracy—interweaving a very wet summer (1848) with a very dry one (1849). If the book is meant as an example, not a reliable scientific document, this compression does not matter. There is no evidence that Cooper kept a comparable journal at any other time in her life, for which reason—along with the evidence of *Elinor Wyllys* that she aspired to a literary career—I theorize that she kept

this journal in the first place to make a book. Her preface, however, makes the ladylike disclaimer that she embarked on the project only for her own amusement (3) and *Rural Hours* editors Johnson and Patterson take her at her word (x).

9. Cooper follows Humboldt only up to a certain point in her history of human attitudes toward nature. In *Cosmos*, Humboldt declares that attitudes toward nature show increasing enlightenment, and Cooper agrees; but he also says that science has superseded poetry as the educated approach to nature, and here Cooper disagrees. She maintains the Natural Theology position that one eventually works up through nature to nature's God, who is outside nature. Her introduction to the *Rhyme and Reason of Country Life* draws on the orthodox Anglican John Keble for the phrase "last form of song." *Rural Hours*, however, is less focused than *Rhyme and Reason* on the theological implications of nature study.

10. Because much recent interest in *Rural Hours* has centered on its contribution to, even initiation of, a distinct women's form of nature writing in the United States, I emphasize that I see the book as an example neither of nature writing that rejects intellection for unmediated communion with nature (see, e.g., Finch and Elder, 19–30; Murray, passim) nor of nature writing that assumes the inherent sacredness of the earth and accepts, even celebrates, the traditional earthiness of women. For this contrasting approach to Cooper, see Norwood, 25–53; for more general issues in ecofeminism and ecocriticism, see Gaard and Murphy; Glotfelty and Fromm; Mellor.

11. Cooper's annotations to John Knapp's journal mainly instruct American readers who might picture the wrong natural object when reading an English book—for example the American, not the English, robin.

12. A huge bibliography, far exceeding my scope in this study, exists of works on English esthetics, the role of discourses about the sublime and the beautiful in creating scenic tourism, and in the political bearings of ideologies of the picturesque.

13. Buell interestingly reads Cooper's hostility to naturalized weeds as a sign of ecological nationalism (407). Possibly the sentence about waging war against weeds inspired Thoreau to depict weeding in *Walden* as epic combat.

14. Ecologists and environmentalists, as well as adherents of the so-called New Geography, increasingly feature the constructedness of the wilderness ideal in U.S. culture. For the idea of all landscape as shaped by the human, and for the idea of landscape itself as a human construction, see especially Cronon, *Changes, Uncommon Ground*; Glacken; Oelschlager; Rackham; Stilgoe, *Common Landscape*; Michael Williams; Worster.

15. Stilgoe says that in this essay Cooper "worried that the rural scenery surrounding her home in Cooperstown, New York, stood a poor second to that of England" (*Borderlands*, 23).

16. For the emergence of, and rationale for, the national parks, see Runte, Sellars. Among denunciations of scientific taxonomy as an attempt to impose Western thinking on an indigenous nature that encompasses traditional cultures, Pratt's *Imperial Eyes* has become a classic.

CHAPTER 6   *Elizabeth Cary Agassiz and Heroic Science*

1. The one reliable biography of Elizabeth Agassiz is Paton; Tharp is novelized but has useful family information. See also Hawkins's account in *Notable American Women*, 1:22–25. Elizabeth Cabot Cary (1822–1907) came from Boston's highest social stratum. Although her parents were not among the wealthiest Cabots and Carys, they enjoyed a privileged life thanks to the generosity of the maternal grandfather, Thomas Perkins. She had only one year of postprimary education in Elizabeth Peabody's progressive school. After that, she studied at home. She met Louis Agassiz through her older sister, who in 1846 had married Cornelius Felton, Harvard's professor of Greek. Marriages between Harvard professors and Boston Brahmins occurred often. Louis Agassiz was fifteen years her senior; after his death in 1873, when she was fifty-one years old, Elizabeth—who never remarried—lent her name to various worthy causes, becoming almost by chance an advocate for the establishment of Radcliffe College and then its first president. In its first decades Radcliffe was a prestigious teachers' college rather than an institution for the socially elite.
2. Women's scientific support of their male kin has been studied, for English botany, by Shteir in "Botany in the Breakfast Room" and *Cultivating Women*.
3. The only comparable woman in England might be Jane Loudon (1807–1858), spouse of John Loudon, a well-known English botanist and horticulturalist. She made a career by writing popular plant books for ladies based on his work.
4. The best account of the school, best because it is not retrospective, comes from Ellen Emerson's letters to her family written while she was a student there.
5. The taxonomic term *radiate*—derived from the classification system of Georges Cuvier (1769–1832), with whom Louis Agassiz had studied—encompasses sea creatures whose anatomical structure radiates from the center: for example, anemones, jellyfish, and starfish. For Alexander Agassiz, see G. R. Agassiz.
6. For details of Louis Agassiz's life, see Lurie, who focuses mainly on his anti-Darwinism and his debate with Asa Gray, Almira Phelps's nemesis and the Harvard botanist who became Darwin's chief scientific advocate in the United States. But, as Numbers (*Darwinism*) has pointed out, Darwin was well received in this country from the first, both by scientists and by the lay public.
7. On the Darwinian controversy in the United States, see Dupree; Lurie; Numbers, *Darwinism*. For Agassiz's views on human speciation see these sources and Gould.
8. Norwood, who inexplicably describes "Actaea" as Elizabeth Agassiz's penname, describes the book as a wonderful example of a true woman's text—that is, one in which, rather than attributing nature's value to its help in developing "reverence for the Creator," "reveres the magical world itself" (23). According to the reading I develop here, in Agassiz this is the difference between a female stress on esthetics and a male stress on reason, not between female earth-worship and male God-worship. I doubt that Norwood means to identify women's writing with writing for children, but the stylistic qualities for which she praises *Actaea* are products of the book's implied audience of young people.
9. On the special generic attributes of nineteenth-century American women's travel writing, see Schriber, who, however, does not discuss Agassiz.

CHAPTER 7   ***Testing Scientific Limits: Emma Willard
and Maria Mitchell***

1. In the 1830s a woman named Mary Griffith achieved a reputation among bee-keepers for her inventions, although her (anonymous) 1836 book attacking Newtonian optics—*Discoveries in Light and Vision*—went unnoticed. Experiments she carried out by shining light on the retinas of dead animals convinced Griffith that the optical image is not inverted on the retina and that white light is not a composite of all colors. She complained that men of science were taking Newton too much on faith (128).

2. According to Stanley, in the eighty-four years between 1809 and 1895 women received 0.75 percent of the primary patents issued by the U.S. government (a total of 3,975 out of more than 535,000); all but 55 date from after 1860 (752). Stanley considers and dismisses the theory that Catherine Greene, not Eli Whitney, invented the cotton gin (796–801). That women did not take out patents, of course, says nothing about their activities behind the scenes.

3. Emma Hart Willard (1787–1870) was born in Berlin, Connecticut, the next youngest (her sister Almira was last) in a farm family of seventeen children. She became a student at the Berlin academy at age fifteen, began teaching there three years later, became preceptress of the female academy in Middlebury, Vermont, in 1808, and married the much older John Willard, a widower with four children, in 1809. In 1814, when John Willard experienced financial problems, she opened a girls' school in their home. Five years later she wrote "A Plan for Improving Female Education," hoping to persuade the New York State legislature to endow a female academy. She failed, but her arguments attracted interest in the city of Troy. Funding from the city council allowed her to open the Troy Female Seminary in 1821. She headed the school until 1838, when she turned it over to her son, John Hart Willard. Her history texts, especially *The Republic of America*, brought her fame and fortune. She made a disastrous second marriage in 1838 (John Willard had died in 1825) and won a divorce decree from the Connecticut legislature in 1843. After working with Henry Barnard on improving the Connecticut common schools, she returned to Troy in 1844. Only Lord, among many analysts and critics, devotes space to her scientific theories and ambitions. For other aspects of her multiform career see Baym, *Feminism* 121–135; *Emma Willard and Her Pupils;* Fowler; Lutz; Scott, 37–88. For Willard as geographer, see Calhoun, "Eyes"; for technology at Troy Female Seminary, see Stevens.

4. For the place of history in women's education, see Baym, *American Women Writers*, especially 1–28, 46–66.

5. A huge critical literature has recently emerged analyzing the role of geography (more specifically, maps) in establishing nations and national subjectivities. Willard saw her role as republican instructor to be that of enforcing U.S. national self-awareness among the citizenry. For the role of maps in U.S. nation formation, see Bruckner.

6. Willard also published a pamphlet in 1861, apparently written by request for the *U.S. Journal of Homeopathy*, called *Theory of Circulation by Respiration: Synopsis of Its Principles and History*. And she wrote letters to diverse medical journals of the day countering criticisms of her theory.

7. There is an uncharacteristic hint of humor in this pun.

8. One of Willard's last publications was an astronomy textbook. Unable to restrict herself wholly to pedagogy, she devises a new name for the subject and includes an original solution (in a footnote) to the intractable problem of the tides (*Astronography,* 160).

9. Maria Mitchell (1818–1889), a Nantucket native, was one of ten children. As an avocation, her father, William Mitchell, made astral observations for the Nantucket whaling fleet. Maria Mitchell helped him from childhood. Later, the two of them (as well as a brother, Henry Mitchell) worked for the U.S. Coast Survey. She never married. Living with her family in Nantucket, she first opened a school, then served as librarian for the Nantucket Athenaeum and contributed computations to Charles Henry Davis's *American Ephemeris and Nautical Almanac,* "a publication designed to render the government the most efficient source of navigational information" (Miller, Voss, and Hussey, 43). After her mother's death in 1861, she kept house with her father, first in Lynn, Massachusetts, and then in Poughkeepsie when she became Vassar's professor of astronomy in 1865. She retired from Vassar in 1888 and returned to Lynn, where she died the next year. Critics disagree whether or not she remained a researcher after accepting the Vassar appointment; according to Wright, "she pioneered in the daily photography of sunspots and faculae" ("Maria Mitchell," 556); but Deborah Warner says her work "was in fact trivial," because she "carried out no organized or sophisticated observing program [and] framed no hypotheses" (*Graceanna Lewis*, 83). For biography, see Dorothy Keller; Kendall; Wright, *Sweeper* and "Maria Mitchell").

10. For the Lazzaroni, see especially Bruce; Miller, Voss, and Hussey; Odgers; and Slotten. The Lazzaroni, a loosely knit and often fractious group, centered on Alexander Dallas Bache, superintendent of the U.S. Coast Survey and eventually a founder and first president of the National Academy of Sciences, and Joseph Henry, secretary of the Smithsonian Institution. Their aims were to establish a national scientific university, involve the national government in the support of science, raise the prestige of science by distinguishing between "quacks" and professional scientists, and form an academy whose membership would recognize scientific accomplishment and thereby control access to scientific patronage. The first of these aims was not fulfilled, but the others were.

11. For numeracy in the early republic and antebellum years, see Cohen. The most important work of original science in the early republic was the *New American Practical Navigator* (1802), by self-taught Salemite Nathaniel Bowditch, who also had translated Laplace.

12. The *Lady's Book*, which at this point opposed gender-neutral instruction (see chapter 3), may well have been targeting Mitchell specifically here.

13. The first was Rebecca Pennell, who taught physics and natural history at Antioch but did not publish and is not known to have done original science. Dorothy Keller has identified some 110 women appointed to various academic college positions between 1850 and 1900, mostly after 1890, and with humanists and social scientists outnumbering scientists by a ratio of 7 to 3 (2, 4). This makes a total of

thirty-three women academic scientists (not all of them appointed as professors) by 1900.

14. The journal in which this article appeared, *Hours at Home,* was folded into the *Century,* which in turn was folded into *Scribner's.*

CHAPTER 8   *Emily Dickinson and Scientific Skepticism*

1. The ubiquity of scientific information in the culture tells against critical claims for Dickinson's extraordinary scientific knowledge—for example, Wolff's assertion that her knowledge of science was "astonishingly broad" (80) or Fred White's that she had an "amazingly comprehensive scientific and technical vocabulary" (121). Sewall says her "knowledge of chemical process, of botanic and especially geologic lore" goes "far beyond the usual nature poet's stock in trade" (345)— an observation perhaps more relevant to the question of whether she is a nature poet than to her use of scientific materials. Not all critics agree that the poetry demonstrates any scientific depth. Rebecca Patterson, who says the poetry shows a "strong intellectual, if untrained, interest in science" (113), traces almost all Dickinson's scientific allusions to Peter Parley's primary school geography (141). St. Armand—who is interested in the signs of popular culture in Dickinson's work and does not think of science as part of popular culture—calls Dickinson a sentimental nature poet whose work rejects elite scientific rigor and specificity (181– 206). Howard, comparing her to other poets of the day *contra* Sewall, finds a standard scientific vocabulary in her work that she might have cribbed from other poets rather than from scientific sources. Watters attributes her scientific references to her reading of Emerson.

2. For Dickinson's life, I use Sewall, Wolff, Leyda, and her correspondence as edited by Thomas H. Johnson.

3. Franklin counts 1,789 poems against Johnson's 1,775; the difference in these numbers affects the percentage by a tenth of a percent. Because scholarship is currently in the process of moving from Johnson's to Franklin's numbering system and text, I use Franklin's texts but cite both numbers: first Franklin's, then Johnson's preceded by J. For a full discussion of the history of Dickinson's texts and the editorial problems they present, see Franklin, *Variorum,* 1:1–43. See also Christianne Miller, Domhnall Mitchell, Smith.

    Fred White, the one earlier critic to have counted and categorized Dickinson's poetry of science, classifies 171 poems under the rubrics of astronomy, botany, chemistry, geology, mathematics, medicine, physics, physiology, and a catchall "general science." But no number can finally be fixed, because it depends on both the critic's own scientific acuity and a series of judgment calls. Rebecca Patterson, Sewall, Sherwood, and Watters, for example, find science in poems that White omits; Patterson and Sewall also discount poems that White includes (for example, they attribute Dickinson's gem vocabulary not to the mineralogy or geology to which White ascribes it, but to her favorite chapter in Revelations; my count also excludes the gem poems).

4. For the ocular sciences in Dickinson and a theorized connection between her tropes of vision and her eye disease, see Greg Johnson.

5. See, e.g., Farr, Guthrie, Howard, Orsini, Patterson, St. Armand, Sewall, Sherwood, Uno, Watters, Fred White, and Wolff.

6. For Hitchcock, see his *Reminiscences*; Guralnick, "Geology"; Gloria Robinson; Sewall, 342–357 passim.

7. Women students, however, were taught mainly by women in the girl's department. Several of these women had studied at Mount Holyoke.

8. The much recited aphorism of early second-wave feminist poet Audre Lorde—that the master's tools would never dismantle the master's house—does not fit Dickinson's project, for which no other tools than the master's could possibly do the job. Her refusal to accept what might now be called "difference feminism" as the basis of a poesis may, obliquely, have qualified her for inclusion in the canon in an era when the specifically feminine was anathema to literary critics. Consequently, a desire to neutralize a masculine reading of the poet may be part of the motivation behind recent celebrations of her same-sex emotional life.

9. In the twentieth century, Mount Holyoke—which did not become a college until 1893—produced "more women who went on for doctorates in the physical sciences from 1910 to 1969, more women who obtained doctorates in chemistry from 1920 to 1980, and more women listed in the 1938 *American Men of Science* than any other undergraduate institution" (Shmurak and Handler, 315). For Lyon's life, see Elizabeth Green; Hitchcock, *Power* and *Reminiscences*; Shmurak and Handler.

10. For textbooks used at Mount Holyoke, see Capps, Lowenberg.

11. My own speculation, based on the fact that Mount Holyoke was equally devoted to producing teachers for the home market and foreign missionaries (Elizabeth Green, 260–265 and passim), conjoined with Dickinson's lifelong prodigality of geographical reference, is that she may have fantasized about becoming a missionary and journeying to faraway places. This was a powerful motivation for many young women, not only in Dickinson's time but until fairly recently, when women's opportunities for traveling were so limited. Throughout her poetry, Dickinson employs geographical allusions both aggressively and defensively to represent the mind's creative powers when faced with an impoverished external environment.

12. The tradition that she was the only student to resist the pressure to convert seems to be inaccurate; apparently some thirty students held out.

13. For more on Dickinson's parents, see Pollak.

14. For a collection of the poems sent to Susan, see Hart and Smith. On Dickinson and mathematics more generally, see Stonum.

15. But there is no external evidence that Dickinson read any work of Hitchcock's or attended any of his lectures or sermons.

16. For the Rochester (or Hydesville) rappings, see chapter 11. If Hitchcock's idea was not her provocation, it is also irrelevant to propose that she writes about it with "a touch of irony" (Sewall, 346; see also Uno). Confusingly, Johnson's edition indexes this poem topically under conservation of energy, not matter.

17. Thanks to Tim Dean for this reading.

CHAPTER 9   *The Sciences in Women's Novels*

1. I must stress, therefore—I return briefly to this point at the end of the chapter—that the absence of science in women's novels says little about the presence of women in the sciences, or their presence in modes of writing that would increasingly be denoted "expository" and therefore "noncreative." Especially when high-flown rhetoric became the women's chosen belletristic style, utilitarian women writers abandoned belles lettres just as women scientists abandoned literature altogether. At a moment when the culture is limiting "literature" to the genres of fiction, poetry, and drama rather than letters more broadly interpreted, belletristic writing cannot be studied as representative of the whole cultural field.

2. In 1868 Evans married Lorenzo Wilson and thereafter published as Augusta Evans Wilson. Because recent reissues of her novels call her Augusta Evans, I will use that name here.

3. For "real" women's reading habits, see especially Baym, *Woman's Fiction* and "Women's Novels"; Richard Brown; Bushman; Gilmore; Susan Harris, "Responding"; Zboray.

4. The Scotsman Hugh Miller's *Footprints of the Creator* (1847) was a popular and influential attempt to reconcile geology with the biblical account of creation.

5. For discussion of early career novels as *Bildungsromane* and *Kunstlerromane* combined, see Huf.

CHAPTER 10   *Women of Letters and Medical Science*

1. Kett estimates that no more than 27 percent of doctors practicing between 1790 and 1840 had studied in medical curricula (23). Morantz-Sanchez says that the curricula of traditional universities were weakened by competition for medical students that included setting entrance requirements low and offering abbreviated programs. Students graduated in some cases after no more than a year of course work (30; see also Bruce, 6; Garrison; Rothstein, 181; Starr, 4, 5; Shryock). Only those with the funds to study in Zurich, London, Vienna, or Paris could have clinical experience with a wide range of diseases.

2. Pasteur (1822–1885) did his work on fermentation in the 1860s; Koch (1843–1910) identified the bacteria responsible for anthrax in 1876, wound infections in 1878, tuberculosis in 1882, and Asiatic cholera in 1884. Standard histories of science exclude medicine from their accounts (e.g., Bruce, 6).

3. Thomsonianism carried forward age-old traditions of herbal healing. Books of herbal advice and recipes sold exceedingly well throughout the century; publicity for diverse therapies and cure-all medicines figured prominently in popular print culture. Magnetism, or mesmerism, had a vogue before the Civil War; it justified itself on scientific grounds by claiming to harness electromagnetism for curative purposes (see Fuller, *Mesmerism*). Phrenology—which inferred character traits from configurations of the skull—involved a moral rather than a medical rhetoric; although the field's assignment of traits to cranial "bumps" proved entirely erroneous, the belief that behaviors correlated with specific sites in the brain foreran various initiatives in neurology and neuropsychology (see John

Davies, Stern). Louisa Folger Fowler, of the firm of Fowler and Wells, also published a textbook on anatomy, physiology, and phrenology. For alternative therapies and associated pseudosciences (practices differentiated even at the time from science proper), see Fuller, *Alternative*, and the essays in Gevitz; on hydropathy, Cayleff and Donegan; on homeopathy, Kaufman. Two women's novels satirizing the range of medical fashion are Hannah Gardner Creamer's delightful *Delia's Doctors* (1852) and Alice Cary's *Married, Not Mated* (1856).

4. A number of feminist scholars discuss nineteenth-century invalidism as a socially constructed female condition or a quasi-hysterical expression of anger and frustration. These are reasonable approaches—invalidism is an excellent evasive strategy, and many women's lives were painfully empty. But there seems to be no doubt that an enormous amount of the recorded suffering of nineteenth-century men, women, and children was somatically "real," that is, many people were often, and seriously, sick or injured. And, if the female invalid is a social construction, what of the female who carries out the demanding and often unpleasant labor of caring for the sick?

5. For antebellum abortion and Madame Restell, see Browder, Allan Keller, Mohr. For abortion in the years between criminalization and *Roe v. Wade*, see Reagan.

6. For health reform, see Verbrugge, Whorton. The number of women doctors dropped 35 percent between 1894 and 1909 and declined another 25 percent between 1909 and 1912 (Walsh, 186). Sartisky (315—combining figures from Ehrenreich and English, Starr, and Walsh) says the percentage of women doctors in Boston dropped from 18.2 percent of the total in 1900 to 8.7 percent in 1930.

7. The one novel I know of in which a woman doctor actually works in a laboratory (her private home laboratory) is by a man—it is Henry James's *The Bostonians*. Most criticism of that novel assumes that James's desexualized Dr. Mary Prance is a hostile satire (Donovan, "Nan Prince," 26; Graham, 154). I disagree.

8. Wittenberg mentions these three memoirs with an emphasis on motifs of piety, women's rights conservatism, and personal exceptionalism, which she reads as attempts to neutralize objections to the transgressive career choice (126–127).

9. Blistering raised a blister on the skin that, when it became infected, was thought to be draining the body of diseased fluids. Mercurials produced vomiting or diarrhea. The term *leeches* encompassed a range of blood-letting procedures.

10. Although Combe was a phrenologist, *The Constitution of Man* is not phrenological. If the "laws of life" theory invited people to take control of their health away from doctors, it also freed them from the theological dictum that pain and disease ought to be accepted as God's punishments for sin. The orthodox went so far as to oppose anesthesia, when it was introduced in 1847, as an attempt to thwart God's dictum that women would bring forth children in pain and suffering.

11. Morris proposes that "Dr. Zay" alludes to Zakrzweska, whose name was typically abbreviated to "Zak" (151, n. 1).

12. Crumpacker interprets Jewett's ideal of doctoring as a holistic denial of the mind-body split, which would be an advanced approach for its time (165).

13. Cinchona is a genus of shrub whose bark is used for medicines such as quinine.

Dr. Zay is a homeopath. Yorke consents to being cared for by her (although actually he has no choice) because his mother consults only homeopaths. The romance transfers the son from mother to wife, showing that Dr. Zay's science is inseparable from her maternal femininity (Bender, 92–97).

14. Morris, however, interprets Dr. Zay as a woman of science, not sentiment (144). He notes her anti-abortion stand but does not interpret it as the commitment to women that Phelps says it is.

15. Jewett's social Darwinism is not eugenicist. On the contrary, doctoring tries to salvage damaged lives that have been brought into existence unwisely. It also works to instruct people how to produce healthier babies in the future by safeguarding their own health. As the orphan child of an alcoholic mother who fled to the big city and died early, Nan herself might be a good candidate for a eugenicist purge. Only Dr. Leslie's careful supervision, disciplining her impulses and helping her turn unruly energies toward worthy ends, rescues Nan from her mother's fate. Bender reads *A Country Doctor* as a reply to Edward H. Clarke's infamous *Sex in Education*, an 1873 tract distorting Darwin's 1871 *Descent of Man* into an argument against higher education for women.

16. For a popular biography of Jacobi, see Truax. See also Jacobi, *Life and Letters*, introduction to *Pathfinder*; Lubove, 263–265.

CHAPTER 11   *Spiritual Science*

1. For science studies, feminist constructionist, and ecofeminist critiques of science, see the bibliographical notes to chapter 1. Especially relevant to my point here are essays in Bleier; essays in Gergen, especially Hubbard; Haraway; Harding, *Science Question* and *Whose Science?;* Evelyn Keller, "Gender/Science System" and *Reflections;* King, "Ecological Feminism"; Kolodny; Latour; Longino; Mackay; Mellor; Merchant; Noble; Norwood; Pratt, "Scratches" and *Imperial*; Schiebinger, *Mind* and *Nature's Body*; essays in Tuana; Wertheim.

2. Ahlstrom perceives Spiritualism as a precursor to diverse "New Age" religious phenomena; see also Albanese. For Christian Science, see especially Fuller, *Alternative Medicine*; Gill; Gottschalk; Podmore, *From Mesmer*; Thomas. For Ellen White and Seventh-Day Adventism see Nichol; Numbers, *Prophetess* and *Darwinism*. For Spiritualism, see especially Ahlstrom; Braude; Slater Brown; Carroll; Goldsmith; Houdini; Moore; Podmore, *Mediums*.

3. Page references are to this edition. For Eddy, in addition to works parenthetically cited, see Lindley; Parker, "Mary Baker Eddy" and *Mind Cure*; Schrager; and Douglas, whose *Terrible Honesty* makes Eddy a paradigm of nineteenth-century cultural feminization—the supposedly dominant Victorian matriarchy—that the moderns strove to overcome (e.g., 6–7). Douglas concedes, however, that in many cases the Christian Scientist "was assuming responsibility for her own health" (138). She also connects Christian Science, as a form of mind cure, to developments in psychology and psychoanalysis.

4. Unlike Mary Baker Eddy, Emerson clearly exaggerated for rhetorical effect. And, also unlike her in the most emphatic way, he resisted all attempts of would-be followers to form a personality cult around him.

5. Even elite media like the *New York Times* have identified the purposes of decoding the human genome as the establishment of genetic bases for disease and the discovery of appropriate cures. (The *Times* has also revised its Tuesday "Science Times" section into a "Science and Health Times," with health articles occupying more than half the space.)

6. A powerful polemic against Christian Science medical theology is Fraser.

7. Especially as a young woman, White went into trance states in public (see Nichol, 51–57); but of course nobody but she saw her visions. Some visions seem to have been soundless pictures, while others included messengers and messages.

8. My summary of White's health initiatives comes from Numbers, *Ellen G. White.*

9. Early in her career, Mary Baker Eddy had advertised for patients and students in Spiritualist journals; but as a Christian Scientist she excoriated Spiritualism for its belief in some kind of attenuated, yet real, materiality in the spirit world. For her part, Ellen White opposed Spiritualism because she found no scriptural authority for spirit appearances at that historical juncture.

10. In an odd conjunction of histories, the individual who seems to have invented the spirit-rapping system—that is, who proposed that the spirits might communicate by rapping out a specific number of times for specific answers—was the renegade Quaker Isaac Post, husband of Amy Post, who counseled and supported Harriet Jacobs when she composed the narrative eventually published as *Incidents in the Life of a Slave Girl.*

11. Hardinge said that eleven million Americans were practicing Spiritualists. Others proposed lower figures—three to four million. In fact, not even a roughly accurate estimate of the number of adherents is possible. There are no membership rolls. Should the mediums "count" as clergy? There is no way to know how many mediums there were, all told. Are those who once or twice tried to reach the spirits in their homes to be counted? Are those who played with the ouija board on occasion to be considered bona fide Spiritualists? Are those who once attended a public mediumistic performance or visited a medium in her rooms for a private seance to be included? If those who favored Spiritualism would likely exaggerate its prevalence, so would those who opposed it. What can be said with confidence is that the traces of Spiritualism are ubiquitous in the nineteenth-century cultural record after 1848.

12. Spiritualist cosmogony drew from the perfectionist writings of Immanuel Swedenborg, whose work also influenced the Transcendentalists. Swedenborg said that he made many guided visits to the spirit world. His work was popularized in lectures and writings by Andrew Jackson Davis (1826–1910) of Poughkeepsie, New York, who also regularly visited the country he influentially called the "summerland." (See especially his *Death and the After-Life.*) Davis's writings also offered a huge array of scientific facts; evolution, geology, and any historical view of natural process fitted well with the Spiritualist belief in a progression toward perfection that was not terminated by death.

13. Ether is making a comeback. An article in the February 2, 1999, *New York Times* titled "Ether Re-emerges as the Je Ne Sais Quoi of Physics" explains why many physicists now think some kind of substance may fill space.

WORKS CITED

Abir-Am, Pnina, and Dorinda Outram, eds. *Uneasy Careers and Intimate Lives: Women in Science, 1789–1979.* New Brunswick: Rutgers University Press, 1987.

Ackmann, Martha. "Biographical Studies of Dickinson." In Grabher et al., *The Emily Dickinson Handbook,* 11–23.

Agassiz, Elizabeth. "A Cruise through the Galapagos." *Atlantic Monthly* 31 (1873): 579–584.

———. *Actaea: A First Lesson in Natural History.* 2d ed. Boston: D. C. Heath, 1888.

———. "A Dredging Excursion in the Gulf Stream." *Atlantic Monthly* 24 (1869): 507–516.

———. "In the Straits of Magellan." *Atlantic Monthly* 31 (1873): 89–95.

———. *Louis Agassiz: His Life and Correspondence.* Boston: Houghton Mifflin, 1885.

Agassiz, Elizabeth, and Alexander Agassiz. *Seaside Studies in Natural History. Marine Animals of Massachusetts Bay: Radiates.* Boston: Houghton Mifflin, 1865.

Agassiz, Elizabeth, and Louis Agassiz. *A Journey in Brazil.* Boston: Ticknor and Fields, 1868.

Agassiz, G. R. *Letters and Recollections of Alexander Agassiz.* Boston: Houghton Mifflin, 1913.

Agassiz, Louis. *Contributions to the Natural History of the United States of America.* 4 vols. 1857–1860. Reprint, New York: Arno Press, 1978.

———. *Geological Sketches.* Boston: James R. Osgood, 1871.

———. *Geological Sketches, Second Series.* Boston: James Osgood, 1875.

———. *Methods of Study in Natural History.* Boston: James R. Osgood, 1863.

Ahlstrom, Sydney E. *A Religious History of the American People.* New Haven: Yale University Press, 1972.

Albanese, Catherine. *Nature Religion in America: From the Algonkian Indians to the New Age.* Chicago: University of Chicago Press, 1990.

Alcott, Louisa May. *Work: A Story of Experience.* 1873. Reprint, New York: Schocken, 1977.

Allen, David Elliston. *The Naturalist in Britain: A Social History.* Princeton: Princeton University Press, 1994.

Allen, John L. "Working the West: Public Land Policy, Exploration, and the

Preacademic Evolution of American Geography." In Blouet, *Origins of Academic Geography,* 57–68.

Apple, Rima D. "'Liberal Arts or Vocational Training': Home Economics Education for Girls." In Stage and Vincenti, *Rethinking Home Economics,* 79–95.

"Aquariums." *Godey's Lady's Book* 54 (1857): 525–527; 55 (1857): 45–47; 56 (1858): 51–54.

Banner, Lois W. *American Beauty.* Chicago: University of Chicago Press, 1983.

Barber, Lynn. *The Heyday of Natural History.* Garden City, N.Y.: Doubleday, 1980.

Barnard, Henry, ed. *Educational Biography: Memoirs of Teachers and Educators.* New York: F. C. Brownell, 1861.

Baym, Nina. *American Women Writers and the Work of History, 1790–1860.* New Brunswick: Rutgers University Press, 1995.

———. "English Nature, New York Nature, and *Walden's* New England Nature." In Charles Capper and Conrad Wright, eds., *Transient and Permanent: The Transcendentalist Movement and Its Contexts,* 168–189. Boston: Massachussetts Historical Society, 1999.

———. *Feminism and American Literary History: Essays.* New Brunswick: Rutgers University Press, 1992.

———. "From Enlightenment to Victorian: Toward a Narrative of American Women Writers Writing History." In Baym, *Feminism,* 105–120.

———. *Novels, Readers, and Reviewers: Responses to Fiction in Antebellum America.* Ithaca, N.Y.: Cornell University Press, 1984.

———. "Onward, Christian Women: Sarah J. Hale's History of the World." *New England Quarterly* 63 (1990): 249–270.

———. "Sarah Hale, Political Writer." In Baym, *Feminism,* 167–182.

———. *Woman's Fiction: A Guide to Novels by and about Women in America, 1820–1870.* 2d ed. Urbana: University of Illinois Press, 1992.

———. "Women and the Republic: Emma Willard's Rhetoric of History." In Baym, *Feminism,* 121–135.

———. "Women's Novels and Women's Minds: An Unsentimental View of Nineteenth-Century American Women's Fiction." *Novel* 31 (1998): 335–350.

Beard, James Franklin. "Cooper, Susan Augusta Fenimore." In James, *Notable American Women,* 1:382–383.

Beaver, Donald de B. *The American Scientific Community, 1800–1860: A Statistical-Historical Study.* New York: Arno Press, 1980.

Beecher, Catharine E. *Educational Reminiscences and Suggestions.* New York: J. B. Ford, 1874.

———. *Letters to the People on Health and Happiness.* New York: Harper and Brothers, 1855.

———. *A Treatise on Domestic Economy, for the Use of Young Ladies at Home and at School.* 1841. Reprint, New York: Shocken, 1977.

———. *Woman Suffrage and Woman's Profession.* Hartford: Brown and Gross, 1871.

Beecher, Catharine E., and Harriet Beecher Stowe. *The American Woman's Home; or, Principles of Domestic Science.* 1869. Reprint, Hartford: Stowe-Day Foundation, 1975.

———. *Principles of Domestic Science: As Applied to the Duties and Pleasures of*

Home. A Text-Book for the Use of Young Ladies in Schools, Seminaries, and Colleges. New York: J. B. Ford, 1870.

Beer, Gillian. *Darwin's Plots: Evolutionary Narrative in Darwin, George Eliot, and Nineteenth-Century Fiction.* 2d ed. Cambridge: Cambridge University Press, 2000.

Belisle, D[avid] W. "Celestial Phenomena." *Godey's Lady's Book* 48 (1854): 60–62, 131–133, 233–234, 315–317, 403, 404, 504, 506; 49 (1854): 28–30, 129–130, 237, 333–334, 407–408, 512–513.

Bender, Bert. "Darwin and 'The Natural History of Doctresses': The Sex War between Howells, Phelps, Jewett, and James." *Prospects* 18 (1993): 81–120.

Bendixon, Alfred. Introduction to *The Amber Gods and Other Stories by Harriet Prescott Spofford.* New Brunswick: Rutgers University Press, 1989.

Benjamin, Marina. "Elbow Room: Women Writers on Science, 1790–1840." In Benjamin, *Science and Sensibility,* 27–59.

———. Introduction to Benjamin, *Science and Sensibility,* 1–23.

———, ed. *Science and Sensibility: Gender and Scientific Enquiry, 1780–1945.* Oxford: Basil Blackwell, 1991.

———, ed. *A Question of Identity: Women, Science, and Literature.* New Brunswick: Rutgers University Press, 1993.

Bergmann, Linda S. "A Troubled Marriage of Discourses: Science Writing and Travel Narrative in Louis and Elizabeth Agassiz's *A Journey in Brazil." Journal of American Culture* 18 (1995): 83–88.

———. "Elizabeth Cary Agassiz." In James Schramer and Donald Ross, eds., *Dictionary of Literary Biography,* vol. 189, 12–17. Detroit: Gale Research, 1998.

———. "Widows, Hacks, and Biographers: The Voice of Professionalism in Elizabeth Agassiz's *Louis Agassiz: His Life and Correspondence." Auto\Biography Studies* 12 (1997): 1–21.

Bevier, Isabel. *Home Economics in Education.* Philadelphia: J. B. Lippincott, 1924.

Bevier, Isabel, and Susannah Usher. *The Home Economics Movement.* Part 1. Boston: Whitcomb and Bartows, 1906.

Biagioli, Mario, ed. *The Science Studies Reader.* New York: Routledge, 1999.

Bianchi, Martha Dickinson. *Emily Dickinson Face to Face.* Boston: Houghton Mifflin, 1932.

Biester, Charlotte E. "Prelude—Catharine Beecher." *Journal of Home Economics* 51 (1959): 549–551.

Bigelow, Jacob. *The Useful Arts, Considered in Connexion with the Applications of Science.* 2 vols. Boston: Marsh, Capen, Lyon, and Webb, 1829.

Blackwell, Elizabeth. *The Laws of Life, with Special Reference to the Physical Education of Girls.* New York: George P. Putnam, 1852.

———. *Pioneer Work in Opening the Medical Profession to Women: Autobiographical Sketches.* 1895. Reprint, New York: Schocken, 1977.

Blake, John B. "Nichols, Mary Sargent Neal Gove." In James, *Notable American Women,* 2:627–629.

Bledstein, Burton J. *The Culture of Professionalism: The Middle Class and the Development of Higher Education in America.* New York: W. W. Norton, 1976.

Bleier, Ruth, ed. *Feminist Approaches to Science.* New York: Pergamon, 1986.

Blouet, Brian W., ed., with Teresa L. Stitcher. *The Origins of Academic Geography in the United States*. Hamden, Conn.: Archon Books, 1981.

Blumin, Stuart M. *The Emergence of the Middle Class: Social Experience in the American City, 1760–1900*. Cambridge: Cambridge University Press, 1989.

Bolzau, Emma Lydia. *Almira Hart Lincoln Phelps: Her Life and Work*. Philadelphia: University of Pennsylvania Press, 1936.

Bordo, Susan R. *The Flight to Objectivity: Essays on Cartesianism and Culture*. Albany: SUNY Press, 1987.

Botting, Douglas. *Humboldt and the Cosmos*. New York: Harper and Row, 1973.

Bowen, Margarita. *Empiricism and Geographical Thought: From Francis Bacon to Alexander von Humboldt*. Cambridge: Cambridge University Press, 1981.

Boydston, Jeanne, Mary Kelley, and Anne Margolis. *The Limits of Sisterhood: The Beecher Sisters on Women's Rights and Women's Sphere*. Chapel Hill: University of North Carolina Press, 1988.

Bozeman, Theodore Dwight. *Protestants in an Age of Science: The Baconian Ideal and Antebellum American Religious Thought*. Chapel Hill: University of North Carolina Press, 1977.

Braude, Ann. *Radical Spirits: Spiritualism and Women's Rights in Nineteenth-Century America*. Boston: Beacon Press, 1989.

Brodhead, Richard H. *Cultures of Letters: Scenes of Reading and Writing in Nineteenth-Century America*. Chicago: University of Chicago Press, 1993.

Browder, Clifford. *The Wickedest Woman in New York: Madame Restell, the Abortionist*. Hamden, Conn.: Archon Books, 1988.

Brown, Marjorie M. *Philosophical Studies of Home Economics in the United States: Our Practical-Intellectual Heritage*. 2 vols. East Lansing: Michigan State University Press, 1985.

Brown, Richard D. *Knowledge Is Power: The Diffusion of Information in Early America, 1700–1865*. New York: Oxford University Press, 1989.

Brown, Slater. *The Heyday of Spiritualism*. New York: Hawthorne Books, 1970.

Bruce, Robert V. *The Launching of Modern American Science, 1846–1876*. New York: Knopf, 1987.

Bruckner, Martin. "Lessons in Geography: Maps, Spellers, and Other Grammars of Nationalism in the Early Republic." *American Quarterly* 51 (1999): 311–343.

Budewig, Flossie Caroline. *Origins and Development of the Home Economics Idea*. Ann Arbor: University Microfilms, 1957.

Buell, Lawrence. *The Environmental Imagination: Thoreau, Nature Writing, and the Formation of American Culture*. Cambridge: Harvard University Press, 1995.

Burritt, Elijah H. *The Geography of the Heavens, and Class-book of Astronomy*. New York: Mason Brothers, 1856.

Burstyn, Joan N. "Catharine Beecher and the Education of American Women." *New England Quarterly* 47 (1974): 386–403.

Bushman, Richard L. *The Refinement of America: Persons, Houses, Cities*. New York: Alfred A. Knopf, 1992.

"Butterfly Vivarium." *Godey's Lady's Book* 59 (1859): 310–312.

Calhoun, Daniel H. "Eyes for the Jacksonian World: William C. Woodbridge and Emma Willard." *Journal of the Early Republic* 4 (1984): 1–26.

Cannon, Susan Faye. *Science in Culture: The Early Victorian Period.* New York: Dawson and Science History Publications, 1978.

Capper, Charles. *Margaret Fuller: An American Romantic Life.* New York: Oxford University Press, 1992.

Capps, Jack L. *Emily Dickinson's Reading, 1836–1886.* Cambridge: Harvard University Press, 1966.

Carroll, Bret E. *Spiritualism in Antebellum America.* Bloomington: Indiana University Press, 1997.

Carter, Elizabeth. *Memoirs of the Life of Mrs. Elizabeth Carter.* 2 vols. 4th ed. London: James Cawthorn, 1825.

Carver, Marie Negri. *Home Economics as an Academic Discipline: A Short History.* Tucson: University of Arizona Press, 1979.

Cary, Alice. *Married, Not Mated; or, How They Lived at Woodside and Throckmorton Hall.* New York: Derby and Jackson, 1856.

Cayleff, Susan E. *"Wash and Be Healed": The Water-Cure Movement and Women's Health.* Philadelphia: Temple University Press, 1987.

"Chemistry for Youth" ["Chemistry for the Young"]. *Godey's Lady's Book* 46 (1853): 283, 377, 471, 568–569; 47 (1853): 90, 187–188, 252–253, 376, 473, 559; 48 (1854): 81, 185, 279, 566; 49 (1854): 85, 380; 52 (1856): 78, 176, 270, 464, 556, and passim.

Chielens, Edward E. *American Literary Magazines: The Eighteenth and Nineteenth Centuries.* New York: Greenwood Press, 1986.

Cohen, Patricia Cline. *A Calculating People: The Spread of Numeracy in Early America.* Chicago: University of Chicago Press, 1982.

Combe, George. *The Constitution of Man, Considered in Relation to External Objects.* 20th ed., revised and enlarged. New York: Fowler and Wells, 1850.

Conrad, Susan Phinney. *Perish the Thought: Intellectual Women in Romantic America, 1830–1860.* New York: Oxford University Press, 1976.

Cooley, Anna Maria, et al. *Teaching Home Economics.* New York: Macmillan, 1919.

Cooper, James Fenimore. *Pages and Pictures, from the Writings of James Fenimore Cooper, with Notes by Susan Fenimore Cooper.* New York: W. A. Townsend, 1861.

Cooper, Susan Fenimore. "A Dissolving View." In *The Home Book of the Picturesque: or, American Scenery, Art, and Literature,* 79–94. New York: G. P. Putnam, 1852.

———. *Rural Hours.* Edited by Rochelle Johnson and Daniel Patterson. Athens: University of Georgia Press, 1998.

———. *Rural Hours.* Rev. ed., 1887. Reprint, edited by David Jones, Syracuse: Syracuse University Press, 1968.

———, ed. *Country Rambles in England; or, Journal of a Naturalist, by John Knapp.* Buffalo: Phinney, 1853.

———. *The Rhyme and Reason of Country Life.* New York: G. P. Putnam, 1855.

Coultas, Harlan. "Animal and Vegetable Physiology." *Godey's Lady's Book* 51 (1855): 341–342, 412–413, 527–528.

———. "Autumnal Vegetation." *Godey's Lady's Book* 49 (1854): 334–335.

———. "Botanical Geography." *Godey's Lady's Book* 49 (1854): 426–427, 514–515.

———. "The Curiosities of the Vegetable Kingdom." *Godey's Lady's Book* 51 (1855): 12–13, 137–138, 224–225.

————. "Vegetable Physiology." *Godey's Lady's Book* 45 (1852): 136–137, 227–228, 346–347; 46 (1853): 25–26, 145–146, 244–245, 398–399, 403–404, 519–520; 47 (1853): 60–61, 229–230, 341–342, 403–404, 513–514; 48 (1854): 148–149, 232–233; 49 (1854): 258; 50 (1855): 250–251.

————. "Wildflowers." *Godey's Lady's Book* 44 (1853): 373–374, 485–486.

————. "Wildflowers of the Month." *Godey's Lady's Book* 48 (1854): 523–524; 49 (1854): 35–36.

Craig, Hazel T. *The History of Home Economics*. New York: Practical Home Economics Press, 1945.

Creamer, Hannah Gardner. *Delia's Doctors; or, a Glance Behind the Scenes*. New York: Fowler and Wells, 1853.

Cronon, William. *Changes in the Land: Indians, Colonists, and the Ecology of New England*. New York: Hill and Wang, 1983.

————. Introduction to *Uncommon Ground*, 23–56.

————. "The Trouble with Wilderness: Or, Getting Back to the Wrong Nature." In *Uncommon Ground*.

————, ed. *Uncommon Ground: Towards Reinventing Nature*. New York: W. W. Norton, 1995.

Cross, Barbara M. "Beecher, Catherine Esther." In James, *Notable American Women*, 1:121–124.

Crumpacker, Laurie. "The Art of the Healer: Women in the Fiction of Sarah Orne Jewett." *Colby Library Quarterly* 19 (1983): 155–166.

Cummins, Maria Susanna. *The Lamplighter*. Edited by Nina Baym. New Brunswick: Rutgers University Press, 1988.

Cutter, Calvin. *First Book on Anatomy, Physiology, and Hygiene, for Grammar Schools and Families*. Boston: Benjamin B. Mussey, 1848.

Dana, Samuel L. *A Muck Manual for Farmers*. Lowell, Mass.: James P. Walker, 1842.

Daniels, George H. *American Science in the Age of Jackson*. New York: Columbia University Press, 1968.

Davies, Charles. *The Logic and Utility of Mathematics, with the Best Methods of Instruction Explained and Illustrated*. New York: A. S. Barnes, 1850.

Davies, John D. *Phrenology, Fad and Science: A Nineteenth-Century American Crusade*. New Haven: Yale University Press, 1955.

Davis, Andrew Jackson. *Death and the After-Life; Eight Evening Lectures on The Summer-Land*. Boston: Banner of Light Publishing Company, 1865.

Deane, Samuel. *The New-England Farmer; or Georgical Dictionary*. 3d ed. Boston: Wells and Lilly, 1822.

Depew, David and Bruce Weber, eds. *Evolution at a Crossroads*. Cambridge: M.I.T. Press, 1985.

Dick, Thomas. *The Sidereal Heavens, and Other Subjects Connected with Astronomy, as Illustrative of the Character of the Deity and of an Infinity of Worlds*. Philadelphia: E. C. and J. Biddle, 1840.

Dickinson, Emily. *The Complete Poems*. Edited by Thomas H. Johnson. Boston: Little, Brown, 1960.

————. *The Letters of Emily Dickinson*. Edited by Thomas H. Johnson. 3 vols. Cambridge: Harvard University Press, 1958.

———. *The Poems of Emily Dickinson: Reading Edition.* Edited by R. W. Franklin. Cambridge: Harvard University Press, 1998.

———. *The Poems of Emily Dickinson: Variorum Edition.* 9 vols. Edited by R. W. Franklin. Cambridge: Harvard University Press, 1998.

Dingwall, E. J. Introduction to *Modern American Spiritualism,* by Hardinge, ix–xviii.

Donegan, Jane B. *"Hydropathic Highway to Health": Women and Water-Cure in Antebellum America.* Westport, Conn.: Greenwood Press, 1986.

Donovan, Josephine. "Nan Prince and the Golden Apples." *Colby Library Quarterly* 22 (1986): 17–27.

———. *New England Local Color Literature: A Women's Tradition.* New York: Frederick Ungar, 1983.

Doten, Lizzie. *Poems of Progress.* Boston: William White, 1871.

Douglas, Ann. *Terrible Honesty: Mongrel Manhattan in the 1920s.* New York: Farrar, Straus and Giroux, 1995.

Douty, Esther M. *America's First Woman Chemist: Ellen Richards.* New York: Julian Messner, 1961.

Dupree, A. Hunter. *Asa Gray, 1810–1888.* Cambridge: Harvard University Press, 1959.

Eddy, Mary Baker. *Science and Health, with Key to the Scriptures.* 44th ed. Boston: By the author, 1889.

Ehrenreich, Barbara, and Dierdre English. *For Her Own Good: 150 Years of the Experts' Advice to Women.* New York: Anchor, 1978.

Ellul, Jacques. *The Technological Society.* Translated by John Wilkinson. New York: Alfred A. Knopf, 1978.

Emerson, Ellen Tucker. *Letters of Ellen Tucker Emerson.* Edited by Edith E. W. Gregg. Kent, Ohio: Kent State University Press, 1982.

Emerson, George, and Charles L. Flint. *Manual of Agriculture, for the School, the Farm, and the Fireside.* Boston: Swan Brewer and Liteston, 1862.

Emma Willard and Her Pupils; or, Fifty Years of Troy Female Seminary, 1822–1872. New York: Mrs. R. Sage, 1898.

Entrikkin, Isabelle Webb. *Sarah Josepha Hale and Godey's Lady's Book.* Philadelphia: Lancaster, 1946.

Evans, Augusta Jane. *Beulah.* Edited by Elizabeth Fox Genovese. 1859. Reprint, Baton Rouge: Louisiana State University Press, 1992.

———. *Macaria; or, the Altars of Sacrifice.* Edited by Drew Gilpin Faust. 1864. Reprint, Baton Rouge: Louisiana State University Press, 1992.

———. *St. Elmo.* Edited by Diane Roberts. 1866. Reprint, Tuscaloosa: University of Alabama Press, 1992.

Fahnestock, Jeanne. "Accommodating Science: The Rhetorical Life of Scientific Facts." In McRae, *The Literature of Science,* 17–36.

Farr, Judith. *The Passion of Emily Dickinson.* Cambridge: Harvard University Press, 1992.

Faust, Drew Gilpin. Introduction to *Macaria,* by Evans, xiii–xxvi.

Fee, Elizabeth. "Critiques of Modern Science: The Relationship of Feminism to Other Radical Epistemologies." In Bleier, *Feminist Approaches to Science,* 42–56.

Feinstein, Howard M. *Becoming William James.* Ithaca, N.Y.: Cornell University Press, 1984.

Fidler, William Perry. *Augusta Evans Wilson, 1835–1909: A Biography.* University: University of Alabama Press, 1951.

"Fifteen Rules for the Preservation of Health." *Godey's Lady's Book* 63 (1860): 364.

Finch, Robert, and John Elder, eds. *The Norton Book of Nature Writing.* New York: W. W. Norton, 1990.

Finley, Ruth. *The Lady of Godey's: Sarah Josepha Hale.* Philadelphia: Lippincott, 1932.

Fowler, Lydia Folger. *Familiar Lessons on Physiology and Phrenology, for Children and Youth.* 2 vols. New York: Fowler and Wells, 1860.

Fowler, William. "Emma Willard." In Barnard, *Educational Biography,* 125–168.

Fraser, Caroline. *God's Perfect Child: Living and Dying in the Christian Science Church.* New York: Metropolitan Books, 1999.

Fuller, Robert C. *Alternative Medicine and American Religious Life.* New York: Oxford University Press, 1989.

———. *Mesmerism and the American Cure of Souls.* Philadelphia: University of Pennsylvania Press, 1982.

Fulton, Valerie. "Rewriting the Necessary Woman: Marriage and Professionalism in James, Jewett, and Phelps." *Henry James Review* 15 (1994): 242–256.

Gaard, Greta, and Patrick D. Murphy, eds. *Ecofeminist Literary Criticism: Theory, Interpretation, Pedagogy.* Urbana: University of Illinois Press, 1998.

Garrison, Fielding H. *An Introduction to the History of Medicine.* 4th ed. Philadelphia: W. B. Saunders, 1929.

Gates, Barbara T., and Ann B. Shteir. Introduction to *Natural Eloquence,* 3–26.

———, eds. *Natural Eloquence: Women Reinscribe Science.* Madison: University of Wisconsin Press, 1997.

Gergen, Kenneth. "Feminist Critique of Science and the Challenge of Social Epistemology." In Gergen, *Feminist Thought and the Structure of Knowledge,* 27–48.

Gergen, Mary McCanney, ed. *Feminist Thought and the Structure of Knowledge.* New York: New York University Press, 1988.

Gevitz, Norman, ed. *Other Healers: Unorthodox Medicine in America.* Baltimore: Johns Hopkins University Press, 1988.

Giedion, Siegfried. *Mechanization Takes Command: A Contribution to Anonymous History.* New York: Oxford University Press, 1948.

Gill, Gillian. *Mary Baker Eddy.* Reading, Mass.: Perseus Books, 1998.

Gilligan, Carol. *In a Different Voice: Psychological Theory and Women's Development.* Cambridge: Harvard University Press, 1982.

Gillispie, Charles. *The Edge of Objectivity: An Essay in the History of Scientific Ideas.* Princeton: Princeton University Press, 1960.

———. *Genesis and Geology: A Study in the Relations of Scientific Thought, Natural Theology, and Social Opinion in Great Britain, 1790–1850.* New York: Harper, 1959.

Gilmore, William J. *Reading Becomes a Necessity of Life: Material and Cultural Life in Rural New England, 1780–1835.* Knoxville: University of Tennessee Press, 1989.

Glacken, Clarence J. *Traces on the Rhodian Shore: Nature and Culture in Western Thought from Ancient Times to the End of the Eighteenth Century.* Berkeley: University of California Press, 1967.

Glotfelty, Cheryll, and Harold Fromm, eds. *The Ecocriticism Reader: Landmarks in Literary Ecology*. Athens: University of Georgia Press, 1996.

"Godey's Course of Lessons in Drawing." *Godey's Lady's Book* 48 (1854): 36–40, 115–118, 216–217, 323–325, 410–412; 50 (1855): 314–316; 408–409, 515–517; 51 (1855): 417–419; 52 (1856): 119–122, 318–320, 506–507; 53 (1856): 117–119; 54 (1856): 322–324, 506–507; passim into the 1870s.

Goetzmann, William H. *Army Exploration in the American West, 1803–1863*. New Haven: Yale University Press, 1959.

————. *Exploration and Empire: The Explorer and the Scientist in the Winning of the American West*. New York: Alfred A. Knopf, 1966.

Goldsmith, Barbara. *Other Powers: The Age of Suffrage, Spiritualism, and the Scandalous Victoria Woodhull*. New York: Alfred A. Knopf, 1998.

Goodwin, Joan W. "A Kind of Botanic Mania." *Arnoldia* 56 (1996–97): 17–24.

————. *The Remarkable Mrs. Ripley: The Life of Sarah Alden Bradford Ripley*. Boston: Northeastern University Press, 1998.

Gottschalk, Stephen. *The Emergence of Christian Science in American Religious Life*. Berkeley: University of California Press, 1973.

Gould, Stephen Jay. *The Mismeasure of Man*. Rev. ed. New York: W. W. Norton, 1981.

Grabher, Gudrun, Roland Hagenbuchle, and Cristanne Miller, eds. *The Emily Dickinson Handbook*. Amherst: University of Massachusetts Press, 1998.

Graham, Wendy. *Henry James's Thwarted Love*. Stanford: Stanford University Press, 1999.

Gray, Alonzo. *Elements of Chemistry; Containing the Principles of the Science, Both Experimental and Theoretical, Intended as a Text-book for Academies, High Schools, and Colleges*. 2d ed. New York: Mark H. Newman, 1841.

Gray, Alonzo, and C. B. Adams. *Elements of Geology*. New York: Harper and Brothers, 1859.

Gray, Asa. *First Lessons in Botany and Vegetable Physiology*. New York: Ivison and Phinney, 1857.

————. *Manual of the Botany of the Northern United States*. 2d ed. New York: Ivison, Blakeman, Taylor, 1856.

Green, Elizabeth Alden. *Mary Lyon and Mount Holyoke: Opening the Gates*. Boston: University Press of New England, 1979.

Green, Marjorie. "Perception, Interpretation, and the Sciences." In Depew and Weber, *Evolution at a Crossroads*, 1–20.

Greene, John C. "Protestantism, Science, and American Enterprise: Benjamin Silliman's Moral Universe." In Leonard Wilson, *Benjamin Silliman*, 11–28.

Griffith, Mary. *Discoveries in Light and Vision: With a Short Memoir Containing Discoveries in the Mental Faculties*. New York: G. and C. Carvill, 1836.

Guralnick, Stanley M. "Geology and Religion before Darwin: The Case of Edward Hitchcock, Theologian and Geologist (1793–1864)." *Isis* 62 (1972): 529–543.

————. *Science and the Ante-Bellum American College*. Philadelphia: American Philosophical Society, 1975.

Guthrie, James R. *Emily Dickinson's Vision: Illness and Identity in Her Poetry*. Gainesville: University Press of Florida, 1998.

Hale, Sarah J. "Appeal to American Christians on Behalf of the Ladies Medical Missionary Society." *Godey's Lady's Book* 44 (1852): 185–188.

———. "Editor's Table." *Godey's Lady's Book* 16 (1838): 284; 42 (1851): 65–66; 44 (1852): 293–294; 46 (1854): 80, 463; 80 (1870): 347–349; 92 (1876): 90; 95 (1877): 258–259.

———. "Female Education in Spain." *Ladies' Magazine* 1 (1828): 529–534.

———. "Fifty Years of My Life." *Godey's Lady's Book* 95 (1877): 522–523.

———. *Flora's Interpreter: or, The American Book of Flowers and Sentiments.* Rev. ed. Boston: B. B. Mussey, 1850.

———. "Ladies' Mentor." *Godey's Lady's Book* 14 (1837): 46–47, 140.

———. *Ladies' New Book of Cookery: A Practical System for Private Families in Town and Country; with Directions for Carving, and Arranging the Tables for Parties, etc. Also, Preparation of Food for Invalids and for Children.* 5th ed. New York: H. Long and Brother, 1850.

———. "Ladies' Record." *Ladies' Magazine* 6 (1833): 142, 176, 552–556; 9 (1836): 116–120.

———. Letter to the editor. *Ladies' Magazine* 6 (1833): 227–228.

———. "Literary Notices: Insect Miscellanies." *Ladies' Magazine* 5 (1832): 383–384.

———. "A Page from the Book of Nature." *Ladies' Magazine* 5 (1832): 71–72, 134–136, 172–175.

———. "Review of Darwin's *Origin of Species.*" *Godey's Lady's Book* 60 (1860): 373.

———. "Science and Sentiment." *Ladies' Magazine* 6 (1833): 272–273.

———. "To American Science." *Godey's Lady's Book* 84 (1872): 93.

———. *Woman's Record.* 2d ed. New York: Harper and Brothers, 1855.

Handlin, David P. *The American Home: Architecture and Society, 1815–1915.* Boston: Little, Brown, 1979.

Haraway, Donna. "Situated Knowledges: The Science Question in Feminism and the Privilege of Partial Perspective." In Biagioli, *The Science Studies Reader,* 234–242.

Harding, Sandra. *The Science Question in Feminism.* Ithaca, N.Y.: Cornell University Press, 1986.

———. *Whose Science? Whose Knowledge? Thinking from Women's Lives.* Ithaca, N.Y.: Cornell University Press, 1991.

Hardinge, Emma. *Modern American Spiritualism: A Twenty Years' Record of the Communion between Earth and the World of Spirits.* 1870. Reprint, New Hyde Park, N.Y.: University Books, 1970.

Harris, Susan K. "The Female Imaginary in Harriet Beecher Stowe's *The Minister's Wooing.*" *New England Quarterly* 66 (1993): 179–198.

———. "Responding to the Text(s): Women Readers and the Quest for Higher Education." In Machor, *Readers in History,* 259–282.

Harris, Thaddeus William. *Report on the Insects of Massachusetts, Injurious to Vegetation.* Cambridge: Folsom, Wells, and Thurston, 1841.

Hart, Ellen Louise, and Martha Nell Smith, eds., *Open Me Carefully: Emily Dickinson's Intimate Letters to Susan Huntington Dickinson.* Ashfield, Mass.: Paris Press, 1998.

Harveson, Mae Elizabeth. *Catharine Esther Beecher, Pioneer Educator.* Philadelphia: University of Pennsylvania Press, 1932.

Hawking, Stephen. *A Brief History of Time: From the Big Bang to the Black Hole*. New York: Bantam, 1988.

Hawkins, Hugh. "Elizabeth Cabot Cary Agassiz." In James, *Notable American Women*, 1:22–25.

Hayden, Dolores. *The Grand Domestic Revolution: A History of Feminist Designs for American Homes, Neighborhoods, and Cities*. Cambridge: M.I.T. Press, 1981.

Hedrick, U. P. *A History of Horticulture in America*. New York: Oxford University Press, 1950.

Herschel, John Frederick William. *A Preliminary Discourse on the Study of Natural Philosophy*. Philadelphia: Cary and Lea, 1831.

———, ed. *A Manual of Scientific Enquiry; Prepared for the Use of Her Majesty's Navy: And Adapted for Travellers in General*. London: John Murray, 1849.

Herschel, John (Mrs.). *Memoir and Correspondence of Caroline Herschel*. London: John Murray, 1876.

Higgins, David. "Mabel Loomis Todd." In James, *Notable American Women*, 3:468–469.

Hinckley, C. T. "Everyday Actualities." *Godey's Lady's Book* 44 (1852): 421–426; 45 (1852): 5–9, 117–121, 213–216, 307–314, 403–412; 46 (1853): 3–11, 197–203; 47 (1853): 295–302, 389–394, 489–494; 48 (1854): 5–25, 101–107, 199–207, 295–300, 393–395, 487–494; 49 (1854): 7–15, 103–111, 199–207, 297–306, 393–394, 489–492.

Hitchcock, Edward. *Outline of the Geology of the Globe, and of the United States in Particular*. Boston: Phillips, Sampson, 1853.

———. *The Power of Christian Benevolence Illustrated in the Life and Labors of Mary Lyon*. Northampton, Mass.: Hopkins, Bridgman, 1852.

———. *The Religion of Geology and Its Connected Sciences*. Boston: Philips, Sampson, 1855.

———. *Religious Lectures on Peculiar Phenomena in the Four Seasons, Delivered to the Students in Amherst College, in 1845, 1847, 1848, and 1849*. Amherst: J. S. and C. Adams, 1849.

———. *Reminiscences of Amherst College, Historical Scientific, Biographical and Autobiographical*. Northampton, Mass.: Bridgman and Childs, 1863.

Hitchcock, Edward, and Edward Hitchcock Jr. *Elementary Anatomy and Physiology for Colleges, Academies and Other Schools*. Rev. ed. New York: American Book Company, 1860.

Holstein, Suzy Clark. "'Offering Up Her Life': Confederate Women on the Altars of Sacrifice." *Southern Studies* 2 (1991): 113–130.

Hooper, Lucy. *The Lady's Book of Flowers and Poetry; To Which are Added a Botanical Introduction, A Complete Floral Dictionary, and A Chapter on Plants in Rooms*. New York: Derby and Jackson, 1860.

Houdini, Harry. *A Magician among the Spirits*. New York: Harper and Brothers, 1924.

Hovenkamp, Herbert. *Science and Religion in America, 1800–1860*. Philadelphia: University of Pennsylvania Press, 1978.

Howard, William. "Emily Dickinson's Poetic Vocabulary." *PMLA* 72 (1957): 225–248.

Howitt, William. *The Book of the Seasons; or, The Calendar of Nature*. London: Henry Colburn and Richard Bentley, 1831.

Hubbard, Ruth. "Some Thoughts about the Masculinity of the Natural Sciences." In M. Gergen, *Feminist Thought,* 1–15.

Huf, Linda. *A Portrait of the Artist as a Young Woman: The Writer as Heroine.* New York: Ungar, 1984.

Hufford, David J. "Contemporary Folk Medicine." In Gevitz, *Other Healers,* 228–264.

Hughes, Linda K. "History in Focus, Part 3, 1870." In Herbert F. Tucker, ed., *A Companion to Victorian Literature and Culture,* 35–50. Malden, Mass.: Blackwell, 1999

Humboldt, Alexander von. *Cosmos.* Translated by E. C. Otte. 2 vols. New York: Harpers, 1850.

Hunt, Caroline L. *The Life of Ellen H. Richards.* Boston: Whitcomb and Barrows, 1912.

Hunt, Harriot K. *Glances and Glimpses; or, Fifty Years Social, including Twenty Years Professional Life.* 1856. Reprint, New York: Source Book Press, 1970.

Huth, Hans. *Nature and the Americans: Three Centuries of Changing Attitudes.* Berkeley: University of California Press, 1957.

Irmscher, Christoph. *The Poetics of Natural History: From John Bartram to William James.* New Brunswick: Rutgers University Press, 1999.

[J.D.] "James Watt, Improver of the Steam-Engine." *Godey's Lady's Book* 44 (1852): 241–248.

Jacobi, Mary Putnam. *Life and Letters.* Edited by Ruth Putnam. New York: G. P. Putnam's Sons, 1925.

———. *A Pathfinder in Medicine, with Selections from Her Writings and a Complete Bibliography.* Edited by Women's Medical Association of New York City. New York: G. P. Putnam's Sons, 1925.

James, Edward T., ed. *Notable American Women.* 3 vols. Cambridge: Harvard University Press, 1971.

Jewett, Sarah Orne. *A Country Doctor.* 1884. Reprint, New York: Library of America, 1994.

Johnson, Greg. *Emily Dickinson: Perception and the Poet's Quest.* University: University of Alabama Press, 1985.

Johnson, Thomas Cary, Jr. *Scientific Interests in the Old South.* New York: D. Appleton, 1936.

Kaplan, Amy. "Manifest Domesticity." *American Literature* 70 (1998): 582–606.

Kasson, John F. *Civilizing the Machine: Technology and Republican Values in America, 1777–1900.* New York: Viking, 1976.

Kaufman, Martin. *Homeopathy in America: The Rise and Fall of a Medical Heresy.* Baltimore: Johns Hopkins University Press, 1971.

Keeney, Elizabeth B. *The Botanizers: Amateur Scientists in Nineteenth-Century America.* Chapel Hill: University of North Carolina Press, 1992.

Keller, Allan. *Scandalous Lady: The Life and Times of Madame Restell, New York's Most Notorious Abortionist.* New York: Athenaeum, 1981.

Keller, Dorothy. "Maria Mitchell, An Early Woman Academician." Ph.D. diss., University of Rochester, 1974.

Keller, Evelyn Fox. *A Feeling for the Organism: The Life and Work of Barbara McClintock.* San Francisco: W. H. Freeman, 1983.

————. "The Gender/Science System; or, Is Sex to Gender as Nature Is to Science?" In Biagioli, *The Science Studies Reader,* 234–242.

————. *Reflections on Gender and Science.* New Haven: Yale University Press, 1985.

Kelly, Lori Duin. *The Life and Works of Elizabeth Stuart Phelps, Victorian Feminist Writer.* Troy, N.Y.: Whitston, 1983.

Kendall, Phebe Mitchell, comp. *Maria Mitchell: Life, Letters, and Journals.* Boston: Lee and Shepherd, 1896.

Kerber, Linda K. "Separate Spheres, Female World, Women's Place: The Rhetoric of Women's History." *Journal of American History* 75 (1988): 9–39.

————*Women of the Republic: Intellect and Ideology in Revolutionary America.* Chapel Hill: University of North Carolina Press, 1980.

Kessler, Carol Farley. *Elizabeth Stuart Phelps.* Boston: Twayne, 1982.

Kett, Joseph F. *The Formation of the American Medical Profession: The Role of Institutions, 1780–1860.* New Haven: Yale University Press, 1968.

King, Ynestra. "Toward an Ecological Feminism and a Feminist Ecolology." In Rothschild, *Machina ex Dea,* 118–129.

Kirkland, Caroline. *A New Home—Who'll Follow?* 1847. Reprint, edited by Sandra Zagarell, New Brunswick: Rutgers University Press, 1990.

Knight, David. *The Age of Science: The Scientific World-View in the Nineteenth Century.* Oxford: Basil Blackwell, 1986.

Kohlstedt, Sally Gregory. *The Formation of the American Scientific Community: The American Association for the Advancement of Science, 1848–1890.* Urbana: University of Illinois Press, 1976.

————. "In from the Periphery: American Women in Science, 1830–1880." *Signs* 4 (1978): 81–96.

————. "Maria Mitchell and the Advancement of Women in Science." In Abir-Am and Outram, *Uneasy Careers,* 129–146.

Kolodny, Annette. *The Land before Her: Fantasy and Experience of the American Frontiers, 1630–1860.* Chapel Hill: University of North Carolina Press, 1984.

Kuhn, Thomas. *The Structure of Scientific Revolutions.* 2d ed. Chicago: University of Chicago Press, 1977.

Lardner, Dionysius. *Popular Lectures on Science and Art; Delivered in the Principal Cities and Towns of the United States.* 2 vols. 11th ed. New York: Greeley and McElrath, 1849.

Latour, Bruno. *Science in Action: How to Follow Scientists and Engineers through Society.* Cambridge: Harvard University Press, 1987.

————. *We Have Never Been Modern.* Cambridge: Harvard University Press, 1993.

Latour, Bruno, and Steve Woolgar. *Laboratory Life: The Social Construction of Scientific Facts.* Beverly Hills, Calif.: Sage, 1979.

Leggon, Cheryl B. "The Scientist as Academic." *Daedalus* 126 (1997): 221–244.

Lerner, Gerda. *The Majority Finds Its Past: Placing Women in History.* New York: Oxford University Press, 1979.

Levine, George, ed. *Realism and Representation: Essays on the Problem of Realism in Relation to Science, History, and Culture*. Madison: University of Wisconsin Press, 1993.

Leyda, Jay. *The Years and Hours of Emily Dickinson*. 2 vols. New Haven: Yale University Press, 1960.

Liebig, Justus Freiherr von. *Familiar Letters on Chemistry, and Its Relation to Commerce, Physiology, and Agriculture*. Edited by John Gardner. New York: C. M. Saxton, 1857.

Lindee, M. Susan. "The American Career of Jane Marcet's *Conversations on Chemistry*." *Isis* 82 (1991): 8–23.

Lindley, Susan Hill. "The Ambiguous Feminism of Mary Baker Eddy." *Journal of Religion* 64 (1984): 318–331.

Livingstone, David N. *The Geographical Tradition: Episodes in the History of a Contested Enterprise*. Oxford: Blackwell, 1992.

Longino, Helen E. *Science as Social Knowledge: Values and Objectivity in Scientific Inquiry*. Princeton: Princeton University Press, 1990.

Loomis, Elias. *Elements of Natural Philosophy*. New York: Harper and Brothers, 1858.

———. *Introduction to Practical Astronomy, with A Collection of Astronomical Tables*. New York: Harper and Brothers, 1855.

———. *Recent Progress of Astronomy, Especially in the United States*. New York: Harper and Brothers, 1851.

Lord, John. *The Life of Emma Willard*. New York: D. Appleton, 1873.

Lowell, James Russell. "Agassiz." *Atlantic Monthly* 33 (1874): 586–596.

Lowenberg, Carlton. *Emily Dickinson's Textbooks*. Lafayette, Calif.: Carlton Lowenberg, 1986.

Lubove, Roy. "Mary Corinna Putnam Jacobi." In James, *Notable American Women*, 2:263–265.

Lurie, Edward. *Louis Agassiz: A Life in Science*. Chicago: University of Chicago Press, 1960.

Lutz, Alma. *Emma Willard, Daughter of Democracy*. Boston: Houghton Mifflin, 1929.

Lyman, Theodore. "Recollections of Agassiz." *Atlantic Monthly* 33 (1874): 221–229.

MacDougall, Hugh. "We Know the Hours, What Was the Year?" *James Fenimore Cooper Society Newsletter* 6 (1995): 2.

Machor, James, ed. *Readers in History: Nineteenth-Century American Literature and the Contexts of Response*. Baltimore: Johns Hopkins University Press, 1993.

Mackay, David. *In the Wake of Cook: Exploration, Science, and Empire, 1780–1801*. London: Croom Helm, 1985.

Maddox, Lucy B. "Susan Fenimore Cooper and the Plain Daughters of America." *American Quarterly* 40 (1988): 131–146.

Magner, Lois N. "Women and the Scientific Idiom: Textual Episodes from Wollstonecraft, Fuller, Gilman, and Firestone." *Signs* 4 (1978): 61–80.

Mahan, D[ennis] H[art]. *An Elementary Course of Civil Engineering, For the Use of the Cadets of the United States Military Academy*. New York: Wiley and Putnam, 1837.

Marcet, Jane. *Conversations on Chemistry; On Which the Elements of That Science Are Familiarly Explained and Illustrated by Experiments*. 15th ed. London: Longman, Brown, Green, and Longmans, 1846.

Marcou, Jules. *Life, Letters and Works of Louis Agassiz*. 2 vols. New York: Macmillan, 1896.

Marx, Leo. *The Machine in the Garden: Technology and the Pastoral Ideal in America*. New York: Oxford University Press, 1964.

Masteller, Jean C. "The Woman Doctors of Howells, Phelps, and Jewett: The Conflict of Marriage and Career." In Gwen L. Nagel, ed., *Critical Essays on Sarah Orne Jewett*, 136–147. Boston: G. K. Hall, 1984.

Mayr, Ernst. *This Is Biology: The Science of the Living World*. Cambridge: Harvard University Press, Belknap Press, 1997.

McAllister, Ethel M. *Amos Eaton: Scientist and Educator, 1776–1842*. Philadelphia: University of Pennsylvania Press, 1941.

McRea, Murdo Williams. Introduction to *The Literature of Science*, 1–13.

———, ed. *The Literature of Science: Perspectives on Popular Scientific Writing*. Athens: University of Georgia Press, 1993.

Mellor, Mary. *Feminism and Ecology*. New York: New York University Press, 1997.

Merchant, Caroline. *The Death of Nature: Women, Ecology, and the Scientific Revolution*. San Francisco: Harper and Row, 1980.

Mikesell, Marvin W. "Continuity and Change." In Blouet, *Origins of Academic Geography*, 1–15.

Miller, Christanne. "Whose Dickinson?" *American Literary History* 12 (2000): 230–253.

Miller, Howard S. *Dollars for Research: Science and Its Patrons in Nineteenth-Century America*. Seattle: University of Washington Press, 1970.

Miller, Lillian B., Frederick Voss, and Jeannette M. Hussey, eds. *The Lazzaroni: Science and Scientists in Mid-Nineteenth Century America*. Washington: Smithsonian Institution Press, 1962.

Mitchell, Domhnall. "Revising the Script: Emily Dickinson's Manuscripts." *American Literature* 70 (1998): 705–738.

Mitchell, Maria. "Astronomical Notes." *Scientific American* 27 (1872): 356–357; and passim until 1881.

———. "Mary Somerville." *Atlantic Monthly* 5 (1860): 568–571.

———. "Other Worlds than Ours." *Hours at Home* 11 (1870): 471–473.

———. "Reminiscences of the Herschels." *Century* 16 (1889): 903–909.

———. "The Total Eclipse of 1869." *Hours at Home* 9 (1869): 555–560.

———. "The United States Coast Survey." *Christian Examiner* 52 (1852): 77–96.

Mitchell, Maria, ed. *Wonders of the Moon, Translated from the French of Amedee Gullemin, by Miss M.G. Mead*. New York: Scribner, Armstrong, 1873.

Mohr, James C. *Abortion in America: The Origins and Evolution of National Policy, 1800–1900*. New York: Oxford University Press, 1978.

Moore, R. Laurence. *In Search of White Crows: Spiritualism, Parapsychology, and American Culture*. New York: Oxford University Press, 1977.

Morantz-Sanchez, Regina Markell. *Sympathy and Science: Women Physicians in American Medicine*. New York: Oxford University Press, 1985.

Morris, Timothy. "Professional Ethics and Professional Erotics in Elizabeth Stuart Phelps' *Doctor Zay*." *Studies in American Fiction* 21 (1993): 141–152.

Mullan, John. "Gendered Knowledge, Gendered Minds: Women and Newtonianism, 1690–1760." In Benjamin, *Question of Identity*, 41–56.

Murray, John A. *The Sierra Club Nature Writing Handbook*. San Francisco: Sierra Club Books, 1995.

Myers, Greg. "Fictionality, Demonstration, and a Forum for Popular Science: Jane Marcet's *Conversations on Chemistry.*" In Gates and Shteir, *Natural Eloquence,* 43– 60.

Nichol, Francis D. *Ellen G. White and Her Critics*. Tacoma Park, D.C.: Review and Herald Publishing Association, 1951.

Nietz, John A. *Old Textbooks*. Pittsburgh: University of Pittsburgh Press, 1961.

Niklas, Karl J. *The Evolutionary Biology of Plants*. Chicago: University of Chicago Press, 1997.

Noble, David F. *A World without Women: The Christian Clerical Culture of Western Science*. New York: Alfred A. Knopf, 1992.

Norwood, Vera. *Made from This Earth: American Women and Nature*. Chapel Hill: University of North Carolina Press, 1993.

Norwood, Vera, and Janice Monk, eds. *The Desert Is No Lady: Southwestern Landscapes in Women's Writing and Art*. New Haven: Yale University Press, 1987.

Numbers, Ronald L. *Darwinism Comes to America*. Cambridge: Harvard University Press, 1998.

———. *Prophetess of Health: A Study of Ellen G. White*. New York: Harper and Row, 1976.

Odgers, Merle M. *Alexander Dallas Bache: Scientist and Educator, 1806–1867*. Philadelphia: University of Pennsylvania Press, 1947.

Oelschlaeger, Max. *The Idea of Wilderness: From Prehistory to the Age of Ecology*. New Haven: Yale University Press, 1991.

Okker, Patricia. *Our Sister Editors: Sarah J. Hale and the Tradition of Nineteenth-Century Editors*. Athens: University of Georgia Press, 1995.

Olmsted, Denison. *An Introduction to Astronomy; Designed as a Text Book for the Students of Yale College*. Rev. ed. New York: Robert B. Collins, 1854.

Orsini, Daniel J. "Emily Dickinson and the Romantic Uses of Science." *Massachusetts Studies in English* 7, 8 (1981): 57–69.

Parker, Gail Thain. "Mary Baker Eddy and Sentimental Womanhood." *New England Quarterly* 43 (1970): 3–18.

———. *Mind Cure in New England: From the Civil War to World War I*. Hanover, N.H.: University Press of New England, 1973.

Parley, Peter (Samuel G. Goodrich). *A Glance at the Physical Sciences; or, The Wonders of Nature, in Earth, Air, and Sky*. Boston: George C. Rand, 1852.

Paton, Lucy Allen. *Elizabeth Cary Agassiz: A Biography*. 1919. Reprint, New York: Arno Press, 1974.

Patterson, Elizabeth Chambers. *Mary Somerville and the Cultivation of Science, 1815–1840*. The Hague: Martinus Nijhoff, 1983.

Patterson, Rebecca. *Emily Dickinson's Imagery*. Edited by Margaret H. Freeman. Amherst: University of Massachusetts Press, 1979.

Perry, Ruth, "Radical Doubt and the Liberation of Women." *Eighteenth-Century Studies* 18 (1985): 472–493.

Pessen, Edward. *Jacksonian America: Society, Personality, and Politics*. Rev. ed. Urbana: University of Illinois Press, 1985.

Phelps, Almira Hart. *Caroline Westerley; or, the Young Traveller from Ohio.* New York: J. and J. Harper, 1844.

————. *Chemistry for Beginners.* Hartford: J. F. Huntington, 1834.

————. *Familiar Lectures on Botany: For the Use of Colleges, Schools, and Private Students.* New York: Mason Brothers, 1860.

————. *Familiar Lectures on Botany, Practical, Elementary, and Physiological: For the Use of Seminaries and Private Students.* Fifth Edition. Hartford: J. F. Huntington, 1836.

————. *Familiar Lectures on Botany, Practical, Elementary, and Physiological...for the Use of Seminaries, Private Students, and Practical Botanists.* New York: Huntington and Savage, 1849.

————. *The Fireside Friend, or Female Student, Being Advice to Young Ladies, on the Important Subject of Education.* Boston: Marsh, Capen, Lyon, and Webb, 1840.

————. *Hours with My Pupils.* New York: A. S. Barnes, 1868.

————. *Ida Norman; or, Trials and Their Uses.* 2 vols. New York: Sheldon, Lamport and Blakeman, 1854.

————. *Natural Philosophy for Beginners.* New York: F. J. Huntington, 1838.

————. *Reviews and Essays on Art, Literature, and Science.* Philadelphia: Claxton, Remsen and Haffelfinger, 1873.

Phelps, Elizabeth Stuart. *Dr. Zay.* 1882. Reprint, New York: Feminist Press, 1987.

————. *The Story of Avis.* 1877. Reprint, edited by Carol Farley Kessler, New Brunswick: Rutgers University Press, 1985.

Phillips, Patricia. *The Scientific Lady: A Social History of Women's Scientific Interests, 1520–1918.* New York: St. Martin's, 1990.

"Physical Training." *Godey's Lady's Book* 48 (1854): 525–526; 49 (1854): 51–53.

Podmore, Frank. *From Mesmer to Christian Science: A Short History of Mental Healing.* 1909. Reprint, New Hyde Park, N.Y.: University Books, 1963.

————. *Mediums of the Nineteenth Century.* 1902. Reprint, New Hyde Park, N.Y.: University Books, 1963. (Orig. title: *Modern Spiritualism*)

Pollak, Vivian R., ed. *A Poet's Parents: The Courtship Letters of Emily Norcross and Edward Dickinson.* Chapel Hill: University of North Carolina Press, 1988.

Porter, Charlotte F. *The Eagle's Nest: Natural History and American Ideas, 1812–1842.* University: University of Alabama Press, 1986.

Pratt, Mary Louise. *Imperial Eyes: Travel Writing and Transculturation.* London: Routledge, 1992.

————. "Scratches on the Face of the Country; or, What Mr. Barrow Saw in the Land of the Bushmen." In *Race, Writing, and Difference,* ed. Henry Louis Gates, 138–162. Chicago: University of Chicago Press, 1986.

Putnam, George Haven. *George Palmer Putnam: A Memoir.* New York: G. P. Putnam's Sons, 1912.

Rackham, Oliver. *The History of the Countryside.* London: J. M. Dent, 1986.

Reagan, Leslie J. *When Abortion Was a Crime: Women, Medicine, and Law in the United States, 1867–1973.* Berkeley: University of California Press, 1997.

Reingold, Nathan, ed. *Science in Nineteenth-Century America: A Documentary History.* Chicago: University of Chicago Press, 1964.

Renker, Elizabeth. "Resistance and Change: The Rise of American Literature Studies." *American Literature* 64 (1992): 347–365.

Richards, Ellen. *Food Materials and Their Adulterations.* Boston: Estes and Lauriat, 1886.

Richardson, Darlene S., Connie J. Sutton, and Karen R. Cercone. "Female-Friendly Geoscience: Eight Techniques for Reaching the Majority." In Rosser, *Teaching,* 183–192.

Ritvo, Harriet. "Zoological Taxonomy and Real Life." In Levine, *Realism,* 235–254.

Robinson, David M. "Fields of Investigation: Emerson and Natural History." In Scholnick, *American Literature and Science,* 94–109.

Robinson, Gloria. "Edward Hitchcock." In Leonard Wilson, *Benjamin Silliman,* 49–84.

Rosenberg, Charles E. *The Cholera Years: The United States in 1832, 1849, and 1866.* Chicago: University of Chicago Press, 1987.

Rosser, Sue. "Applying Feminist Theories to Women in Science Programs." *Signs* 24 (1998): 171–200.

————. Introduction to *Teaching the Majority,* 1–21.

————, ed. *Teaching the Majority: Breaking the Gender Barrier in Science, Mathematics, and Engineering.* New York: Teachers College Press, 1995.

Rossiter, Margaret W. *Women Scientists in America: Struggles and Strategies to 1940.* Baltimore: Johns Hopkins University Press, 1982.

————. *Women Scientists in America: Before Affirmative Action, 1940–1972.* Baltimore: Johns Hopkins University Press, 1995.

Rothschild, Joan, ed. *Machina ex Dea: Feminist Perspectives on Technology.* New York: Pergamon Press, 1983.

Rothstein, William G. *American Physicians in the Nineteenth Century: From Sects to Science.* Baltimore: Johns Hopkins University Press, 1972.

————. "The Botanical Movements and Orthodox Medicine." In Gevitz, *Other Healers,* 29–51.

Rudolph, Frederick. "Almira Hart Lincoln Phelps." In James, *Notable American Women,* 3:58–60.

Runte, Alfred. *National Parks: The American Experience.* 2d ed. Lincoln: University of Nebraska Press, 1987.

St. Armand, Barton Levi. *Emily Dickinson and Her Culture: The Soul's Society.* New York: Cambridge University Press, 1984.

Sartisky, Michael. Afterword to Phelps, *Dr. Zay,* 259–321.

Schiebinger, Londa. *The Mind Has No Sex? Women in the Origins of Modern Science.* Cambridge: Harvard University Press, 1989.

————. *Nature's Body: Gender in the Making of Modern Science.* Boston: Beacon Press, 1993.

Schoepflin, Rennie B. "Christian Science Healing in America." In Gevitz, *Other Healers,* 192–214.

Scholnick, Robert J., ed. *American Literature and Science.* Lexington: University Press of Kentucky, 1992.

Schrager, Cynthia D. "Mark Twain and Mary Baker Eddy: Gendering the Transpersonal Subject." *American Literature* 70 (1998): 29–62.

Schriber, Mary Suzanne. *Writing Home: American Women Abroad, 1830–1920.* Charlottesville: University Press of Virginia, 1997.

"The Science of Cooking Meat." *Godey's Lady's Book* 77 (1868): 445.

Scott, Ann Firor. *Making the Invisible Woman Visible*. Urbana: University of Illinois Press, 1984.

Sellars, Richard West. *Preserving Nature in the National Parks: A History*. New Haven: Yale University Press, 1997.

Sellers, Charles. *The Market Revolution: Jacksonian America, 1815–1846*. New York: Oxford University Press, 1991.

Seton, Kate. "The Brown Canvas Bag." *Godey's Lady's Book* 41 (1850): 222– 228.

Sewall, Richard. *The Life of Emily Dickinson*. New York: Farrar, Straus and Giroux, 1974.

Shapiro, Laura. *Perfection Salad: Women and Cooking at the Turn of the Century*. New York: Farrar, Straus and Giroux, 1986.

"Shells for the Ladies, and Where They Come From." *Godey's Lady's Book* 53 (1856): 203–206, 299–302, 395–400.

Sherwood, William R. *Circumference and Circumstance: Stages in the Mind and Art of Emily Dickinson*. New York: Columbia University Press, 1968.

Shmurak, Carole B., and Bonnie S. Handler. "'Castle of Science': Mount Holyoke College and the Preparation of Women in Chemistry," *History of Education Quarterly* 32 (1992): 315–341.

Shryock, Richard Harrison. *Medicine and Society in America, 1660–1860*. New York: New York University Press, 1960.

Shteir, Ann B. "Botany in the Breakfast Room: Women and Early Nineteenth-Century British Plant Study." In Abir-Am and Outram, *Uneasy Careers*, 31–43.

———. *Cultivating Women, Cultivating Science: Flora's Daughters and Botany in England, 1760 to 1860*. Baltimore: Johns Hopkins University Press, 1996.

Sigourney, Lydia H. *Select Poems*. Philadelphia: L. C. and J. Biddle, 1847.

Silliman, Benjamin, Jr. *First Principles of Chemistry, for the Use of Colleges and Schools*. Philadelphia: Theodore Bliss, 1845.

———. *Principles of Physics, or Natural Philosophy; Designed for the Use of Colleges and Schools*. Philadelphia: Theodore Bliss, 1858.

Sinfield, Alan. *The Wilde Century: Effeminacy, Oscar Wilde, and the Queer Moment*. New York: Columbia University Press, 1994.

Sklar, Kathryn Kish. *Catharine Beecher: A Study in American Domesticity*. New Haven: Yale University Press, 1973.

Slack, Nancy G. "Nineteenth-Century American Women Botanists: Wives, Widows, and Work." In Abir-Am and Outram, *Uneasy Careers*, 77–103.

Slotten, Hugh Richard. *Patronage, Practice, and the Culture of American Science: Alexander Dallas Bache and the U.S. Coast Survey*. Cambridge: Cambridge University Press, 1994.

Smallwood, William Martin, and Mabel Sarah Smallwood. *Natural History and the American Mind*. New York: Columbia University Press, 1941.

Smith, Martha Nell. "Dickinson's Manuscripts." In Grabher et al., *The Emily Dickinson Handbook*, 113–137.

Somerville, Mary. *On the Connexion of the Physical Sciences*. 7th ed. London: John Murray, 1834.

———. *Physical Geography*. 2d American ed. Philadelphia: Lea and Blanchard, 1850.

Spofford, Harriet Prescott. *Azarian*. Boston: Ticknor and Fields, 1864.

Stage, Sarah. "Home Economics, What's in a Name." In Stage and Vincenti, *Rethinking Home Economics,* 1–17.

Stage, Sarah, and Virginia B. Vincenti, eds. *Rethinking Home Economics: Women and the History of a Profession*. Ithaca, N.Y.: Cornell University Press, 1997.

Stanley, Autumn. *Mothers and Daughters of Invention: Notes for a Revised History of Technology*. Metuchen, N.J.: Scarecrow Press, 1993.

Starr, Paul. *The Social Transformation of American Medicine*. New York: Basic Books, 1982.

Stern, Madeleine B. *Heads and Headlines: The Phrenological Fowlers*. Norman: University of Oklahoma Press, 1971.

Stevens, Edward G., Jr. *The Grammar of the Machine: Technical Literacy and Early Industrial Expansion in the United States*. New Haven: Yale University Press, 1995.

Stevenson, David. *Sketch of the Civil Engineering of North America*. London: John Weale, Architectural Library, 1838.

Stevenson, Louise L. *Scholarly Means to Evangelical Ends: The New Haven Scholars and the Transformation of Higher Learning in America, 1830–1890*. Baltimore: Johns Hopkins University Press, 1986.

Stilgoe, John R. *Borderland: Origins of the American Suburb, 1820–1939*. New Haven: Yale University Press, 1988.

———. *The Common Landscape of America, 1580–1845*. New Haven: Yale University Press, 1982.

Stoddard, Elizabeth. *The Morgesons*. 1862. Reprint, edited by Lawrence Buell and Sandra Zagarell, Philadelphia: University of Pennsylvania Press, 1984.

Stonum, Gary. *The Dickinson Sublime*. Madison: University of Wisconsin Press, 1990.

Struick, Dirk J. *Yankee Science in the Making*. Rev. ed. New York: Collier, 1962.

Swift, Mary A. *First Lessons on Natural Philosophy, for Children*. Hartford: Hamersley, 1845. Part 2, Hartford: Hamersley, 1852. Expanded ed., Philadelphia, Hamersley and Lippincott, 1859.

Taylor, Alan. *William Cooper's Town: Power and Persuasion on the Frontier of the Early American Republic*. New York: Alfred A. Knopf, 1995.

Tharp, Louise Hall. *Adventurous Alliance: The Story of the Agassiz Family of Boston*. Boston: Little, Brown, 1959.

Thomas, Robert David. *"With Bleeding Footsteps": Mary Baker Eddy's Path to Religious Leadership*. New York: Alfred A. Knopf, 1994.

Thornton, Tamara Plakins. *Cultivating Gentlemen: The Meaning of Country Life among the Boston Elite, 1785–1860*. New Haven: Yale University Press, 1989.

Tomes, Nancy. *The Gospel of Germs: Men, Women, and the Microbe in American Life*. Cambridge: Harvard University Press, 1998.

Tompkins, Jane. *Sensational Designs: The Cultural Work of American Fiction, 1790–1865*. New York: Oxford University Press, 1985.

Tonkovich, Nicole. *Domesticity with a Difference: The Nonfiction of Catharine Beecher, Sarah J. Hale, Fanny Fern, and Margaret Fuller*. Jackson: University Press of Mississippi, 1997.

Toqueville, Alexis de. *Democracy in America*. 1831. Reprint, New York: Vintage, 1960.

Townsend, Mary [anon]. *Life in the Insect World; or, Conversations Upon Insects, Between an Aunt and Her Nieces.* Philadelphia: Lindsay and Blakiston, 1844.

Truax, Rhoda. *The Doctors Jacobi.* Boston: Little, Brown, 1952.

Tuana, Nancy, ed. *Feminism and Science.* Bloomington: Indiana University Press, 1989.

Tuckerman, Henry T. "Alexander Von Humboldt." *Godey's Lady's Book* 40 (1850): 133–138.

"Turning an Honest Penny." *Godey's Lady's Book* 86 (1873): 50–51.

Tyler, Alice Felt. "Davis, Paulina Kellogg Wright." In James, *Notable American Women,* 1:444–445.

Tyndall, John. *Faraday as a Discoverer.* 5th ed. London: Longmans, Green, 1894.

Underhill, Ann Leah Fox. *The Missing Link in Modern Spiritualism, Revised and Arranged by a Literary Friend.* New York: Thomas R. Knox, 1885.

Uno, Hiroko. "'Chemical Conviction': Dickinson, Hitchcock, and the Poetry of Science." *Emily Dickinson Journal* 7 (1998): 95–111.

Valian, Virginia. *Why So Slow? The Advancement of Women.* Cambridge: M.I.T. Press, 1998.

Van Leer, David. "Nature's Book: The Language of Science in the American Renaissance." In Andrew Cunningham and Nicholas Jardine, eds., *Romanticism and the Sciences,* 307–321. Cambridge: Cambridge University Press, 1990.

Verbrugge, Martha H. *Able-Bodied Womanhood: Personal Health and Social Change in Nineteenth-Century Boston.* New York: Oxford University Press, 1988.

Vincenti, Virginia Bramble. "A History of the Philosophy of Home Economics." Ph.D. diss., Pennsylvania State University, 1981.

Viola, Herman J., and Carolyn Margolis, eds. *Magnificent Voyagers: The United States Exploring Edition, 1838–1842.* Washington: Smithsonian Institution Press, 1985.

Walls, Laura Dassow. *Seeing New Worlds: Henry David Thoreau and Nineteenth-Century Natural Science.* Madison: University of Wisconsin Press, 1995.

Walsh, Mary Roth. *Doctors Wanted: No Women Need Apply: Sexual Barriers in the Medical Profession.* New Haven: Yale University Press, 1977.

Waples, Rufus. "The Electricity of the Heart." *Godey's Lady's Book* 46 (1853): 71.

Warner, Deborah Jean. *Graceanna Lewis: Scientist and Humanitarian.* Washington, D.C.: Smithsonian Institution Press, 1979.

———. "Science Education for Women in Antebellum America." *Isis* 69 (1978): 58–67.

Warner, Susan. *The Wide, Wide World.* 1850. Reprint, edited by Jane Tompkins, New York: Feminist Press, 1987.

Watters, David. "Emerson, Dickinson, and the Atomic Self." *Dickinson Studies* 32 (1977): 122–134.

Welch, Margaret. *The Book of Nature: Natural History in the United States, 1825–1875.* Boston: Northeastern University Press, 1998.

Wells, Susan. "Women Write Science: The Case of Hannah Longshore." *College English* 58 (1996): 176–191.

Wertheim, Margaret. *Pythagoras' Trousers: God, Physics, and the Gender Wars.* New York: Times Books, Random House, 1995.

Whewell, William. *Astronomy and General Physics, Considered with Reference to Natural Theology.* London: William Pickering, 1833.

————. *History of the Inductive Sciences, From the Earliest to the Present Time.* 2 vols. New York: D. Appleton, 1837.

————. *Philosophy of the Inductive Sciences, Founded Upon Their History.* 2 vols. London: John W. Parker, 1840.

White, Andrew Dickson. *Warfare of Science.* New York: D. Appleton, 1876.

White, Ellen G. *Education.* Oakland, Calif.: Pacific Press, 1903.

————. *Principles of True Science.* Tacoma Park, D.C.: Washington College Press, 1929.

White, Fred C. "'Sweet Skepticism of the Heart': Science in the Poetry of Emily Dickinson." *College Literature* 19 (1992): 121–128.

White, Richard. "'Are You an Environmentalist or Do You Work for a Living?': Work and Nature." In Cronon, *Uncommon Ground*, 171–185.

Whorton, James C. *Crusaders for Fitness: The History of American Health Reformers.* Princeton: Princeton University Press, 1982.

Willard, Emma. *Astronography, or Astronomical Geography.* Troy: Merriam, Moore, 1854.

————. *Respiration and Its Effects: More Especially in Relation to Asiatic Cholera, and Other Sinking Diseases.* New York: Huntington and Savage, 1849.

————. *Theory of Circulation by Respiration: Synopsis of Its Principles and History.* New York: Francis Hart, 1861.

————. *A Treatise on the Motive Powers Which Produce the Circulation of the Blood.* New York: Wiley and Putnam, 1846.

Williams, L. Pearce. *Michael Faraday: A Biography.* New York: Basic Books, 1965.

Williams, Michael. *Americans and Their Forests: A Historical Geography.* Cambridge: Cambridge University Press, 1988.

Wilson, John. "Health Department." *Godey's Lady's Book* 64 (1862): 94; 65 (1852): 402.

Wilson, Leonard G., ed. *Benjamin Silliman and His Circle: Studies on the Influence of Benjamin Silliman on Science in America.* New York: Science History Publications, 1979.

Wittenberg, Judith B. "Challenge and Compliance: Textual Strategies in *A Country Doctor* and Nineteenth-Century American Women's Medical Autobiographies." In Karen L. Kilcup and Thomas S. Edwards, eds., *Jewett and Her Contemporaries: Reshaping the Canon,* 123–136. Gainesville: University Press of Florida, 1999.

Wolff, Cynthia Griffin. *Emily Dickinson.* New York: Alfred A. Knopf, 1987.

Woody, Thomas. *History of Women's Education in the United States.* Vol. 1. New York and Lancaster: Science Press, 1929.

Worster, Donald. *Nature's Economy: A History of Ecological Ideas.* 2d ed. Cambridge: Cambridge University Press, 1994.

Wright, Helen. "Mitchell, Maria." In James, *Notable American Women*, 2:554–556.

————. *Sweeper in the Sky: The Life of Maria Mitchell, First Woman Astronomer in America.* New York: Macmillan, 1949.

Youmans, Edward L. *The Hand-Book of Household Science: A Popular Account of Heat, Light, Air, Aliment, and Cleansing in Their Scientific Principles and Domestic Applications.* New York: D. Appleton , 1857.

Youmans, Eliza A. *The First Book of Botany. A Practical Guide in Self-Teaching. Designed to Cultivate the Observing and Reasoning Powers of Children.* New York: D. Appleton, 1889.

Zakrzweska, Marie. *A Practical Illustration of "Woman's Right to Labor": A Letter from Marie E. Zakrzewska, M.D.* Edited by Caroline H. Dall. Boston: Walker, Wide, 1860.

Zboray, Ronald J. *A Fictive People: Antebellum Economic Development and the American Reading Public.* New York: Oxford University Press, 1993.

INDEX

Property of:
Henry County Library System
1001 Florence McGarity Blvd.
McDonough, GA 30252

Assigned to:
☐ Cochran Public Library
☐ Fairview Public Library
☐ Fortson Public Library
☐ Locust Grove Public Library
☒ McDonough Public Library

ABOUT THE AUTHOR

Nina Baym is Swanlund Chair and Center for Advanced Study Professor of English, as well as Jubilee Professor of Liberal Arts and Sciences, at the University of Illinois in Urbana. She has written many books and essays about various aspects of American literature, focusing particularly on the nineteenth century and on writing by and about women. Among earlier works are *Feminism and American Literary History* (1992) and *American Women Writers and the Work of History, 1790–1860* (1995), both published by Rutgers University Press. She is general editor of the *Norton Anthology of American Literature*. In the year 2000 she was awarded the annual Hubbell Lifetime Achievement Medal by the American Literature Section of the Modern Literature Association.